The Methuen Modern Plays series has always been at the forefront of modern playwriting. Since 1959, the series has reflected the most exciting developments in modern drama, making the most significant plays widely available in paperback.

### Blithe Spirit

*Blithe Spirit*: 'Without a single lapse into improbability it achieves the impossible . . . The author's light, easy amusing way with ectoplasm, poltergeists, hypnotic trances and the like is so adroitly sustained that we are surprised only as we are meant to be surprised when at the bidding of the briskly fantastic, madly sincere Mme. Arcati the first Mrs Condomime returns after death to make herself scandalously at home in her husband's pleasant country house.' *The Times* 1941

'Riotously witty stuff.' *Daily Mail* 1941

**Noël Coward** was born in 1899 in Teddington, Middlesex. He made his name as a playwright with *The Vortex* (1924), in which he also appeared. His numerous other successful plays included *Fallen Angels* (1925), *Hay Fever* (1925), *Private Lives* (1933), *Design for Living* (1933), and *Blithe Spirit* (1941). During the war he wrote screenplays such as *Brief Encounter* (1944) and *This Happy Breed* (1942). In the fifties he began a new career as a cabaret entertainer. He published volumes of verse and a novel, *Pomp and Circumstance* (1960), two volumes of autobiography and four volumes of short stories: *To Step Aside* (1939), *Star Quality* (1951), *Pretty Polly Barlow* (1964) and *Bon Voyage* (1967). He was knighted in 1970 and died three years later in Jamaica.

*also by Noël Coward*

**Coward**

**Collected Plays: One**
(Hay Fever, The Vortex, Fallen Angels, Easy Virtue)

**Collected Plays: Two**
(Private Lives, Bitter-Sweet, The Marquise, Post-Mortem)

**Collected Plays: Three**
(Design for Living, Cavalcade, Conversation Piece,
*and* Hands Across the Sea, Still Life, Fumed Oak
*from* To-night at 8.30)

**Collected Plays: Four**
(Blithe Spirit, Present Laughter, This Happy Breed,
*and* Ways and Means, The Astonished Heart, 'Red Peppers'
*from* To-night at 8.30)

**Collected Plays: Five**
(Relative Values, Look After Lulu!
Waiting in the Wings, Suite in Three Keys)

**Collected Plays: Six**
(Semi-Monde, Point Valaine, South Sea Bubble,
Nude With Violin)

**Collected Plays: Seven**
(Quadrille, 'Peace in Our Time',
*and* We Were Dancing, Shadow Play, Family Album, Star Chamber
*from* To-night at 8.30)

**Collected Revue Sketches and Parodies**

**The Complete Lyrics of Noël Coward**

**Collected Short Stories**

**Pomp and Circumstance**
*A Novel*

**Autobiography**

*in the same series*

**Private Lives**

**Semi-Monde**

**Star Quality**

**Hay Fever**

his way to Damanhour. His friend was from Nashawy, and while they were talking about the crops and the fields, who had planted what and whose cotton was doing well, his friend had told him an amazing tale—a story about a recent event in his village.

There was a parcel of land in one of the village's fields that was owned by one of the sons of the old 'omda, Ahmed Badawy Effendi, a highly-placed civil servant who lived in Cairo. It was one of the few pieces of land that had been left to the family after the Land Reforms; a tiny fraction of what they had once owned, admittedly, but still a very large area in relation to the landholdings of the ordinary fellaheen.

One morning, quite unexpectedly the civil servant's car was seen driving into Nashawy. Everyone was taken by surprise, because he very rarely came to visit the village: he was afraid of getting mud on his clothes, or so people said. But there was yet another surprise in store for the people of the village. When the car stopped and the 'omda's son stepped out, the people who were watching assumed that he would go straight to his .ather's old house. But no: to their utter astonishment, he headed in the opposite direction—towards a tumbledown mud hut that belonged to the fellah family that had share-cropped his land for the last so many years.

Those members of the family who were at home were astonished when they saw the 'omda's son knocking on their door: it was years since they had last seen him, for he always sent one of his minions to pick up his share at harvest-time. But they threw their doors open and welcomed him in, and it was a good hour or so before he emerged again.

No one knew exactly what the 'omda's son had said while he was in that house, but everyone agreed later that it was something like this: 'I am soon going to buy a new apartment in Cairo, insha'allah (or perhaps a car), and for that reason I need to raise a large sum of money quickly. Pray to the Prophet! I have given the matter much thought, and after speaking to my children I have decided to sell my land. So, as law and custom demands, I have come to your family first, because you have worked on that land for so long, to ask whether you can raise the money to buy it. If you can, you will be welcome to it—everything good is the work of God—but if you cannot, I must tell you that I shall put my land on the market, with God's permission.'

Now, it so happened that this family was both very poor and very large, and between all of them together they probably had no more than a couple of pounds in savings. But it was many, many years since such good land had been put up for sale in Nashawy, and they knew that they would never again be presented with such an opportunity. So they took their chance and said to him: 'Give us a month, ya Effendi, to see if we can raise the money, insha'allah, and if at the end of that time we do not succeed, you will be free to dispose of the land as you please, and we shall not stand in your way, by God.'

The moment the Effendi left, the brothers began to run around the village—even the youngest one, who was just a boy. They went from house to house, from distant cousins to far relatives, borrowing a few pounds here and a few piastres there. They sold their cattle, they sold parts of the house they lived in, they even sold their ploughshares, but on the day the Effendi came back they had the money ready and were able to take possession of the land. They were heavily in debt by this time, but still, from that day onwards they could be counted amongst the largest landowners in the village. They had realized the secret dream that every fellah inherits from his ancestors: they had succeeded in expanding their family's landholdings.

'That was six years ago,' said Shaikh Musa, 'just a couple of years after you left. It took only three or four harvests for your friend Khamees and his family to pay off their debts, and now they're so well-to-do they've built a new brick-and-cement house on their own land, outside the village.'

'What about Busaina?' I asked. 'What's become of her?'

Her life had changed too, Shaikh Musa said, but not quite so dramatically as her brothers'. She had decided to set up on her own, with her two sons, when her brothers moved to their new house. She had managed to save a fair bit of money in the meanwhile, because she had become a seasoned businesswoman, trading regularly in the market in Damanhour. With her savings she had bought a little two-room house in the centre of Nashawy, right beside the square. People said she made her two sons study late into the night, and they were both doing quite exceptionally well at school, although they were still very young.

'What about her husband?' I asked. 'The boys' father?'

Shaikh Musa laughed. 'He went away to Iraq,' he said. 'And no one's heard from him for years.'

Shaikh Musa recalled the story's ending later in the night, while talking of something else.

'I forgot to tell you,' he said cutting himself short. 'There's another piece of news about Khamees and his family: I heard it from Jabir.'

A few months ago, Shaikh Musa said, a large truck had driven past Lataifa, piled high with suitcases and cardboard boxes, of the kind that were used for television sets and such like. It took just one glance at that truck to see that somebody had returned from Iraq, or the Gulf, or some place like that, having made a lot of money. Jabir had seen the truck go past from a window in his house, and had gone off at once to make inquiries about who it was that had driven past in such state. He'd soon discovered that the returning hero was none other than Khamees's brother, 'Eid.

'Do you remember him?' said Shaikh Musa. 'You mentioned him sometimes, when you were living in Nashawy. He was a little boy then, of course, but now he's taller than any of his brothers.'

'Eid had been away in Saudi Arabia for some three or four years, and had done very well for himself, working in construction. He had come home with a colour television set, a fridge, a washing-machine, and many other things of that kind. On top of that, he had also saved a lot of money and was soon going to buy his family a new tractor.

'And not long ago,' said Shaikh Musa, 'we heard that 'Eid is soon to be married. He is going to pay a large sum of money as a marriage-payment, and he's going to have an educated wife. Can you imagine! And him a Jammal, and an unlettered fellah!'

Shaikh Musa shook his head in wonderment.

'He's marrying a Badawy girl,' he said. 'They say it's a real love-match, and the two of them have been waiting for years.'

# 16

THERE IS GOOD reason to believe that soon after moving—or being forced to move—to Mangalore Ben Yiju contracted a liaison which eventually led to his marriage. The evidence lies in the earliest documents that can be dated to Ben Yiju's stay in India: two unusual and intriguing fragments which can fortunately be dated without fear of inaccuracy.

The first actually specifies both the day and the place where it was drawn up, for it happens to be a legally attested deed. The second, which is closely linked to the first, is a rough draft of another legal document, written in Ben Yiju's handwriting, on one of those scraps of paper which he used for making notes.

Of the two, the first is the more important, but it has long been relatively inaccessible being lodged in a collection in the erstwhile Leningrad. Fortunately, there can be no doubt about the nature of its contents, for Goitein chanced upon it during his researches there and referred to it frequently in his later writings: it is a deed of manumission which records that on 17 October 1132, in Mangalore, Ben Yiju publicly granted freedom to a slave girl by the name of Ashu. The second fragment, which is now in the Taylor-Schechter Collection in Cambridge, is a supporting document: the draft of a deposition backing up the deed of manumission.

The date on the deed of manumission establishes it as the earliest document that can be reliably dated to the period of Ben Yiju's stay in India. It is uncertain how long he had been in Mangalore at the time of its writing; it must, at any rate, have been long enough for him to acquire slaves and set up a household. This could mean that Ben Yiju had left Aden and moved to India as early as 1130 or 1131; in any event the date must have preceded Ashu's manumission by a good few years.

It is probably not a coincidence that the first dated document from Ben Yiju's stay in India has to do with the woman who probably bore his children. Indeed, he may well have expected to contract a marital or sexual liaison soon after his arrival, for amongst the people of the Middle East, India then bore a reputation as a place notable for the ease of its sexual relations. Had Ben Yiju read the works of his contemporary, the Sharif al-Idrisi, for example, he would have discovered that in India 'concubinage is permitted between everyone, so long as it is not with married women.' A couple of centuries before Ben Yiju's lifetime, a chronicler in the Persian Gulf port of Siraf had professed shock upon hearing of the duties of Indian temple dancers. 'Let us thank God,' he had written, in pious disapproval, 'for the Qur'ân which he has chosen for us and with which he has preserved us from the sins of the infidels.' Some travellers, such as the Italian Nicoló Conti, who visited India in the fifteenth century, were struck by the number of courtesans. 'Public women are everywhere to be had,' he wrote, 'residing in particular houses of their own in all parts of the cities, who attract the men by sweet perfumes and ointments, by their blandishments, beauty and youth; for the Indians are much addicted to licentiousness.' A contemporary of his, a Persian ambassador called 'Abd al-Razzâq al-Samarqandî who travelled to the kingdom of Vijaynagar in 1442, appears to have acquired a much closer acquaintance with the customs of courtesans. Soon after his arrival in the capital, he was taken by his hosts to visit the area in which the women lived, and discovered that: 'Immediately after midday prayer they place before the doors of the chambers...thrones and chairs, on which the courtesans seat themselves...Each one of them has by her two young slaves, who give the signal of pleasure, and have the charge of attending to everything which can contribute to amusement. Any man may enter into this locality, and select any girl that pleases him, and take his pleasure with her.'

It could well be that Ben Yiju encountered Ashu on just such a visit, soon after moving to Mangalore.

The fact that Ben Yiju manumitted Ashu a short while after having acquired her custody indicates that his intentions towards her were anything but casual. Since he also appears to have celebrated her manumission with some fanfare, it is possible that he made use of the occasion to issue public notice of a wedding, or betrothal.

At any rate, before three years were over Ben Yiju was the father of a young son. The proof of this lies in a letter written to him by his mentor, Madmun, in 1135: 'I have also sent a piece of coral for your son Surûr,' wrote Madmun, listing the presents he had sent for Ben Yiju in Mangalore, along with a shipment of cargo.

There is no particular reason to connect Ashu's manumission with Ben Yiju's fatherhood yet it is difficult not to. The connection seems so obvious that Goitein, for one, was persuaded that Ben Yiju had married Ashu, and that Ashu was 'probably beautiful'.

About Ashu's origins there is only a single clue. In a set of accounts scribbled on the back of one of Madmun's letters, Ben Yiju refers to a sum of money that he owed to his 'brother-in-law', who bears the name 'Nâîr'. The lucky accident of that reference provides Ashu with a semblance of a social identity: it links her to the matrilineal community of Nairs, who still form a substantial section of the population of the southern part of the Malabar coast.

Ashu is not mentioned anywhere else in the entire corpus of Ben Yiju's documents, although her children figure in it frequently. Ben Yiju did not once refer to her in his letters or jottings, and his correspondents in Aden, who were always careful to send their good wishes to his children, never mentioned her either, not even by means of the euphemisms customary in their time, and nor did they send her their greetings. This haunting effacement may in fact be proof that Ben Yiju did indeed marry Ashu, for only a marriage of that kind—with a slave girl, born outside the community of his faith—could have earned so pointed a silence on the part of his friends. Ben Yiju probably converted Ashu to Judaism before their marriage, but the conversion may have signified very little, either to Ashu or to Ben Yiju's friends and relatives. It is also possible that their liaison was modelled upon the institution of 'temporary marriage', a kind of marital union that was widely practised by expatriate Iranian traders.

There were certain marital choices open to Ben Yiju in India that may well have been more acceptable to his friends. For instance, he could well have married into the ancient sect of the Jews of Malabar—a community so well-known for its strictness in religious matters, that it had even found favour with Ben Yiju's near contemporary, the strict and learned Spanish Rabbi, Benjamin of Tudela, who wrote after his visit to the Malabar: 'And throughout the [land] including all the towns there, live several thousand Israelites. The inhabitants are all black, and the Jews are also. The latter are good and benevolent. They know the law of Moses and the prophets, and to a small extent the Talmud and the Halacha.'

Yet, since Ben Yiju chose, despite the obvious alternative, to marry a woman born outside his faith, it can only have been because of another overriding and more important consideration.

 If I hesitate to call it love it is only because the documents offer no certain proof.

EVEN THOUGH KHAMEES never mentioned the subject himself, everyone around him seemed to know that he was haunted by his childlessness.

Once, on a cold winter's day, I dropped in to see him and found him sitting with his father in the guest-room of their house—one of the shabbiest and most derelict in the village. His father was sitting in a corner, huddled in a blanket, hugging his knees and shivering whenever a draught whistled in through the crumbling walls. He smiled when I stepped in, and motioned to me to sit beside him—a thin, frail old man with absent, wandering eyes. He had worked as a labourer in Alexandria during the Second World War, and he had met many Indians among the soldiers who had passed through the city at the start of the North African campaign. They had made a deep impression on his memory and at our first meeting he had greeted me as though he was resuming an interrupted friendship.

Now, after I had seated myself beside him, he leant towards me and ran his hands over my wool sweater, examining it closely, rubbing the material carefully between finger and thumb.

'That's the right thing to wear in winter,' he said. 'It must be really warm.'

'Not as warm as your blanket,' interjected Khamees.

His father pretended not to hear. 'I've heard you can get sweaters like that in Damanhour,' he said to me.

'You can get anything if you have the money,' said Khamees. 'It's getting the money that's the problem.'

Paying him no attention, his father patted my arm. 'I remember the Indian soldiers,' he said. 'They were so tall and dark that many of us Egyptians were afraid of them. But if you talked to them they were the most generous of all the soldiers; if you asked for a cigarette they gave you a whole packet.'

'That was then,' Khamees said, grinning at me. 'Now things have changed.'

'Do you see what my children are like?' his father said to me. 'They won't even get me a sweater from Damanhour so I can think of the winter without fear.'

At that Khamees rose abruptly to his feet and walked out of the room. His father watched him go with an unblinking stare.

'What am I to do with my children?' he muttered, under his breath. 'Look at them; look at Busaina, trying to rear her two sons on her own; look at Khamees, you can't talk to him any more, can't say a thing, neither me, nor his brothers, nor his wife. And every year he gets worse.'

He pulled his blanket over his ears, shivering spasmodically. 'Perhaps I'm the one who's to blame,' he said. 'I married him off early and I told him we wanted to see his children before we died. But that didn't work, so he married again. Now the one thought in his head is children—that's all he thinks about, nothing else.'

A few months later, in the spring, after nearly a year had passed and the time for my departure from Egypt was not far distant, I was walking back from the fields with Khamees and 'Eid one evening, when we spotted Imam Ibrahim sitting on the steps of the mosque.

Khamees stopped short, and with an uncharacteristic urgency in his voice he said: 'Listen, you know Imam Ibrahim, don't you? I've seen you greeting him.'

I made a noncommittal answer, although the truth was that ever after that ill-fated meal at Yasir's house the Imam had scarcely deigned to acknowledge my greetings when we passed each other in the village's narrow lanes.

'My wife's ill,' said Khamees. 'I want the Imam to come to my house and give her an injection.'

His answer surprised me, and I quickly repeated what Nabeel and his friends had said about the Imam's blunt needles, and told him that if his wife needed an injection there were many other people in the village who could do the job much better. But Khamees was insistent: it was not just the injection, he said—he had heard that Imam Ibrahim knew a lot about remedies and medicines and things like that, and people had told him that maybe he would be able to do something for him and his wife.

I understood then what sort of medicine he was hoping the Imam would give him.

'Khamees, he can't help in matters like that,' I said, 'and anyway he's stopped doing remedies now. He only does those injections.'

But Khamees had grown impatient by this time. 'Go and ask him,' he said, 'he won't come if I ask; he doesn't like us.'

'He doesn't like me either,' I said.

'That doesn't matter,' said Khamees. 'He'll come if you ask him—he knows you're a foreigner. He'll listen to you.'

It was clear that he had made up his mind, so I left him waiting at the edge of the square, and went across, towards the mosque. I could tell that the Imam had seen me—and Khamees —from a long way off, but he betrayed no sign of recognition and carefully kept his eyes from straying in my direction. Instead, he pretended to be deep in conversation with a man who was sitting beside him, an elderly shopkeeper with whom I had a slight acquaintance.

I was still a few steps away from them when I said 'good evening' to the Imam, pointedly, so he could no longer ignore me. He paused to acknowledge the greeting, but his response was short and curt, and he turned back at once to resume his conversation.

The old shopkeeper was taken aback at the Imam's manner; he was a pleasant man, and had often exchanged cordial salutes with me in the lanes of the village.

'Please sit down,' he said to me, in embarrassment. 'Do sit. Shall we get you a chair?'

Without waiting for an answer, he glanced at the Imam, frowning in puzzlement. 'You know the Indian doktór, don't you?' he said. 'He's come all the way from India to be a student at the University of Alexandria.'

'I know him,' said the Imam. 'He came around to ask me questions. But as for this student business, I don't know. What's he going to study? He doesn't even write in Arabic.'

'That's true,' said the shopkeeper judiciously, 'but after all, he writes his own languages and he knows English.'

'Oh those,' said the Imam scornfully. 'What's the use of those languages? They're the easiest languages in the world. Anyone can write those.'

He turned to face me now, and I saw that his mouth was twitching with anger and his eyes were shining with a startling brightness.

'Tell me,' he said, 'why do you worship cows?'

Taken by surprise I began to stammer, and he cut me short by turning his shoulder on me.

'That's what they do in his country,' he said to the old shopkeeper. 'Did you know? They worship cows.'

He shot me a glance from the corner of his eyes. 'And shall I tell you what else they do?' he said. He let the question hang in the air for a moment, and then announced, in a dramatic hiss: 'They burn their dead.'

The shopkeeper recoiled as though he had been slapped, and his hands flew to his mouth. 'Ya Allah!' he muttered.

'That's what they do,' said the Imam. 'They burn their dead.'

Then suddenly he spun around to face me and cried: 'Why do you allow it? Can't you see that it's a primitive and backward custom? Are you savages that you permit something like that? Look at you: you've had some education; you should know better. How will your country ever progress if you carry on doing these things? You've even been to Europe; you've seen how advanced they are. Now tell me: have you ever seen them burning their dead?'

A small crowd had gathered around us now, drawn by the Imam's voice, and under the pressure of their collective gaze, I found myself becoming increasingly tongue-tied.

'Yes, they do burn their dead in Europe,' I managed to say, my voice rising despite my efforts to control it. 'Yes, they have special electric furnaces meant just for that.'

The Imam turned away and laughed scornfully. 'He's lying,' he said to the crowd. 'They don't burn their dead in the West. They're not an ignorant people. They're advanced, they're educated, they have science, they have guns and tanks and bombs.'

Suddenly something seemed to boil over in my head, dilemmas and arguments I could no longer contain within myself.

'We have them too!' I shouted back at him. 'In my country we have all those things too; we have guns and tanks and bombs. And they're better than anything you've got in Egypt—

we're a long way ahead of you.'

'I tell you, he's lying,' cried the Imam, his voice rising in fury. 'Our guns and bombs are much better than their theirs. Ours are second only to the West's.'

'It's you who's lying,' I said. 'You know nothing about this. Ours are much better. Why, in my country we've even had a nuclear explosion. You won't be able to match that even in a hundred years.'

It was about then, I think, that Khamees appeared at my side and led me away, or else we would probably have stood there a good while longer, the Imam and I: delegates from two superseded civilizations, vying with each other to establish a prior claim to the technology of modern violence.

At that moment, despite the vast gap that lay between us, we understood each other perfectly. We were both travelling, he and I: we were travelling in the West. The only difference was that I had actually been there, in person: I could have told him a great deal about it, seen at first hand, its libraries, its museums, its theatres, but it wouldn't have mattered. We would have known, both of us, that all that was mere fluff: in the end, for millions and millions of people on the landmasses around us, the West meant only this—science and tanks and guns and bombs.

I was crushed, as I walked away; it seemed to me that the Imam and I had participated in our own final defeat, in the dissolution of the centuries of dialogue that had linked us: we had demonstrated the irreversible triumph of the language that has usurped all the others in which people once discussed their differences. We had acknowledged that it was no longer possible to speak, as Ben Yiju or his Slave, or any one of the thousands of travellers who had crossed the Indian Ocean in the Middle

Ages might have done: of things that were right, or good, or willed by God; it would have been merely absurd for either of us to use those words, for they belonged to a dismantled rung on the ascending ladder of Development. Instead, to make ourselves understood, we had both resorted, I, a student of the 'humane' sciences, and he, an old-fashioned village Imam, to the very terms that world leaders and statesmen use at great, global conferences, the universal, irresistible metaphysic of modern meaning; he had said to me, in effect: 'You ought not to do what you do, because otherwise you will not have guns and tanks and bombs.' It was the only language we had been able to discover in common.

For a while, after Khamees and 'Eid had led me back to their house, I could not bring myself to speak; I felt myself a conspirator in the betrayal of the history that had led me to Nashawy; a witness to the extermination of a world of accommodations that I had believed to be still alive, and, in some tiny measure, still retrievable.

But Khamees and his family did not let me long remain in silence. They took me back to their house, and after 'Eid had repeated the story of my encounter with Imam Ibrahim, Khamees turned to me, laughing, and said: 'Do not be upset, ya doktór. Forget about all those guns and things. I'll tell you what: I'll come to visit you in your country, even though I've never been anywhere. When you leave, I'll come with you; I'll come all the way to India.'

He began to scratch his head, thinking hard, and then he added: 'But if I die there you must remember to bury me.'

# MANGALORE

# 1

SEEN FROM THE sea, on a clear day, Mangalore can take a newcomer's breath away. It sits upon the tip of a long finger of steeply rising land; a ridge of hills which extends out of a towering knuckle of peaks in the far distance. Two rivers meet around the elliptical curve of the fingertip to form a great palm-fringed lagoon, lying tranquil under a quicksilver sky. Between the lagoon and the sea, holding back the waves, are two thin elbows of sand. They strain towards each other, but stop just short of touching, and through the gap between them flows a narrow channel, joining the lagoon to the open sea.

The boats that pass through that channel today are mainly small fishing craft; the lagoon's ancient functions as a harbour have now been delegated to a modern, artificially-dredged port a little to the north of the city. But it was the lagoon that first granted Mangalore its charter as a port, and it is from there that Ben Yiju would have had his first glimpse of the city he was to live in for close on two decades.

The geographical location is all that remains of the Mangalore that Ben Yiju saw: the city was sacked several times in the sixteenth century and afterwards, and today almost no trace of its medieval incarnation remains. The area that is now known as 'the old port' lies forgotten below the city's bustling business centres and market-places, at the bottom of a steep slope. It still bears the Persian name Bandar, 'port', but today its few moments of life are provided by a ferry that connects it to the fishing-villages on the sand-spit across the lagoon. Otherwise its docks are largely untenanted and its wharfs empty, except for a handful of barges and river-boats.

When Ben Yiju arrived in Mangalore there was probably a stretch of sand where the docks stand now: the ships that plied the Indian Ocean appear to have been designed to be beached rather than docked—the better to profit from the fine sands that lined those waters. The merchants of the city, including the large community of expatriate Middle Easterners, would have had their offices and godowns close to the Bandar, probably on the hillside above, from where they could keep an eye on incoming ships.

The expatriate merchant community of Mangalore was a large one, by all accounts. The Moroccan traveller Ibn Battuta, who visited the city some two hundred years after Ben Yiju, reports that it was the practice of most merchants from the Yemen and Persia to disembark there; the Sumatrans, on the other hand, along with others from the eastern reaches of the Indian Ocean, seem to have preferred other cities, such as Calicut and 'Fandarîna', a little further to the south. At the time of Ibn Battuta's visit the Muslims of Mangalore (and by implication) the foreign merchants, together formed a community of about 4,000 people, 'living in a suburb alongside the town.'

The settlement of foreigners at Mangalore was by no means the largest or the most cosmopolitan on the coast: Calicut, a couple of hundred miles to the south, appears to have housed an even larger and more diverse merchant community. There were thirteen 'Chinese' vessels in the harbour when Ibn Battuta's ship docked there, and he reports that the city regularly had visitors from 'China, Sumatra, Ceylon, the Maldives, Yemen, and Fars [Iran]...' A Portuguese sailor, Duarte Barbosa, who visited the city early in the sixteenth century, noted that the city's merchants included 'Arabs, Persians, Guzarates, Khorasanys, and Decanys', who were known collectively as pardesis, or foreigners. The pardesi merchants were not all itinerant traders; many of them were expatriates who had settled in Malabar for considerable lengths of time. '[They] possess in this place wives and children,' noted Barbosa, 'and ships for sailing to all parts with all kinds of goods.'

The lifestyle of these merchants was so sumptuous that even sophisticated travellers and courtiers, accustomed to the refinements of great royal courts, were taken by surprise upon being admitted into their circle. The Persian ambassador 'Abd al-Razzaq al-Samarqandi, for instance, was greatly impressed by their style of living when he passed through Malabar in 1442AD. 'They dress themselves in magnificent apparel,' he wrote, 'after the manner of the Arabs, and manifest luxury in every particular...' Duarte Barbosa was to echo those observations a few decades later: 'They have large houses and many servants: they are very luxurious in eating, drinking and sleeping...'

There is nothing now anywhere within sight of the Bandar to lend credence to the great mansions and residences that Ibn Battuta and Duarte Barbosa spoke of. Now the roads and lanes around the wharfs fall quiet after sunset; shipping offices shut their doors, coffee-shops pull down their shutters, and only a few passengers waiting to cross to the sand-spit remain. The imagination baulks at the thought that the Bandar once drew merchants and mariners from distant corners of the world.

For many hundreds of years, however, large numbers of foreign visitors congregated in the cities of this region, and it was Middle Eastern travellers who gave this part of the coast the Arabic name 'Malabâr'. In their usage, the name was applied loosely to the southern third of the west coast, an area that shares many aspects of a common culture. But Malabar is also divided into several smaller sub-regions, among which the district around Mangalore is perhaps the most distinctive. Being the northernmost frontier of the Malabar region, it forms a kind of double-headed causeway, between the south and the north on the one hand, and between the seaboard and the interior on the other. With its southerly neighbours it shares certain distinctive cultural institutions, as well as legacies bequeathed by a parallel history—forms of personal law based on principles of matrilineal descent, for instance, are common to many groups throughout the area. But in other respects its affiliations lie with the adjoining districts of the north and the east, and with the state of Karnataka, of which it is a part. Its speech, for example, while forming a distinct language in its own right, is also closely akin to Kannada, the majority language of the state.

The language of Mangalore is called Tuḷu, and it is one of the five siblings of the Dravidian family of languages: it is rich in folk traditions and oral literature, but it does not possess a script of its own and is usually transcribed in Kannada. It is this language that has given the area around Mangalore its name, Tuḷunâḍ: like so many other parts of the the subcontinent, it forms a cultural area which is distinctive and singular, while being at the same time closely enmeshed with its neighbours in an intricate network of differences.

Tulunad is not large—it is contained today within a single district—yet it has had a distinct identity since antiquity. Writing in Alexandria in the second century AD, the Greek geographer Ptolemy referred to it as 'Olokhoira'—a term which is thought to have been derived from 'Alupa', the name of Tulunad's long-lived ruling dynasty. For several hundreds of years, until the beginning of the fifteenth century, Tulunad's Alupa rulers succeeded in preserving a measure of autonomy for their small kingdom by picking allies judiciously among the various dynasties that followed each other to power in the hinterlands. It was during their rule that Mangalore became one of the principal ports of the Indian Ocean, and it was in the reign of the king Kavi Alupendra that Ben Yiju came to the city.

Ben Yiju, like so many other Middle Eastern merchants, was drawn to Mangalore because of the economic opportunities it offered as one of the premier ports of an extremely wealthy hinterland: a region that was well endowed with industrial crafts, apart from being one of the richest spice-producing territories of the medieval world. Later the area's wealth was to attract the much less welcome attention of the European maritime and colonial powers and it was in the course of the struggles that ensued that Mangalore came to lose virtually every trace of its extraordinary past.

But appropriately, Mangalore does not treat its lost history as a matter of crippling melancholy: it has always been a busy, bustling kind of place, and today it is again a thriving, relatively prosperous city. Its ancient connections with the Arab world have bequeathed it a more useful legacy than a mere collection of artefacts: thousands of its residents are now employed in the Persian Gulf, and its suburbs are awash with evidence of the extravagant spending of its expatriates.

In this, as in many other intangible ways, Mangalore remains perfectly true to its medieval heritage.

# 2

THE MORNING AFTER I arrived in Mangalore, one day in the summer of 1990, I found myself sitting in a coffee-shop, waiting eagerly to make the acquaintance of a scholar whose name I had heard mentioned several times on the way to the coast. I had been told on excellent authority, that this, if anyone, was the person who might be able to help me with the riddle of the Slave of MS H.6: his name was Professor B. A. Viveka Rai and he was one of the world's foremost experts on Tulu folklore and philology. For me a great deal depended on this meeting, for my unravelling of the Slave's history had been blocked by an intractable etymological puzzle: the mystery of his name.

My introduction to the puzzle had come from Goitein's translation of the letter that Khalaf ibn Ishaq wrote to Ben Yiju in 1139: at the end of the letter Khalaf happened to mention the Slave's name while sending him 'plentiful greetings'. In the translated version of the letter, the name was spelt 'Bama' and it was accompanied by a footnote which explained that Goitein had been informed by a specialist on Indian history that 'Bama' was 'vernacular for Brahma'.

At the time, captivated as I was by the letter's contents, I had not given the name any further thought. Years later, when I began working directly with the Geniza material, I discovered that the name occurred in some half-dozen documents, written by various different people—Madmun, Khalaf, and of course Ben Yiju himself. The name was always spelt in exactly the same way, with three characters: B-M-H. But of these, the last, 'H', was actually not a consonant at all, but rather an open vowel that is known in Arabic as the 'teh marbûta'. The three characters of the Slave's name were therefore, properly speaking, B-M-A. Clearly there was another vowel between the first and second characters, but it was never specified in the documents, for in Judæo-Arabic, as in written Arabic and Hebrew, short vowels are not usually indicated in handwritten texts. The vowel could have been 'u', 'o' or any other—one guess was about as good as another. In spelling the name as 'Bama', Goitein had taken it to be 'a', on the plausible assumption, as his footnote explained, that the word was derived from 'Brahma'.

My first doubts about the exact nature of the relationship between the letters 'B-M-A' and the word 'Brahma' arose while reading some medieval accounts of India written by Arab travellers and geographers. The word 'Brahma' and its cognates occurred often in those texts and it soon became clear to me that it had been well-known amongst educated people in the Middle East and North Africa since long before Ben Yiju's time. Indeed, it seemed possible that there had been an accepted way of spelling the word in Arabic through much of the Middle Ages.

Against that background it began to seem increasingly improbable that Ben Yiju and his friends would spell the Slave's name as B-M-A if it were actually 'Brahma'. If other Arabic-speakers, many of whom had never even visited India, could spell the term accurately, then surely Ben Yiju, who lived so many years in Mangalore, would have been able to do just as well, or better.

Clearly then, the Slave's name was not 'Brahma'. But it might of course have been a diminutive or a shortened form of that word. Yet if that were so, I began to suspect, the word would probably have had a slightly different shape: as a diminutive 'Bama' did not have a very convincing sound to my ear. I could think offhand of several other forms, from various Indian languages, which sounded a great deal more persuasive.

At this point I realized that finding an acceptable solution to the puzzle of the Slave's name was a crucial step in determining his identity—indeed, it was the one clue that could provide some indication of where he was born and what his background and social circumstances were. But the moment that door swung open, a fresh host of problems appeared. The first among them was that there was no indication anywhere about what language the Slave was named in: after all the B-M-A of the documents could have had its origins in any one of several different languages.

Such information as I was able to find about slavery in the region of the Indian Ocean during the Middle Ages only served to complicate the matter further. The slave trade in Ben Yiju's time was a wide-ranging transcontinental phenomenon, with substantial numbers of slaves being brought into the region from distant parts of the world: from as far away as Central Asia, the Russian steppes, the Transcaucasus and Europe. Mangalore, as a major port, would certainly have been a way station for many of the slave-traders, and it was entirely conceivable that the Slave of MS H.6 had been brought there from the Middle East. Indeed, an obscure reference in one of Ben Yiju's letters suggested that he himself may have had occasional dealings with certain slave-traders from the Yemeni town of Zabid.

At the same time, there were good reasons to believe that the Slave of MS H.6 was in fact from the region of Mangalore rather than the Middle East: the spelling of his name for one. The slaves who were traded in the markets of Egypt were usually given Arabic names of a distinctive kind—Lu'lu ('Pearl'), for instance, and Jawhar ('Jewel')—names that served to locate them on the margins of human society. But the Slave's name, whatever it was, did not bear any resemblance to the usual run of Middle-Eastern slave-names, and indeed it did not appear to be of Arabic, or even Semitic origin. While the evidence was not conclusive by any means, it was certainly strong enough to suggest that Goitein was right in assuming that the Slave's origins lay in India.

But that only served to bring me back to that mysterious acrostic: B-M-A. After puzzling over those three characters for a long time, one last possibility suggested itself to me. In Judæo-Arabic (as in Arabic) a doubled letter is often represented by a single character. It was possible then that the single 'M' in the name was actually doing duty for two of its kind. If that were so, it would mean that there were actually four letters in the name: 'B-M-M-A'. If I then filled in a short vowel after the first letter, the result was 'Bomma' or 'Bamma', names which I knew to be common in certain parts of India.

Proceeding on that premise I began to look through the names in medieval inscriptions from Tulunad and its surrounding regions. The results were immediately gratifying. I discovered, for instance, that a man called Mâsaleya Bamma, who had worked as a servant for a group of warriors, had been killed, not far from Tulunad, just a few years before Ben Yiju arrived in India. His masters had caused an inscription to be carved in his memory: it was dated 15 June 1126, and it was discovered in a village about two hundred miles north-east of Mangalore. Another inscription from the same region records the name of one Seṭṭi Bamma, a man from a merchant family, who married a pious wife. From those, as well as other sources, it was soon clear to me that 'Bamma' had been a common name in that region in the Middle Ages.

Slowly the indications mounted, and just before leaving for Mangalore I came to be convinced that the Slave's name was actually 'Bamma' or something of the sort. Exciting as the discovery was, it also brought me to a standstill: I did not know whether the name was derived from the Sanskrit word 'Brahma' or from some other source, and I had no idea at all whether it might reveal anything about the Slave's origins by linking him to any particular caste, religion or social group.

And so it was not without reason that I found myself balancing on the edge of my seat, as I waited for Professor Viveka Rai that morning in Mangalore: it was as though the identity of an elusive and mysterious acquaintance were soon to be revealed.

# 3

PROFESSOR RAI PROVED to be a soft-spoken, youngish man, tall and bespectacled, with an air of gentle abstraction that hid a precise and immensely erudite mind. He quickly became absorbed in my account of my unravelling of the Slave's name, and it was not till I reached the end of the story that he broke in to correct me.

I had come very close, he said, in fact I was only fractionally off the mark: the Slave's name was probably 'Bomma' rather than 'Bamma'.

The name Bomma had once had wide currency within Tulu culture, he explained, and even until a generation or so ago it was commonly encountered in and around Mangalore. Over the last few decades it had passed out of general use as a personal name, but it was still preserved in the titles of various groups and clans in Tulunad. As for the derivation of the word, he said, it was a matter of critical importance to the story of the Slave, but the trail that led to its source was a circuitous one, traversing a wide swathe of Tulu culture and history.

The people of Tulunad were divided, by tradition, into several castes, ranging over a broad expanse of the social hierarchy— from immensely rich and powerful landlords, to poor peasants and Untouchables. But divided as they were by rank and occupation, the Tuluva still shared certain aspects of a common culture: they all spoke Tulu, for one, and they also followed matrilineal rules of inheritance for certain kinds of property. Equally, they shared in the worship of certain spirit-deities known as Bhûtas.

By tradition, each of the Tuluva castes and communities played a designated role in the Bhuta-cult, one providing financial support, for instance, one tending the shrines, others performing the ritual dances and so on. The cult was closely tied to the land, and those who did not own or work on the land—Brahmins, for example—were generally excluded from its rituals and celebrations. These rites were not just occasional events; they followed closely upon each other, even weekly in some seasons, and so the people who participated in them were thrust together at frequent and regular intervals. As a result they stood apart, in some ways, from the other people in the region: their rites, their language, and their matrilineal institutions gave them a distinct identity within the diverse population that had drifted into Tulunad over the centuries.

The Brahmins, on the other hand, played an important role in an altogether different aspect of the religious life of the region;

they were the standard-bearers of the Pan-Indian Hindu tradition which formed the complementary other half of the folk-religion of Tulunad. As in much of India, the religious fabric of Tulunad was woven from an equal mixture of local forms of worship (the Bhuta-cult, in this case) and the high Sanskritic tradition. Along with its innumerable Bhuta shrines, Tulunad had its fair share and more of temples dedicated to the gods of the Sanskritic pantheon, and most of the Tuluva people participated enthusiastically in the worship of both sets of deities. There was no contradiction in this, of course, for to them Bhutas and Sanskritic deities represented aspects of divine and supernatural power that shaded gently and imperceptibly into each other. Indeed, under the benign cover of that shade, there was a good deal of trafficking between the two pantheons: some Bhuta deities would occasionally appear within the mists of high Sanskritism, while others fell from favour and vanished into the netherworld.

It is somewhere in those dark and shaded regions that the pedigree of the name Bomma takes a sudden and unexpected turn and leads away from the Brahma of classical Hindu mythology towards a deity of an altogether different character.

And, by an extraordinary coincidence, said Professor Rai, I could, if I wanted, have a glimpse of that deity, a darshan, that very night.

'How?' I asked, imagining a night-time vigil at a lonely shrine in a deserted and wind-tossed palm-grove. 'Is there going to be a secret exorcism?'

Professor Rai cast me a quizzical glance. 'On television,' came the laconic answer. 'In a film that's going to be broadcast this evening.'

The film was in black and white; it had been made some ten or fifteen years earlier by some friends of Professor Rai's, and besides serving as an advisor for it, he had also written some of the songs. It was one of a small number of films made in the Tulu language, and it was based upon the most celebrated folk-epic of Tulunad, a legend that recounted the deeds of two heroic brothers, Koti and Chennaya.

When the heroes appeared on the screen, I noticed they were carrying small sickles around their waists. The sickles were symbols of their caste, Professor Rai explained, for the brothers were Billavas, whose traditional occupation was that of brewing and extracting palm-wine or toddy.

Through no fault of their own, Koti and Chennaya eventually ran afoul of the ruler of their area—a man of the Bant caste, which was traditionally the landowning community of Tulunad. Soon their enmity became very bitter, and the brothers were sentenced to exile and sent away from their native region. Before setting out on their travels, however, they managed to go to the shrine of their personal deity to seek his succour and protection.

'Now watch this scene,' said Professor Viveka Rai with a smile, as the two heroes went up to the shrine and began to sing a devotional song, their hands joined in prayer.

Listening carefully, I soon recognized a name that was repeated over and over again; it was the only word I could understand, for the song was, of course, in Tulu. This particular word, however, was instantly familiar: it was none other than 'Brahma'.

Having recognized the name of the deity, I thought I knew exactly what I would see when the camera turned towards the shrine's interior: a four-headed, four-armed image, accompanied by a goose—the traditional representation of the god Brahma according to the rules of classical iconography. But instead, to my great surprise, the camera revealed an elongated wooden figure, with curling moustaches, holding a sword in one hand. It was an image of a warrior-deity, wholly unrelated to the Brahma of the Sanskritic pantheon.

I knew now why Professor Rai had smiled so enigmatically: the deity of the Tulu myth was evidently not the same as the Brahma of classical Sanskritic mythology.

Later, he explained that the god depicted in the film had originally had a wholly different name: he was Berme or Bermeru, the principal figure in the pantheon of Tuluva Bhuta-deities. Over time, with the growth of Brahminical influence, the Tulu deity Berme had slowly become assimilated to the Sanskritic deity 'Brahma'.

So the pedigree of the name Bomma in the Tulu language probably stretched back to a time before the deities of Tulunad had begun to assume Sanskritic incarnations: in all likelihood it was a diminutive of 'Berme', the figure who stood at the pinnacle of the Tuluva pantheon of Bhuta-spirits.

It took me a long time afterwards to check the steps in the argument and to work out the consequences that this derivation would have for the history of the Slave. Speculative though it was, the argument seemed to lead to the conclusion that the Slave of MS H.6 had been born into one of the several matrilineal communities which played a part in the Bhuta-cult of Tulunad.

It was thus that Bomma finally came of age and was ready at last to become a protagonist in his own story.

# 4

THERE IS ONLY one incident in Bomma's life of which we have direct knowledge. By yet another odd coincidence this story also happens to be the one with which Bomma entered the annals of the Geniza: the letter which recounts it is the earliest known document in which his name is mentioned.

The principal reason why the story has been preserved is that it was set in Aden, and thus earned a mention in a letter written by Madmun. The letter in question is one of the most important that Madmun ever wrote, for he included in it a description of an unusual and dramatic event: a piratical raid on Aden by the ruler of a small kingdom in the Persian Gulf. Yet in the letter, Bomma's doings actually took precedence over the raid and from the pattern of Madmun's narrative it seems possible that Bomma was actually present, on his very first appearance in the Geniza, at the enactment of a full-blooded historical event, more than a thousand miles from his home in Mangalore.

The events which Madmun described in his letter are known to have occurred in 1135, so the letter must have been written soon afterwards. Bomma happened to be in Aden at the time because Ben Yiju had sent him there on an expedition that appears to have been partly a business trip and partly a shopping jaunt. When he returned to Mangalore, he brought back a large consignment of goods, including a whole array of clothes, household utensils and presents for Ben Yiju and his family. Altogether, the purchases that Bomma made in Aden added up to about ninety-three dinars. It is worth adding— since it is only human to be curious about other people's shopping expenses—that this sum of money could have paid the wages of a mason or builder for more than two and a half years, or it could have bought somewhere in the region of 2,000 kilograms of meat or 3,000 kilograms of olive oil. Alternatively, with the addition of a mere seven dinars it would even have served to ransom the lives of three adult Spaniards at the going rates.

Ben Yiju gave Bomma a fairly generous monthly allowance while he was in Aden—two dinars a month, or about the wage of any artisan—but the figure was a paltry one compared to the sums of money that Bomma was handling in Aden. Madmun's accounts show that the consignment of goods that Bomma took with him to Aden fetched about 685 dinars on the market: a sum that would have been large enough to buy Ben Yiju a splendid mansion in Fustat. But of course, Bomma for his part must have been accustomed to dealing with sums of that kind, for it is worth remembering that this small fortune represents the value of just a single consignment of goods sent from Mangalore to Aden—probably no more than a season's earnings, and that, too, for a newly established merchant with a business of relatively modest size.

The volume of goods and money that flowed through Aden was evidently huge and it was the prospect of those rich pickings that made the city the object of a raid in the year of Bomma's visit.

The expedition was not perhaps an event that properly deserves to be called 'historic', yet it did make a deep enough impression to earn a mention in a chronicle written by the historian Ibn Mujawwir a century and a half later. As for Ben Yiju's friends in Aden, at least two of them were moved to describe it at length in their correspondence: Madmun, when he wrote to Ben Yiju, and Khalaf ibn Ishaq, in a letter to their common friend, the traveller Abu Sa'id Halfon.

The villains of the piece, by common agreement, were the rulers of Kish (or, properly speaking, Qaiṣ), an island at the mouth of the Straits of Hormuz, which by virtue of its location commanded the sea routes to the Persian Gulf. The Amirs of that tiny kingdom were amongst the most ambitious representatives of a breed that proliferated in the Indian Ocean: pirates, who made their living by preying on the rich merchant vessels that plied the trade-routes.

Pirate attacks were fairly frequent occurrences throughout the Indian Ocean, and there are several references to them in the Geniza documents. The Amirs of Kish, for example, had sent raiding expeditions up and down the coasts of Africa and India, and even so distant a port as Cambay in Gujarat had to take special precautions to guard against their depredations. But an attack such as the raid on Aden was unusual, for generally the pirates tried not to invite the attention of the stronger rulers of the region. Even at their worst, they were a nuisance rather than a serious threat to commerce, and neither they nor any of the powers of the Indian Ocean, no matter how large or well-armed, ever tried to gain control of the seas or to take over the trade routes by force.

But clearly, on this occasion the pirates of Kish decided that they would try to expand their horizons. First, at the beginning of the seafaring season, the Amir's son sent an expedition to Aden demanding a part of the city in payment for protection against a raid. When the demand was refused he sent a fleet of fifteen ships which forced their way into the city's harbour and took up positions there. The raiding party did not attempt a landing; their intention was to capture a merchant vessel on its way back from India.

As it turned out, their plan failed. Aden's soldiers gave the pirates no respite in the time they spent waiting in the harbour; they were constantly attacked and harried, many were killed in skirmishes, while others died of hunger and thirst. At length, when a prize of the kind they had been waiting for finally did appear on the horizon, it happened to be a convoy of two ships that belonged to one of the most powerful merchants in the Indian Ocean—a trader called Abû'l Qâsim Râmisht, who was based in the Persian Gulf port of Sirâf.

Ramisht of Siraf was rich beyond computation: a contemporary writer relates that one of his clerks alone was worth half a million dinars, while the silver plate his family ate out of weighed approximately one ton. Ramisht's trading empire stretched as far as China, and the traders of Aden and Mangalore, including Ben Yiju and his friends, frequently used his ships for transporting their merchandise.

The pirates from Kish attacked Ramisht's ships as soon as they appeared in the harbour. But the city sent troops to their rescue and eventually the pirates were driven back to the open sea where they quickly dispersed. 'Thus God did not give them victory,' wrote Madmun in his letter, 'and they made off in the most ignominious way, after having suffered great losses and humiliation...'

But despite his obvious delight in the pirates' defeat, it was not the raid that was uppermost in Madmun's mind when he wrote the letter: that honour was kept for Bomma. It appears that Bomma, determined to enjoy his trip to the full, had spent his wages on an extended drinking bout during which he had presented himself several times in Madmun's office, demanding money.

This is how Madmun put it:

And after that he [Bomma] started on other things. He said: Give me more money, [what I have] is not enough. He took 4 months money from me, eight dînârs. Often he would come here, very drunk, and would not listen to a word I said.'

We cannot be sure of course, but it is not impossible that the Adenese soldiers were cheered into battle by a drunken Bomma, standing on the shore and waving a flask.

## 5

THE GENIZA DOCUMENTS provide no indication at all about how Bomma's path came to cross Ben Yiju's. From certain references in Ben Yiju's papers it seems likely that he took Bomma into his service as a business agent and helper soon after he had established himself as a trader in Mangalore.

Whatever the circumstances of their meeting, the terms under which Bomma entered Ben Yiju's service were probably entirely different from those suggested by the word 'slavery' today: their arrangement was probably more that of patron and client than master and slave, as that relationship is now understood. If this seems curious, it is largely because the medieval idea of slavery tends to confound contemporary conceptions, both of servitude and of its mirrored counter-image, individual freedom.

In the Middle Ages institutions of servitude took many forms, and they all differed from 'slavery' as it came to be practised after the European colonial expansion of the sixteenth century. In the lifetimes of Bomma and Ben Yiju, servitude was a part of a very flexible set of hierarchies and it often followed a logic completely contrary to that which modern expectations suggest. In the Middle East and northern India, for instance, slavery was the principal means of recruitment into some of the most privileged sectors of the army and the bureaucracy. For those who made their way up through that route, 'slavery' was thus often a kind of career opening, a way of gaining entry into the highest levels of government.

At a more modest level, merchants and traders often used slavery as a means of finding apprentices and agents; the 'slaves' who entered employment in this way often took a share of their firm's profits and could generally be sure of obtaining manumission, and even of attaining the rank of partner or shareholder.

In the medieval world, slavery was also often used as a means of creating fictive ties of kinship between people who were otherwise unrelated. Amongst the Jewish merchants of medieval Cairo, for instance, as with many tribes in Africa, slaves were sometimes gradually incorporated into their masters' households and came to be counted as members of their families. Equally, in some vocations, the lines of demarcation between apprentice, disciple and bondsman were so thin as to be invisible: to be initiated into certain crafts, aspirants had to voluntarily surrender a part of their freedom to their teachers.

Perhaps the most elusive aspect of medieval slavery is its role as spiritual metaphor, as an instrument of the religious imagination. In south India, amongst the pietist and fiercely egalitarian Vachanakara saint-poets of Bomma's own lifetime, for example, slavery was often used as an image to represent the devotee's quest for God: through the transforming power of metaphor the poets became their Lord's servants and lovers, androgynous in their longing; slaves, searching for their master with a passion that dissolved selfhood, wealth, caste and gender, indeed, difference itself. In their poetry it was slavery that was the paradoxical embodiment of perfect freedom; the image that represented the very notion of relationship, of human bonds, as well the possibility of their transcendence.

This imagery would not have been unfamiliar to Ben Yiju. He and his friends were all orthodox, observant Jews, strongly aware of their distinctive religious identity. But they were also part of the Arabic-speaking world, and the everyday language of their religious life was one they shared with the Muslims of that region: when they invoked the name of God in their writings it was usually as Allah, and more often than not their invocations were in Arabic forms, such as inshâ'allâh and al-ḥamdul-illâh. Distinct though their faith was, it was still a part of the religious world of the Middle East—and that world was being turned upside down by the Sûfis, the mystics of Islam.

Judaism too soon felt the impact of Sufism. Shortly before Ben Yiju's lifetime the Jewish mystic Baḥya Ibn Paqûda composed The Duties of the Heart, a treatise culled largely from Sufi sources, which was to have a powerful impact on the world of Mediterranean Judaism, infusing generations of readers with Sufi ideas. Egypt, in particular, was a fertile ground for mystical beliefs and over the centuries, many members of the congregation of the Synagogue of Ben Ezra in Fustat were to be greatly influenced by Sufism. Abraham Maimonides (1186–1237), a son of the great Talmudist Moses Maimonides, even composed a Sufi text of his own, and he is known to have remarked once that the Sufis were 'worthier disciples of the Prophets of Israel than were the Jews of his time.'

Trve?

Most Sufis would have regarded the Vachanakara saint-poets as pantheistic and blasphemous in their desire to merge themselves in their Lord. Their own conceptions of extinction (fanâ) and subsistence (baqâ) always assumed an utterly transcendent God. Yet they would probably have acknowledged a commonality in the nature of their quest, and they would certainly have perceived a similarity in their use of poetic imagery.

For the Sufis as for the Vachanakaras, the notion of being held by bonds was one of the central metaphors of religious life. They too drew some of their most powerful images from the institution of slavery: metaphors of perfect devotion and love strung together in an intensely charged, often erotic, spiritual imagery. Thus, in Sufi tradition, Sultan Mahmud of Ghazni, the eleventh-century soldier who built an immense empire in Central Asia, was not the fearsome and bloodthirsty conqueror that he is often depicted to be, but rather a symbol of mystical longing, because of the ties that bound him to his soldier-slave, Ayaz. A Sufi parable relates that once when the mythical bird, Huma, the touch of whose shadow was said to confer kingdoms, appeared in the skies above Mahmud's army, the emperor found himself suddenly alone, abandoned by his most faithful courtiers—all except one, Ayaz. While the others went chasing after Homa's shadow, Ayaz stepped instead into the shadow of Mahmud, so that his master might know that for him the world contained no better kingdom. In the telling of the Sufis, that perfect act of love works a miraculous spiritual transformation and the world-conquering Mahmud becomes 'the slave of his slave'.

The imagery of the Vachanakaras and the Sufis would seem to be far distant from Bomma and Ben Yiju, and the workaday relations of a trader and his business agent. But even the most mundane institutions have their life-giving myths and against the setting of that distant backdrop of legend and metaphor, the elements of slavery in the ties that bound an apprentice to a master craftsman, an accountant to a merchant, would have appeared, perhaps, not as demeaning bonds, but rather as links that were in some small way ennobling—human connections, pledges of commitment, in relationships that could just as well have been a matter of a mere exchange of coinage.

Bomma may never have known of the saint-poets of his time and their teachings, but he would certainly have been intimately acquainted with some of that great range of popular traditions and folk beliefs which upturn and invert the categories of Sanskritic Hinduism. Ben Yiju, for his part, as a man of wide education, would probably have read something of the Sufis, and he may well have shared in some of the beliefs and practices that have always formed the hidden and subversive counter-image of the orthodox religions of the Middle East: the exorcism cults, the magical rites, the customs of visiting saints' graves and suchlike. Amongst the members of his community in Cairo, those ideas and practices formed almost as important a part of daily observance as the orthodox aspects of their religion: a very large number of the documents in the Geniza, for example, consist of magical formulae, and treatises related to esoteric rites.

It was probably those inarticulate counter-beliefs, rather than the formal conversion that Bomma probably had to undergo while in Ben Yiju's service, that eventually became a small patch of level ground between them: the matrilineally-descended Tulu and the patriarchal Jew who would otherwise seem to stand on different sides of an unbridgeable chasm.

## 6

WHILE MAKING MY way around Mangalore, I often had Bhuta-shrines pointed out to me: there seemed to be dozens of them dotted around the city and its outskirts, small, modest structures, perched on columns, gazing serenely over gardens and palm-groves. They were always brightly-painted and well-tended, and often there were flowers and offerings lying upon their thresholds.

As the days passed I became increasingly curious about the religious practices that were enshrined in those structures. But when I began to look for material I discovered that as far as most of the standard authorities were concerned the Bhuta-cult did not count as 'religion' at all: it fell far beneath the Himalayan gaze of canonical Hindu practice. Such detailed studies as there were, I found, were mainly carried out by anthropologists and folklorists; it was otherwise often dismissed as mere 'devil worship' and superstition.

Then, one day, quite unexpectedly, I was presented with an opportunity to visit a shrine when a taxi I was travelling in stopped beside one, on the outskirts of the city. The driver apologized for the delay and said it would only be a matter of minutes: it was just that he always made it a point to stop there, when he was passing by, to say a quick prayer and make an offering. The shrine was a very famous one, he explained, and visitors were always welcome.

The shrine stood on top of a mound, a small tiled enclosure surrounded by ricefields, with the sand-dunes of the coastline visible in the near distance. The image inside was a very simple one, a white, circular mask with an emblematic face depicted on it in bold black lines: a pair of curling moustaches were its most striking features. On either side of the mask was a sword, propped upright against the wall.

The spot was tended by a Pujari, a large, friendly man with gold rings in his ears, who touched our foreheads with sandalwood and gave us handfuls of prasad. He explained, through the taxi-driver, who translated into Hindi for my benefit, that once every year the Bhuta who dwelt in the shrine emerged to take possession of him. A great festival was held then, and after a long cycle of dances and rituals the spirit was ceremonially restored to its proper place within the shrine.

It was an extraordinary experience, the Pujari said, to feel the Bhuta within him, for the spirit of that shrine was greatly renowned for his powers. Many stories surrounded the shrine, he said, and one of them had become famous throughout the region. Years ago, when Mangalore's new port was completed, the government's engineers had started building a road to connect it with the city, some fifteen miles to the south. But soon, to general consternation, it was discovered that if the work were to go ahead as planned, the road would cut straight through the shrine. The people of the area had protested mightily, but the government had ignored them and sent out notices of eviction to all the farmers who owned land in the area. Sure enough, one day, the engineers arrived with their machines to begin the work of demolition. But then there was a miracle: their bulldozers were immobilized soon after they had begun to move; they were frozen to the ground before they could touch the shrine's walls. Completely confounded, the engineers called in high-ranking government officers, and technicians with yard-long degrees. But there was nothing anyone could do and eventually, admitting defeat, they agreed to divert the road so that it skirted around the shrine.

This was a story everyone knew, said the Pujari, and every year at the time of the festival, people would tell it over and over again.

Later, when we got back into the car, the driver asked me to look through the rear window. I watched the road carefully as we drove away, and from the angle of its curve it did indeed look as though it had made a loop to spare the shrine.

Smiling, the driver said: 'Have you ever heard of anything like that?'

A recollection suddenly stirred in my mind.

'Yes,' I said, 'I heard a very similar story once. In Egypt.'

He nodded politely, but disbelief was written all over his face.

## 7

BOMMA WAS NOT to remain long in Aden: he came back carrying the very letter in which Madmun described his drunken revelries to Ben Yiju. Madmun's complaints, however, do not appear to have excited an excess of wrath in Ben Yiju, and nor did Madmun himself bear a grudge for long—in his later letters he was always careful to include a word of friendly greeting for Bomma. Over the years, as Bomma's role as business agent grew in importance, Ben Yiju's friends in Aden came to regard him with increasing respect, and in time Khalaf ibn Ishaq even began to prefix his name with the title of 'Shaikh'.

Ben Yiju, for his part, seems to have reposed a great deal of trust in Bomma from the very beginning of their association.

When Bomma went to Aden in 1135, for example, he was responsible not only for delivering a quantity of merchandise, but also for bringing back a large shipment of goods for Ben Yiju and his household. Among the items he brought back were four ḥaṣîra-s or mats from Berbera (in modern Somaliland), a leather table cloth of a special kind on which chess and other games could be played, an iron frying-pan, a sieve, a large quantity of soap, two Egyptian gowns, and several presents from Madmun, such as sugar, raisins, 'a quire of white paper', as well as a piece of coral for Ben Yiju's son, Surur.

The two 'gowns' that Bomma brought back with him were almost certainly intended for Ben Yiju himself, because it is clear from other references in his correspondence that he, like his fellow expatriates, continued to wear the customary garments of the Middle East—robes, turbans and the like—all the while that he was in India. The people of Malabar, on the other hand, generally left the upper parts of their bodies bare, men and women alike—their preferred markers of class distinction being ornaments and jewellery rather than articles of clothing. 'They wear only bandages around the middle,' wrote 'Abd al-Razzaq al-Samarqandi, '[garments] called lankoutah, which descend from the navel to above the knee.'

To Middle Eastern merchants like Ben Yiju, on the other hand, being properly dressed meant wearing a double layer of clothing, first a loose undergarment and over that a robe, a garment that covered the covering, so to speak, of the body's nakedness and rendered it fit to be seen in public: anything less they would have considered immodest.

Ben Yiju, for one, was clearly fastidious about his clothing. Several of his letters and accounts mention imported Egyptian robes and fine Alexandrian cloaks, while others refer to lengths of cloth and kerchiefs that may have served as turbans. He clearly had a reputation as a careful dresser amongst his friends; Madmun, for instance, when sending him a shawl once, thought it prudent to extol its qualities: 'I have also for my own part, sent for you...a fine new Dîbîqî shawl, with nicely worked borders—an appropriate garment for men of eminence.'

The most important of his imports, as far as Ben Yiju was concerned, was paper. In the Malabar, as in most parts of India, the material most commonly used for writing at that time was the palm-leaf—paper appears to have been rare and difficult to obtain. In the Middle East, on the other hand, paper was being produced on a large scale by the eleventh century, and like most of his contemporaries Ben Yiju must have grown accustomed to it in his youth. Once he moved to India his friends went to great pains to keep him well-supplied and packages of paper were included in virtually every shipment sent to him from Aden.

Ben Yiju's friends evidently knew of the great importance that writing played in his life, and they often showed a touching concern for the quality of the paper they bought on his behalf. Madmun, for example, once assured him that the Egyptian Ṭalḥî paper he had acquired for him was 'the best available', and on another occasion he proudly assured him that his two large quires of Sulṭânî paper were so fine that 'no one has its like'. Madmun was not exaggerating: the paper he and his friends sent to Ben Yiju was of so matchless a quality that even today, eight hundred years later, a surprising number of those sheets are still marvellously well-preserved, despite the heat and humidity they have endured in the course of their travels between Egypt and India.

That Ben Yiju was a man with a taste for good living is also evident in many of his household purchases. Much of his kitchenware for instance, was imported from Aden—even such things as frying-pans and sieves—and he also regularly had crockery, soap, goblets and glasses sent out from the Middle East. For his mats he looked to the Horn of Africa, and he is known to have purchased at least one velvet-like carpet, made in Gujarat.

Ben Yiju also seems to have had something of a sweet tooth. His friends often sent him raisins and other delicacies such as nougat and dates. The various kinds of palm-sugar that were in use in Malabar were clearly not to his taste, and his friends seem to have had standing instructions to dispatch Middle Eastern cane-sugar with every consignment of goods.

If it seems curious today that somebody should import sugar into sweet-besotted India, it would not have appeared so in Ben Yiju's time. In the Middle Ages, it was Egypt that pioneered the large-scale production of cane-sugar and its exports of that commodity were such that in many parts of Asia to this day some sugar products bear names that link them to an Egyptian source. No matter that the Arabic word sukkar (hence the English 'sugar') is itself ultimately derived from a Sanskrit source: today, throughout north India, crystallized sugar is still known as misri in commemoration of traders like Ben Yiju and the tastes they imported from Masr.

# 8

I HAD NOT been in Mangalore long when Bomma provided me with an insight into the uses of History.

Among the many castes and religious communities of the Malabar coast few have a past as interesting as that of a small group of fisher-folk, known variously by the name of 'Magavîra' or 'Mogêra'. The sixteenth-century Portuguese traveller, Duarte Barbosa, left a brief description of them in his account of his travels on the Malabar coast. He referred to them as 'another sect of people still lower [than the others]...which they call moguer...These people for the most part get their living at sea, they are mariners and fishermen.' But although the Magavira were traditionally linked with fishing, Barbosa notes that many amongst the group had also prospered in trade: 'They are some of them very rich men who have got ships with which they navigate, for they gain much money with the Moors.'

According to tradition, the Magaviras have always been closely linked with the foreign merchants and mariners who came to trade in Malabar. As fishermen they would perhaps have been the natural associates of Middle Eastern sailors and seafarers, partly because of their expertise in sailing, and partly because of their position on the margins of the caste-structure of Hindu society which would have rendered them free of the restrictions that might have hampered other groups in trade and travel. Some amongst them were clearly successful traders and ship-owners in their own right, but there must also have been a great many others who entered the maritime trade in different ways—by becoming seamen on trading vessels, for example, or by apprenticing themselves or their children to foreign merchants and traders.

Soon after I reached Mangalore, I discovered that the Magavira's links with the foreign merchants were commemorated in the traditional symbol of their distinctive identity—a deity known as the Bobbariya-bhuta, deemed by legend to be the spirit of a Muslim mariner and trader who died at sea. No Magavira settlement, I learnt, was without its Bobbariya-shrine: usually a simple pillar and platform of stone, with a wooden mace propped up beside it.

On hearing of this I was immediately seized with curiosity, and I soon succeeded in prevailing upon a friend, Father D'Souza—a Jesuit priest and a specialist in the religious traditions of Tulunad—to take me to visit a Bobbariya-shrine. Being from the region himself, it was a relatively easy matter for my friend to arrange a visit, particularly because, as a teacher in one of Mangalore's best-known colleges, he had many Magavira students. The nearest Bobbariya-shrine, he told me, was in the fishing-village on the sand-spit that lay directly across the lagoon from Mangalore's old port. A few days later, after he had told his students to expect us, we boarded the ferry together and crossed the lagoon.

Two of my friend's students were waiting for us when the ferry docked at the jetty. They received us with a shy, schoolboy deference, clearly overcome with both delight and apprehension at the prospect of a visit from a teacher. The village lay behind them, tranquil in the shade of a thick awning of coconut palms, its pathways cool and sandy, the open sea visible on the far side of the sand-spit.

I soon discovered that this village was quite unlike the fishing-villages I had seen in other parts of the country: there were no shanties, no palm-leaf huts—everything around us, the well-tended gardens and the pastel-coloured bungalows with their thickets of TV aerials, spoke of quietly prosperous, suburban lives. The walls of the houses around us were painted prominently with the letter 'Om' and other symbols of Hindu piety, and it was hard to tell that this had once been a fishing-village whose inhabitants had been relegated to the bottom edge of orthodox caste society. It was clear that this was a community whose fortunes had soared in recent years.

After walking through the village, we were led to one of the students' houses: a large new bungalow, with an 'Om' painted prominently on its walls. Chairs had been set out in the garden in expectation of our arrival, and we were greeted at the gate by a group of our host's female relatives. The family was a large one, our host explained—his mother was the senior member of her matrilineal clan, so several of her sisters and aunts shared their house. His mother was a small, capable-looking woman, with an air of quiet command: within a few minutes of our arrival she had orchestrated the presentation of several trayloads of snacks and coconut water.

Towards the end of our visit, I prompted my Jesuit friend to ask her a question, in Tulu: had she ever encountered the name Bomma amongst people of the Magavira caste?

She was taken by surprise at the question. No, she said, shaking her head vigorously, you would never hear a name like that in the village nowadays; all the boys here had names like Ramesh and Vivek now, proper names, like you heard on the radio and TV.

But then, casting her mind back, she smiled and said, well, yes, in the old days, sometimes, you would hear names like that. But not now, never: everybody had good Sanskritic names nowadays—names like 'Bomma' belonged to a time when very few people in the community had been educated and fishermen had ranked at the bottom of the social ladder.

She broke off to say a few words to her son, and he ran into the house and fetched an illustrated pamphlet. She opened it reverently, to the first page, her face lit by a smile of intense pride: it was a short history of the village, financed and published by community subscription.

Towards sunset we bid the family goodbye and set out to visit the Bobbariya-shrine. It was almost dark now and silver television-shadows flickered across the lanes as we walked past. With glares of disapproval, our guides led us quickly past a small but boisterous crowd that had gathered at a corner toddy-shop: there had been a lot of drinking in the community once, they explained, but now the younger people were trying to put an end to the sale of alcohol in their village.

When we were still a fair distance away, one of the students pointed towards the lights of the shrine. It looked nothing like any of the simple Bhuta-temples that dotted the countryside around Mangalore: it was a large, modern building, modelled after a classical Hindu temple. When we approached it, I noticed that its walls bore the posters of a fundamentalist Hindu political organization, an upper-caste group notorious for its anti-Muslim rhetoric: it was a clear indication that this community, so long relegated to the peripheries of the Hindu order, had now resolved to use a political short-cut to break into the Sanskritic fold. Having transformed its social and economic position it was now laying claim to the future, in the best tradition of liberalism, by discovering a History to replace the past.

Leading us into the shrine, the students told us how the old structure had been torn down and the new one built, at great expense, by community subscription. It was not really a Bhuta-shrine any more, they explained proudly: it had become a real

Hindu temple, and the main place in it was now reserved for Vishnu, the most Brahminical of gods.

Once we went inside, however, it turned out that one small aspect of the past had ingeniously escaped re-invention: the spirit of the Bobbariya-bhuta still remained in the temple although in a wholly altered guise. The students pointed him out to us; he stood beside the image of Vishnu, but at a slightly lower level. The old symbols, the mace and the pillar, had been dispensed with: he was now represented by an image, like a Hindu god.

I had to struggle with myself to keep from applauding the ironies enshrined in that temple. The past had revenged itself on the present: it had slipped the spirit of an Arab Muslim trader past the watchful eyes of Hindu zealots and installed it within the Sanskritic pantheon.

As we walked away, I was glad to think that in Bomma's lifetime the inhabitants of that sand-spit would have had no need of a temple to lay claim to the future: they would in fact have been witnesses to a great revival in an entirely different aspect of Hinduism—the tradition of personal devotion which, time and time again, has confronted the hierarchical ideology of caste with a critique of millenarian power.

In Bomma's own lifetime, no more than a few hundred miles from his home town, one of the most remarkable of those egalitarian devotional movements was being sung into existence by the Vachanakara saint-poets, who had set about creating fraternal communities of artisans and working people, defying the rules of caste and kinship.

Had Bomma passed his childhood on that sand-spit, as he may well have done, he might have heard one of the Vachanakara's songs being sung where today that brand-new temple projects its shadow into the future and the past:

> With a whole temple
> in this body
> where's the need
> for another?
>
> No one asked
> for two.

# 9

BEN YIJU'S LIFE in Mangalore was extraordinarily rich in relationships: his connection with Ashu, for one, brought an entire constellation of relatives with it. Dealing with this newly-acquired family was not always easy for Ben Yiju: indeed, on the one occasion on which he is known to have called down God's curses it was on someone who was probably connected to him through Ashu's family.

The person in question was a kârdâr, an agent or middleman who helped traders in the buying of spices and other commodities. But the story of this particular kardar, as it develops in Ben Yiju's papers, is a good deal more complex than an account of the dealings between an exporter and his agent.

The plot begins with a set of accounts (reckoned in coins called mithqâls and units of weight called bahârs). 'The kâ(r)dâr, may God curse him,' Ben Yiju scribbled, 'owed...14 mithqâls, for two bahârs of cardamom. He did not deliver the cardamom, so I bought...two bahârs from Fandarîna as a substitute, for 17 mithqâls.'

What had happened, evidently, is that the kardar had offered to procure a consignment of cardamom at unusually low rates, and Ben Yiju, in the hope of making a quick killing, had given him an advance to make the purchase. But when the time came to send the consignment on to Aden, the kardar defaulted, and Ben Yiju was caught in the classic bind of a futures speculator: he had gambled on a commodity that hadn't turned up in time.

In fact, Ben Yiju had committed not just his own but some of his partners' money too, and they took a dim view of the matter when they found out. Yusuf ibn Abraham wrote to say: 'You, my master, mentioned that you approached the kârdâl gently in order to get something for us back for him. Perhaps you should threaten him that here in Aden we [disgrace] anyone that owes us something and does not fulfil his commitments...If he does not pay, we shall issue an official letter of [censure] and send it to him, so that he will become aware of his crime.'

Even Khalaf ibn Ishaq, the closest of Ben Yiju's friends, reacted sharply on this occasion. 'As for the delay [in the delivery of the kârdâr's cardamom],' he wrote to Ben Yiju, 'may God curse him. I have spoken to some people about the matter, and they said to me that the cardamom was yours, and we had no share in it. It is a matter between you and the kârdâr: deal with this thing individually with him, separately from us.' Clearly Khalaf had a suspicion that there was something in Ben Yiju's relationship with the kardar that did not quite meet the eye, and he was evidently resentful of the way Ben Yiju had involved him in a set of private arrangements. He and Yusuf continued to press Ben Yiju for several years, but to no avail: there is no indication that they ever recouped their losses in this affair.

The clue that gives away the nature of Ben Yiju's connection with the kardar lies in a throwaway line on a tiny scrap of paper: it suggests that the kardar was a close relative of Ashu's brother, the man whom Ben Yiju referred to as 'Nair'.

Nair is mentioned only twice in all of Ben Yiju's papers, and in both cases the references consist of little more than the name and a couple of brief words. Yet, if there was anyone who was located at the precise juncture where Ben Yiju's instilled responses could be expected to run into conflict with Ashu's, it was none other than her brother, Nair. By the matrilineal reckoning of the Nairs the bond between brother and sister was far more important than the tie between husband and wife; in their practice it was a woman's brother and not her husband who was entitled to the guardianship of her children. Thus, by the customs of Ashu's community it would have been Nair who held the reins of authority over her progeny; it would have been he—not Ben Yiju—who played Laius to their Oedipus.

It was not without reason therefore that Khalaf suspected that the relationship between Ben Yiju and the kardar extended beyond their business dealings: it could well be that Ben Yiju had given him the advance principally because Ashu or Nair had asked him to make a loan to their relative. It is even possible that the reason why the money was never returned was that her family saw it as their compensation for forgoing their rights over her children. But of course the simplest of solutions is also the most likely: that the kardar had effected a clever swindle by exploiting a family connection.

Fortunately for Ben Yiju, his social and professional life in Mangalore extended far beyond his family. The names that are sprinkled through his papers speak of a startlingly diverse network of associations: entered into a file, the list would yield nothing to the Rolodex of an international businessman today.

Some of Ben Yiju's closest business connections, for instance, lay with a group of merchants whom he and his friends in Aden referred to as the 'Bâniyân of Mangalore'—Hindu Gujaratis of the 'Vania' or trading caste. Long active in the Indian Ocean trade, Gujarati merchants had plied the trade routes for centuries, all the way from Aden to Malacca, and they exerted a powerful influence on the flow of certain goods and commodities. They evidently played a significant role in the economy of Malabar in Ben Yiju's time, and were probably instrumental in the management of its international trade. Madmun, for one, was on cordial terms with several members of the Gujarati trading community of Mangalore, whom he kept informed of trends in the markets of the Middle East. He, in turn, appears to have handed on those connections to Ben Yiju when he set up his business in Mangalore. Over the years, Ben Yiju often served as a courier for Madmun, delivering letters as well as messages and greetings to the 'Bâniyân of Manjalûr', and on occasion he even brokered joint entrepreneurial ventures between them and Madmun.

In matters of business, Ben Yiju's networks appear to have been wholly indifferent to many of those boundaries that are today thought to mark social, religious and geographical divisions. Madmun, for instance, is known once to have proposed a joint venture between himself and three traders in Mangalore, each of different social or geographical origins—one a Muslim, one a Gujarati Vania, and the third a member of the landowning caste of Tulunad. Equally, the ships that Ben Yiju and his friends used for transporting their goods were owned by a wide variety of people. Among the many nâkhudas or ship-owners who are mentioned in Ben Yiju's papers, there is one Pattani-Swami, probably the head of a merchant guild or caste, a man called Nambiar, evidently from Kerala, and many others, including of course 'Abd al-Qasim Ramisht of Siraf. The ties forged by trade were so close that Madmun's kinsman, the nakhuda Mahruz (in a letter written for him by Ben Yiju), once remarked of a ship-owner called 'Tinbu', probably of Tamil extraction, that, 'between him and me there are bonds of inseparable friendship and brotherhood.'

Ben Yiju's closest affiliations in Mangalore would of course have lain with the community with which he shared his spoken language and his taste in food and clothing: the expatriate Muslim Arabs who were resident in the city—indeed, for most purposes he would have counted himself as one of them. Muslim traders figure frequently in his papers, as do the names of the Arab sailors and ships' captains who carried his letters and brought him news from other parts of the world.

Ben Yiju's business interests also brought him into contact with a large number of agents and retailers, and those relationships seem to have often overlapped with the kinship networks of his household. In addition, Ben Yiju was also closely connected with a group of metalworkers specializing in certain bronze objects and utensils which were much in demand in Aden. The names of these craftsmen, who appear to have been Brahmins from Tamilnad, often figure in Ben Yiju's household accounts, and it is possible that their workshop was attached to his warehouse.

The vast network of relationships that Ben Yiju fitted himself into in Mangalore was clearly not a set of random associations: on the contrary, it appears to have had a life of its own, the links being transmitted between generations of merchants, just as they were from Madmun to Ben Yiju. Membership in the network evidently involved binding understandings of a kind that permitted individuals to commit large sums of money to joint undertakings, even in circumstances where there was no legal redress—understandings that clearly presuppose free and direct communications between the participants, despite their cultural, religious and linguistic differences.

But here lies a mystery into which Ben Yiju's papers offer no insight at all: the question of what language the merchants used in their dealings with each other. Madmun's letters, for instance, leave no doubt that he wrote regularly to his friends amongst the 'Bâniyân' of Mangalore. But what neither Madmun nor Ben Yiju ever reveal is what language they used in communicating with their Indian associates.

As far as their letters are concerned, the most likely solution is that they conducted their correspondence largely in Arabic, making liberal use of scribes and translators. But that still leaves a host of other questions unanswered: what language did Ben Yiju speak with Ashu, for instance? Or for that matter, how did he communicate with Bomma, or with the merchants from various regions in India and beyond, with whom, given the nature of his occupation, he must have had to do business? On the evidence of his papers there is no reason to suppose that he ever acquired fluency in Tulu or any other south Indian language: such Indian words that found their way into his writings were all of northern derivation. Indeed, learning any one language would not have solved Ben Yiju's problems of communication, for the Indians he dealt with evidently came from several different linguistic regions.

Common sense suggests that in an area as large and as diverse as the Indian Ocean, business could not possibly have been conducted in Tulu, Arabic, Gujarati or indeed any tongue that was native to a single group of traders; to function at all the language of everyday business would have had to be both simpler and much more widely dispersed than any ordinary language. Given what we know about the practices of Arab traders in other multilingual areas (the Mediterranean for example) it seems likely that the problem was resolved by using a trading argot, or an elaborated pidgin language. The Arab geographer Mas'ûdî refers, in fact, to a language called 'Lâriyya', which he describes as being spoken along much of the length of the Malabar Coast. Since no language corresponding to that name is known to exist, it is possible that he was referring to a pidgin, one that was possibly compounded largely of Perso-Arabic and north Indian elements, and was in use amongst merchants and traders all along the coast.

It is easy enough to imagine that Ben Yiju used a specialized trade language to communicate with his fellow merchants in Mangalore: the difficulties lie in imagining how he and Ashu adapted that argot to the demands of a marital bedroom.

## 10

IN ALL THE eighteen years or more that Ben Yiju spent in India he appears never to have ventured away from the Malabar coast; it would seem that he had no interest at all in the peninsular mainland, on the other side of the mountains. Yet Ben Yiju and his circle did not conceive of Malabar as a region separate from the mainland; as far as they were concerned Mangalore fell squarely within a loosely defined entity that covered most of the subcontinent, a territory which they referred to in their letters, as al-Hind, or bilâd al-Hind, 'the country of India.' Thus to speak of Ben Yiju living in 'India', or to refer to Bomma as an 'Indian' is not to anticipate the borders and the political vocabulary of the twentieth century: those words are merely direct translations of the terms used by Ben Yiju and his friends.

Ben Yiju's usage, in this regard, was entirely in keeping with the academic geography of the Arabic-speaking world, in which the Indian subcontinent, beginning at the eastern border of Sind and extending as far as Assam and even beyond, was generally referred to as one unit, al-Hind, just as China was al-Ṣîn. There is of course, an intriguing asymmetry in this coupling, for China was recognizably a single state, an empire whose provinces were merely constituent parts of a larger political unity. India, on the other hand, as the Arab geographers well knew, was divided into several kingdoms, large and small, and in their descriptions they were always careful to demarcate the various regions and principalities of the subcontinent. Yet, at the same time, Arab travellers and geographers appear to have believed that al-Hind had a centre, recognized by all its kings and its various different regions. For several centuries they seem to have been more or less in agreement on this subject: al-Hind, as they knew it, was centred in the domain of a king called the Ballahrâ, whose capital lay in the city of 'Mankîr'.

The names are puzzling, for they do not correspond to any known political entity, and they occur even in periods when there were frequent shifts in the centres of power in the subcontinent. An eminent scholar of Arabic, Doctor S. M. H. Nainar, has suggested that 'Mankîr' corresponded to the town of Malkhed, now in Andhra Pradesh, and that 'Ballahrâ' was an Arabic representation of 'Vallabharaja' (Supreme King), a title assumed successively by the rulers of several dynasties in the region of south-west India. But if those were indeed the original

282

referents of those terms, in time they seem to have drifted away from their roots until they eventually became metaphors which represented, in a fashion easily comprehensible within Arab culture, India's idiosyncratic ways of giving shape to its luxuriant diversity.

In any event, there can be no doubt that in the Middle Ages, for much of the outside world, the geographical centre of India lay somewhere in the southern peninsula; to Ben Yiju in Mangalore, the northern reaches of the subcontinent may have seemed much like a distant and unruly frontier, on the outer edge of the country. For his own part he appears to have been perfectly content to stay within the Malabar coast, an area that was itself divided into a number of small kingdoms and principalities. It was within the interlinked principalities of the coast that Ben Yiju conducted his business: scattered references in his papers link him with a handful of towns, all in the Malabar—places with names such as 'Fandarîna', 'Dahfattan' and 'Jurbattan', all within easy reach of Mangalore.

Today the names of those towns carry not the faintest resonance, but in the Middle Ages they were well-known all along the trade routes of the Indian Ocean and even beyond, to scholars, geographers and travellers throughout the Arabic-speaking world. They have long since vanished from the map, at least in their earlier incarnations, but unlike many other medieval ports of the Indian Ocean 'Fandarîna', 'Jurbattan' and 'Dahfattan' did not quite disappear: they still exist, not as spectacular ruins, but in the most unexpected avatar of all; as small towns and villages which have prospered, once again, because of their connections with the far side of the Indian Ocean—in this instance the oil-producing countries of the Arab world. They lie hidden in quiet anonymity within the hills and palm-shaded lagoons of the coast, amongst some of the most beautiful landscapes in the Indian subcontinent.

The place that was known as 'Jurbattan' in medieval Arabic texts has been identified as Srikandapuram, a small town in the foothills of the Western Ghats, about a hundred miles south of Mangalore. The hills around it fall amongst the richest pepper- and spice-producing areas in Malabar, and in the Middle Ages the town probably served as a major market where traders could buy directly from producers. The hills possess other attractions as well: a cool, fresh climate and streams and valleys of a kind which even then, long before romanticism made nature an object to marvel at, could not have failed to capture the attention of those who saw them for the first time.

'Jurbattan's' combination of blessings was clearly an attractive one, and Ben Yiju appears to have visited it regularly—partly to buy spices and partly, no doubt, for pleasure. For Ashu the town may have held an added allurement: being a Nair, it is more than likely that she had relatives in the area and it may have been at her insistence that those visits were undertaken.

For Ashu, Ben Yiju, and their children, the journey would have begun with a voyage down the coast from Mangalore, for a distance of a hundred miles or so. After about two days at sea, their boat would have entered a harbour whose Arabic name, 'Budfattan', was probably a garbled rendition of Baliapatam.

Today a quiet palm-fringed road leads north towards Baliapatam from the nearby city of Cannanore, past large houses, some new, with sharp geometric lines and bright pastel colours that speak eloquently of their owners' affiliations with the Persian Gulf. Dotted between them are a few older and gentler dwellings, with carved wooden doorposts and tall red-tiled roofs that sweep high above the palm-tops. The road comes to a halt beside what appears to be a small duck-pond, with two diesel-pumps perched inexplicably on its edge. A wharf lies hidden under weeds on the bank, and on the far side there is a channel that connects it to a wide expanse of water: a great river-mouth that was once the harbour of 'Budfattan'.

From there Ashu and her family would probably have travelled upstream on river-boats as far as the current permitted, before beginning the overland journey into the hills, along the pathway to 'Jurbattan'. For much of the distance they would have used palanquins carried by porters—then the preferred mode of travel amongst those who could afford it.

Today the road that leads to Srikandapuram runs through vast plantations of cashew and rubber, with low-slung motels and lavish residences dotted along its curves and bends. In the valleys, crops seem to grow in two layers, thriving on the exuberant fertility of the land, with coconut and areca palms soaring above long rows of velvety green pepper-vines. Srikandapuram, when it arrives, proves to be a thriving little town: the houses on the outskirts are bright and new, with sleek shops and sparkling clinics dotted between them. The bazaar at the centre, however, seems to belong to another time; the shops are crammed with sacks of spices, and their owners sit cross-legged behind low counters, bargaining at leisure with their customers.

A narrow road leads south from Srikandapuram, at a precipitous angle, and, after a rapid descent to the coast, it passes through several places that would have been well-known to Ben Yiju, long before he came to India. The 'Dahfattan' of his correspondence lies at the junction of two rivers, a small cluster of Gulf-gilded houses known to the world today as Dharmadam. A little further down the coast is Pantalayini Kollam, the 'Fandarîna' of the Arabs, and the 'Pandarene' of the Portuguese, a quiet town on the sea, a little to the north of Calicut.

The journey ends on a beach between 'Fandarîna' and Calicut, at a small fishing-village, hidden behind the shelter of a sand-dune. It is a quiet spot: a few catamarans and fishing-boats lie on a great crescent of sand, a vast beach that is usually empty, except when the fishing-boats come in. The village is called Kappkadavu and on one side of it beside the road is a worn white marker which tells the passer-by that this was where Vasco da Gama landed, on his first voyage to India, on 17 May 1498—some three hundred and fifty years after Ben Yiju left Mangalore.

Within a few years of that day the knell had been struck for the world that had brought Bomma, Ben Yiju and Ashu together, and another age had begun in which the crossing of their paths would seem so unlikely that its very possibility would all but disappear from human memory.

A bare two years after Vasco da Gama's voyage a Portuguese fleet led by Pedro Alvarez Cabral arrived on the Malabar coast. Cabral delivered a letter from the king of Portugal to the Samudri (Samudra-raja or Sea-king), the Hindu ruler of the city-state of Calicut, demanding that he expel all Muslims from his kingdom as they were enemies of the 'Holy Faith'. He met with a blank refusal; then as afterwards the Samudri steadfastly maintained that Calicut had always been open to everyone who wished to trade there—the Portuguese were welcome to as much pepper as they liked, so long as they bought it at cost price. The Portuguese fleet sailed away, but not before Calicut had been subjected to a two-day bombardment. A year or so later Vasco da Gama returned with another, much more powerful Portuguese fleet and demanded once again that all Muslim traders be expelled from Calicut.

During those early years the peoples who had traditionally

participated in the Indian Ocean trade were taken completely by surprise. In all the centuries in which it had flourished and grown, no state or king or ruling power had ever before tried to gain control of the Indian Ocean trade by force of arms. The territorial and dynastic ambitions that were pursued with such determination on land were generally not allowed to spill over into the sea.

Within the Western historiographical record the unarmed character of the Indian Ocean trade is often represented as a lack, or failure, one that invited the intervention of Europe, with its increasing proficiency in war. When a defeat is as complete as was that of the trading cultures of the Indian Ocean, it is hard to allow the vanquished the dignity of nuances of choice and preference. Yet it is worth allowing for the possibility that the peaceful traditions of the oceanic trade may have been, in a quiet and inarticulate way, the product of a rare cultural choice—one that may have owed a great deal to the pacifist customs and beliefs of the Gujarati Jains and Vanias who played such an important part in it. At the time, at least one European was moved to bewilderment by the unfamiliar mores of the region; a response more honest perhaps than the trust in historical inevitability that has supplanted it since. 'The heathen [of Gujarat]', wrote Tomé Pires, early in the sixteenth century, 'held that they must never kill anyone, nor must they have armed men in their company. If they were captured and [their captors] wanted to kill them all, they did not resist. This is the Gujarat law among the heathen.'

It was because of those singular traditions, perhaps, that the rulers of the Indian Ocean ports were utterly confounded by the demands and actions of the Portuguese. Having long been accustomed to the tradesman's rules of bargaining and compromise they tried time and time again to reach an understanding with the Europeans—only to discover, as one historian has put it, that the choice was 'between resistance and submission; co-operation was not offered.' Unable to compete in the Indian Ocean trade by purely commercial means, the Europeans were bent on taking control of it by aggression, pure and distilled, by unleashing violence on a scale unprecedented on those shores. As far as the Portuguese were concerned, they had declared a proprietorial right over the Indian Ocean: since none of the peoples who lived around it had thought to claim ownership of it before their arrival, they could not expect the right of free passage in it now.

By the time the trading nations of the Indian Ocean began to realize that their old understandings had been rendered defunct by the Europeans it was already too late. In 1509AD the fate of that ancient trading culture was sealed in a naval engagement that was sadly, perhaps pathetically, evocative of its ethos: a trans-continental fleet, hastily put together by the Muslim potentate of Gujarat, the Hindu ruler of Calicut, and the Sultan of Egypt was attacked and defeated by a Portuguese force off the shores of Diu, in Gujarat. As always, the determination of a small, united band of soldiers triumphed easily over the rich confusions that accompany a culture of accommodation and compromise.

The battle proved decisive; the Indian and Egyptian ships were put to flight and the Portuguese never again had to face a serious naval challenge in the Indian Ocean until the arrival of the Dutch. Soon, the remains of the civilization that had brought Ben Yiju to Mangalore were devoured by that unquenchable, demonic thirst that has raged ever since, for almost five hundred years, over the Indian Ocean, the Arabian Sea and the Persian Gulf.

# GOING BACK

# 1

LOOKING BACK, IT seems to me now that until I returned in 1988, Shaikh Musa had not realized himself quite how dramatically things had changed in Lataifa since my departure, seven years ago. As we sat talking on that rainy evening when I arrived at his door, I had the impression that he was looking back with new eyes, as though the sharp edges of my memories had served to strip away a dense layer of accretions that had gathered upon his surroundings, like bark.

But it was not long before he entered gleefully into the spirit of my wonderment, and soon enough he even began to manufacture little surprises of his own for our mutual delectation. The morning after I arrived, for example, he sent his grandson scampering out of the room on a secret errand while we were eating our breakfast. When the boy returned he had a tray in his hands, and sitting in the middle of it, like a crown on a cushion, was a richly-beaded glass of iced water.

Shaikh Musa paused to listen to the tinkling of the ice as he handed me the glass. 'You see,' he said, 'even my brother's house is full of wonders now.'

It was a couple of years since his brother's refrigerator had arrived: it had been bought for him by Mabrouk, his eldest son, who was away working in Iraq. He had come home at the end of Ramadan and one afternoon he and some other boys had hired a truck and gone off to Damanhour without telling anyone. When they returned in the evening, the truck was carrying a refrigerator, hidden under a sheet of tarpaulin.

That was two years ago, of course, when refrigerators were still a novelty. Now, every other house in Lataifa had one: many people had iced water sent out to them in the fields while they were working, and some families froze the meat they sacrificed at 'Eid so that it lasted for weeks on end.

Shaikh Musa's was one of the few houses that had neither a refrigerator nor a television set. Being deprived of something that other people took for granted was a novel and unaccustomed experience for Shaikh Musa's family: they had never really felt the lack of anything before since they owned more land than most. But of course, you couldn't buy things like refrigerators with earnings that came solely from the land: for money of that kind you had to go away, to Iraq, or Libya, or the Gulf.

Once, on his way to the market in Damanhour, Shaikh Musa had stopped to look at the showroom where his nephew Mabrouk had bought his refrigerator. It was near the centre of the city, a huge place, with glass windows, and salesmen dressed in suits and ties. He looked in through the window, but he hadn't felt like walking in, dressed in his fellah's jallabeyya and cap. It had come as a shock to think that boys like Mabrouk thought nothing of going into places like that, no matter what they were wearing: they went straight in and sent those effendis running around, in their suits and ties, obeying their orders.

Shaikh Musa laughed when I reminded him how Mabrouk had once come running up to my room to take me to see the

'Indian machine' his father had just bought; how everyone had been taken by surprise because Mabrouk was thought to be one of the shyest boys in the hamlet.

'You wouldn't know him now,' said Shaikh Musa. 'He's so smart, he can paint the air with his talk.'

Most of the young men of Mabrouk's generation were gone now, all but a handful of the eager schoolboys who had never tired of asking me questions; those who had stayed back had done so only because they hadn't been able to find a job 'outside', or because their families needed them on the land. There had always been a fair number of people from the area working 'outside' of course, but now it was different; it was as though half the working population had taken leave of the land and surged into Iraq.

The flow had started in the early 1980s, a couple of years after the beginning of the war between Iraq and Iran; by then Iraq's own men were all tied up on one front or another, in Iran or Kurdistan, and it was desperately in need of labour to sustain its economy. For several years around that time it had been very easy for an Egyptian to find a job there; recruiters and contractors had gone from village to village looking for young men who were willing to work 'outside'. People had left in truckloads: it was said at one time that there were maybe two or three million Egyptian workers in Iraq, as much as a sixth of that country's population. It was as if the two nations had dissolved into each other.

But after the war with Iran ended the Iraqis had immediately changed their policies; their demobilized soldiers had wanted jobs and in order to encourage the migrant workers to go home the government had made new rules and regulations, restricting the flow of currency and suchlike. Over the last couple of years it had become hard to find jobs 'outside' and some of the young men who had left had begun to trickle back to their villages.

Ahmed, Shaikh Musa's son, had often talked of going to work in Iraq: he'd wanted to give his wife and children some of those things that other people had in their houses—a television set, a fridge, perhaps a washing-machine. But Shaikh Musa had refused to hear of it—he had told him to put the idea out of his head, at least so long as he was alive. The reports he had heard about Iraq had made him anxious: the boys who went there often came back with frightening stories—about how they had been mistreated by their employers and sometimes even attacked on the streets by complete strangers for no apparent reason. The Iraqis resented immigrants, he had been told, because they took their jobs away while they were fighting on the front: their 'souls had sickened', as the saying went, through their long years of war, and they often vented their rage on foreigners.

After hearing those stories Shaikh Musa had resolved not to let Ahmed go. What if something were to happen to him while he was away, far from home? He had already lost one son; he couldn't bear to think of another picture hanging on his guest-room wall, next to Hasan's. He would not let Ahmed go, no matter how many things other people had in their houses; it would have been good to have those things, but it was better to live in peace and fear God.

Of my younger friends in Lataifa, only one still remained in Egypt—Jabir. Shaikh Musa had sent word to his family early that morning, knowing that I would want to see him, but Jabir had gone to Damanhour and wouldn't be back till later.

'Why hasn't Jabir "gone outside"?' I asked. 'Didn't he ever want to leave?'

'Oh yes,' said Shaikh Musa. 'He went once for a few months

while he was in college and he's wanted to go back again, ever since. All his friends are outside; even Mohammad, his younger brother, has gone away to Jordan. Jabir has been trying to go for a long time, but it just hasn't worked out, that's all. But I heard recently that he's found something and might be on his way soon; they say he's even cut his beard in preparation.'

'His beard!' I said in surprise. 'Did Jabir have a beard?'

Shaikh Musa laughed perfunctorily.

Yes, he said, Jabir had sported a beard for a while; he had grown it while he was away in college, in the city of Tanta. Everybody was amazed when he came back for the holidays one summer, wearing a beard cut in a distinctively Muslim style. It wasn't surprising of course, for Jabir was always a bright boy, and all the brightest young men had beards now, and many wore white robes as well. Jabir sometimes delivered the Friday sermon in the mosque nowadays, and he too wore white robes for those occasions. He surprised everyone the first time, including his uncle Ustaz Mustafa: he had looked very impressive in his flowing robes and beard, and he had spoken very well too, in beautiful language, with many quotations and polished phrases. Ustaz Mustafa, who had studied in Alexandria himself, said later that Jabir had spoken well even by the standards of the best orators in colleges and universities.

There was a touch of awe in Shaikh Musa's voice now, as though he could barely imagine the courage and daring it would cost a fellah boy, from a tiny hamlet like Lataifa, to throw himself into the flamboyantly public world of religious debate in cities and universities. Even though he was as devout and strictly observant a Muslim as any, he would not have dreamed of entering that milieu: he considered himself far too ignorant to enter into learned arguments on matters of religion.

After breakfast we set off to visit Abu-'Ali: Shaikh Musa had decided that since he was the person who had first introduced me to Lataifa, it was only fitting that I go to see him before visiting any other house in the hamlet. The prospect of meeting Abu-'Ali was not one that I had looked forward to, yet once we set out for his house I was suddenly curious, eager to know how he and his family had fared.

From what I knew of Abu-'Ali, I was fairly sure that his fortunes had more than kept pace with his neighbours', but I was still taken by surprise when I entered his compound. A large soaring new carapace had sprouted upon the dilapidated, low-slung house of my memories: the room on the roof, where I had gone to live, years ago, was now a part of a brightly-painted, three-storeyed mansion. The spindly old moped that had so miraculously borne Abu-'Ali to and from Damanhour had vanished, and in its place was a gleaming new Toyota pick-up truck.

But Abu-'Ali himself was exactly where he had always been, stationed at a vantage point overlooking the road. The moment we stepped into his compound, he thrust his head out of a window, sidewise, like the MGM lion. 'Come in, come in,' he roared. 'Where have you been all these years, my son? Come in, come in and bring blessings upon my house.'

At the sound of his voice his wife rushed out to the veranda to greet us, followed closely by several new additions to her family. Smiling warmly, sweet-natured as ever, she welcomed me into the house, and after we had gone through a long list of salutations, she introduced me to three recently-recruited daughters-in-law, pointing out each of their children, one by one.

I had half-expected, from the unforeseen vigour of Abu-'Ali's roar of welcome, that he too would come hurrying out to the veranda to greet us; in my imagination I had already pictured our meeting, quailing at the thought of exchanging hugs and kisses across the billowing expanse of his stomach. But although Abu-'Ali's roars continued unabated, he failed to materialize in person. I discovered why when his wife led us to him. He had grown even fatter than I remembered; the image of an engorged python that I had carried away with me seemed pitifully inadequate for the sight I was now confronted with: his stomach now soared above him like a dirigible in flight as he lay on his back, intermittently flapping his hands and feet as though to propel himself through the air.

His voice had not been diminished by his body's spectacular enlargement however, and as soon as we were seated he began to chronicle the growth of his family's fortunes in an earth-shaking roar. Much as I had expected, he had been one of the first people in the area to become aware of the opportunities that were opening up in Iraq, during the war with Iran. He had sent his eldest son there soon after I left, and the others had followed, one by one. He had taken care, however, to make sure that they were never all away at the same time; he needed at least one of them at home, to help with the running of his business in Lataifa. There was a lot to take care of, for he was no longer just a shopkeeper now—with the money his sons had sent back from Iraq, he had bought two pick-up trucks and gone into transportation. So successful had the venture been that he was now thinking of setting up yet another business, a flour-mill, or maybe even a modern poultry-farm.

While telling us the story, Abu-'Ali broke off from time to time to order his daughters-in-law and grandchildren to fetch some of the things his sons had brought back from Iraq.

Following his instructions, they filed obediently through the guest-room, carrying by turns a TV set, a food processor, a handful of calculators, a transistor radio, a couple of cassette-players, a pen that was also a flashlight, a watch that could play tunes, a key-ring that answered to a handclap and several other such objects. Shaikh Musa and I stared awestruck as these possessions floated past us like helots gazing at the spoils of Pharaoh.

When the parade was complete, at Abu-'Ali's instructions his wife led us upstairs to show us their newly built apartments. Following her up the staircase I was assaulted by a sudden sensation of dislocation, as though I had vaulted between different epochs. The dirt and chaos of the ground floor, where Abu-'Ali and his wife lived, the flies, the grime, and the scattered goats' droppings, stopped abruptly halfway up the staircase: above that point the floors were meticulously clean, covered in mosaic tiles. Where my room, the old chicken-coop, had once stood, there was now a large kitchen, adjoining an opulently furnished bedroom. It had been incorporated into a complex of four apartments, one for each of Abu-'Ali's sons. The three who were married had already moved in, but the youngest, a bachelor, still lived downstairs whenever he came home on visits from Iraq.

We visited the apartments of her three married sons in turn. They were very alike, each with a drawing-room appointed with ornate furnishings of a kind often seen in the windows of shops in Cairo and Alexandria. It was evident that the drawing-rooms were rarely used, and even Abu-'Ali's wife seemed hesitant to step past their curtained doorways. Neither Shaikh Musa nor I could bring ourselves to go in, despite her repeated urgings: it was clear that Abu-'Ali had now risen to an estate where neither his family nor his neighbours were fit to use his furniture.

Such were his gleanings from that distant war.

2

IT WAS PROBABLY in the mid-1140s or so that Ben Yiju began to think seriously of returning to the Middle East. At about that time, after many years of silence, he finally received news about a member of his family—his younger brother Mubashshir, who as far as he knew was still living in their homeland, Ifriqiya.

The news probably arrived in the wake of a long series of distressing reports from Ifriqiya: travelling merchants and friends had probably kept Ben Yiju informed of how the region had been laid waste by Sicilian armies over the last several years, and of how its people had been stricken by famine and disease. Thus Ben Yiju was probably already in a state of severe anxiety when his friend Khalaf wrote to him from Aden, relaying a brief message from his brother.

'Shaikh Abû Isḥâq ibn Yûsuf arrived here this year,' wrote Khalaf. 'He reports that your brother Mubashshir has arrived in Egypt. He has asked for passage to join you: you should know this.'

Ben Yiju's papers provide only indirect signs of the impact this message had on him. His immediate response was probably to write to his friends to beg for more news, and to ask them to make arrangements for the payment of his brother's onward passage to India. As it turned out, however, his efforts were to no avail: his brother proved more elusive than he had expected and his inquiries met with nothing more than comforting generalities. 'Concerning the news of your brother Mubashshir,' Khalaf wrote back, 'he is well, but he has not arrived here [in Aden] yet.'

But Ben Yiju must have continued to write to his friends at regular intervals, asking them to persist in their inquiries, and to do what they could to send Mubashshir on to Mangalore. For their part, they appear to have exerted themselves on both counts, but despite their efforts Mubashshir continued to absent himself from Aden. Eventually, despairing of success, Yusuf ibn Abraham wrote back to say: 'My master [Ben Yijû] mentioned Mubashshir, his brother [in his letter]: he has not arrived here in all this time, and nor have I seen a letter for my master from Egypt. If such a letter for my master appears his servant will send it to him.' Later in the same letter he added the ominous comment: 'As for the news of Egypt, my master will hear it from the traders…'

Such news as Ben Yiju received from the Middle East could only have given him further cause for anxiety. From 1143 onwards, for several successive years, his homeland, Ifriqiya, had been the target of attacks launched by King Roger II of Sicily. Disease and famine had followed upon these raids and large numbers of people fled the region. Along with a substantial section of the Jewish population of Ifriqiya, the Ben Yiju family was swept away from Mahdia at about this time and deposited in Sicily—unbeknownst to their brother Abraham, living in quiet, untroubled prosperity in distant Mangalore.

At the same time other, still more sombre, portents were taking shape on the two mirrored rims of the Mediterranean. In western Europe the sermons of Bernard of Clairvaux had aroused a frenzy of religious fervour, and preparations for a new

Crusade were under way amidst widespread massacres of Jews. In Germany things had come to such a pass that the despairing Jews of Cologne had begun to lament: 'Behold the days of reckoning have come, the end has arrived, the plague has begun, our days are completed, for our end is here.' At about the same time, in the far west of North Africa the al-Muwaḥḥid (Almohad) dynasty was gaining in strength, and its armies were advancing steadily through the Maghreb, towards Ifriqiya. Between 1145 and 1146 they took the cities of Oran, Tlemcen and the oasis of Sijilmasa, on the north-western border of the Sahara. For seven months they tried peaceably to convert Sijilmasa's large Jewish population to Islam. When their efforts went unrewarded they put a hundred and fifty Jews to the sword. The rest, led by their judge, quickly converted. They were relatively lucky: at about the same time a hundred thousand Christians and Jews were massacred by the Almohads in Fez, and a hundred and twenty thousand in Marrakesh.

Far away though he was, Ben Yiju was probably not unaware of the bloodshed and turmoil that had stricken his homeland: it so happens that the Geniza has yielded a letter addressed to Ben Yiju's friend, the indefatigable traveller Abu Zikri ha-Kohen Sijilmasi, which contains a detailed account of the events in North Africa. The letter was written by Abu Zikri's son, in Cairo, and sent to him in Aden, in 1148. Not long before, in about 1145, Abu Zikri Sijilmasi had been stranded in Gujarat after being captured by pirates. On that occasion Ben Yiju had penned a letter to him, on behalf of his brother-in-law, the 'nakhoda' Mahruz, from Mangalore. Now, three years later, upon learning of the events in North Africa, Abu Zikri would certainly have made an effort to pass the news on to Ben Yiju in Mangalore.

As luck would have it, there was more bad news in store for

Ben Yiju: his friend Khalaf had come to know that Mubashshir was now thinking of travelling to Syria, rather than India, and in 1148 he wrote to Ben Yiju to let him know that his hopes for a reunion with his brother were unlikely to be soon fulfilled.

'I asked [some people] about your brother Mubashshir,' Khalaf wrote. 'They said that he is in good health and that everything is well with him. I asked them about his departure for Syria and they said they knew nothing of it, but that all is well with him. Should he happen to come to Aden your servant will do his best for him, without my master's asking because he esteems him [my master] greatly.'

It may have been this piece of news, following hard upon other events, that finally made up Ben Yiju's mind. He had probably already written to Madmun to sort out whatever tangle it was that had kept him so long absent from Aden. From his friends' letters it would seem that he had written to others as well, mentioning thoughts of return. 'Every year you speak of coming to Aden,' wrote Khalaf in his letter of 1148, 'but you never do it.'

This time Ben Yiju did do it: a year later, in 1149, he was back in Aden, with all his worldly goods and his two adolescent children.

On 11 September 1149, Ben Yiju wrote his brothers a long letter from Aden. His return had stirred many long-settled memories, and he was now overcome with a desire to reclaim his family and the remembered landscapes of his childhood: 'I do not know what to write,' the letter begins, 'so strong is my longing and so ardent my yearning.'

The thought uppermost in Ben Yiju's mind at the time of writing was of providing reassurance and succour to his family. He had heard, he wrote, that their circumstances were now so dire that they had been reduced 'to a single loaf of bread' and he had tried to send them some goods to tide them over the worst, but the shipment had gone astray because of the uncertainty of their present location. He was writing now to offer them whatever else he could; to let them know that he had returned from India and arrived safely in Aden, 'with my belongings, life, and children well preserved', and money 'enough to live on for all of us'. '[Therefore], I ask you, my brother[s],' he urged, 'come to me under any circumstances and without delay...I have a son and a daughter, take them and take with them all the money and riches—*may God fulfil my wishes and yours for the good.* Come quickly and take possession of this money; this is better than strangers taking it.'

But he had another reason too for urging his brothers to join him in Aden 'under any circumstances and without delay': with his departure from India his yearning for his family had grown so powerful that he now longed to reaffirm his bonds with them through a familial union of another kind. 'Also, find out,' he directed them, 'who is the best of the sons of my brother [Yûsuf] or the sons of your sister Berâkhâ, so that I may marry him off to my daughter.'

But it was not until he penned the last lines of the letter that Ben Yiju gave expression to the anxiety that the recent events in North Africa had caused him: 'I heard of what happened on the coast of Ifriqiya, in Tripoli, Jerba, Kerkenna, Sfax, al-Mahdia and Sousse. But I have had no letter to tell me who lives and who is dead. For God's sake, write to me about it and send the letter in the hands of trustworthy people so that I may have some peace of mind. Shalom.'

The address that Ben Yiju wrote on the back was every bit as expressive of the uncertainties of the time as the letter itself. It was sent to al-Mahdia, 'if God will, or anywhere else in Ifriqiya.'

In the event, the letter did not fulfil the destiny Ben Yiju had intended for it. As luck would have it, it fell into the hands of his brother Mubashshir, in the port of Messina, in northern Sicily. His other brother, the pious and unworldly Yusuf, was then living at the far end of the island, in Mazzara, along with his wife and his three sons, Surûr, Moshe and Shamwâl. Disobeying his brother's instructions, Mubashshir chose not to inform Yusuf's family about the letter: as Ben Yiju was to learn to his cost, Mubashshir was a man who had few scruples where money was concerned.

Ultimately rumour proved more conscientious than kinship, and somehow Yusuf did eventually learn that a letter from his brother Abraham had made its way to Sicily. Yusuf's sons were all well-educated and dutiful young men, and none more so than the eldest, Surur. Having heard rumours of the letter, and possibly also of the proposal of marriage contained in it, Surur appears to have taken the task of locating his uncle on his own shoulders. A letter that he wrote at that time to a family acquaintance in Mahdia bears witness to the painstaking thoroughness with which he conducted his inquiries.

'I wished to ask,' Surur wrote, 'whether [my master] has any news of my father's brother, Abraham, known as Ben Yijû, for we have not heard from him [for some time]...Last year...a letter of his reached Messina, where it fell into the hands of my uncle Mubashshir, who took it with him. We have not seen it, and do not know what was in it. So our minds are in suspense, as we wait to hear news of how he is. May I request my Master, to kindly write us a brief note, to let us know whether he has heard any news of him and where he is...'

But the times were hard: the entire region was in turmoil, devastated by war. It would be a long time before Surur and his family next heard news of their uncle 'Abraham, known as Ben Yiju.'

# 3

WITHIN MINUTES OF leaving Abu-'Ali's house, I was brought to a halt by the sound of a familiar voice calling out my name. A moment later Jabir was beside me, and we were pounding each other on the back, exchanging handshakes, slapping our hands together, sending echoes down the lanes.

Jabir was greatly changed and looked much older than his twenty-five years: his face had grown considerably rounder and heavier; the hair at the top of his head had receded and at his temples there were two very prominent patches of grey (mere spots, as he was quick to point out, compared to mine). Once the greetings were over, we quickly agreed that we had a great deal to talk about, so we took leave of Shaikh Musa and headed towards his house. He had a room to himself now, Jabir said, and we could sit there in peace and talk as long as we liked.

On reaching the house, he led me quickly down a corridor, past his cousins and aunts, to a small room furnished with a desk and a bed. After ushering me in, he slammed the door and turned the key, locking out the troop of children who were following close behind us.

I was astonished: in all the time I had spent in Lataifa and Nashawy, I had never seen anyone shut a door upon people in their own house. But when I remarked on this it was Jabir's turn to be surprised.

'You used to shut your door,' he said. 'Have you forgotten or what? We had to bang on it if we wanted to come in.'

Gesturing to me to seat myself on the bed, he cocked his head at the door. 'There's too much noise outside,' he said. 'Too many people: I was away in college for such a long time that now it's become very hard for me here, with so many people in the house.'

He had first left Lataifa in 1982, he said, the year after my departure from Egypt. He had gone to Tanta, a large town about sixty miles from Cairo, to do a degree in commerce at the university there.

'It was wonderful,' he said wistfully. 'I lived on the campus, sharing a room with other students, and we all became close friends. We spent most of our time together, in class and afterwards.'

'Did you find it hard?' I asked. 'Being away from your cousins, your family?'

He threw me a look of surprise. 'No,' he said. 'Not at all, and anyway I saw them from time to time. I was very busy, I was learning so many things, seeing new places, it was so exciting to be there…'

Cutting himself short, he reached under his bed and pulled out a green plastic suitcase. A few shirts and trousers were neatly packed away inside, along with some books and several small packets, carefully wrapped in paper. Picking out one of those packages, he handed it to me and watched, smiling, as I undid the string.

'It's the wallet you gave me before you left Lataifa and went to Nashawy,' he said. 'You brought it back from Cairo—do you remember? I always use it when I go to the city, and if people ask me about it, I tell them about the Indian who gave it to me, and how he once mistook the moon for Ahmed Musa's torch.'

Laughing, he reached into his suitcase again, thumbed through a wad of photographs and handed me one. It was a picture I had taken myself, years ago, of Jabir, in a field near Lataifa; I had sent it to him later, from India, with one of my letters. I was proud of the picture, for I had succeeded in catching him at an unguarded moment, looking towards the camera in the way that came most naturally to him, with an expression that was at once challenging and quizzical, something between a smile and scowl. Seeing that picture again, after so many years, I realized that it was neither Jabir's grey hair nor the shape of his face that was responsible for the difference in his appearance: the real change lay somewhere else, in some other, more essential quality. In the Jabir who was sitting in front of me I could no longer see the sly, sharp-tongued ferocity my camera had captured so well that day—its place had been taken by a kind of quiet hopelessness, an attitude of resignation.

Jabir explained the other photographs in the pile as he handed them to me, one by one: they had been taken later, mainly in the gardens and buildings of his university. In the earlier photographs he was always with the same group of friends, classmates with whom he had shared a room for a couple of years. Most of them were working 'outside' now, so they had lost touch with each other. But they had been inseparable for the first couple of years; they had studied together and gone on holidays together, to Cairo, Aswan and the Sinai. It was clear from the tone of Jabir's voice that the memories of those friendships meant a great deal to him, yet I couldn't help noticing that in many of the pictures he looked like the odd man out, standing straight and looking fixedly into the camera, while the others around him threw themselves into attitudes of exuberant student horseplay. It was easy to see that they were all city boys, from middle-class families: they wore different clothes in each picture, pastel-coloured running-shoes, jeans and T-shirts. Jabir's clothes, on the other hand, looked as though they had been bought in the bazaar at Damanhour, and the same few shirts and trousers recurred in several pictures in succession, as though to prove that he had stayed true to his frugal village upbringing.

The beard that Shaikh Musa had mentioned appeared about three-quarters of the way through the pile of photographs. At first it had the look of cotton fluff, but later it took on a quite impressive appearance, reaching down to the line of his collar.

'It took me a long time to grow that beard,' he said. 'I looked much better when I had it—more respectable. I never had to bargain when I went to the market—no one would try to cheat me.'

I made no comment and, after turning over a few more pictures, he added that it was in college that he had begun to learn the real meaning of Islam, from talking to some of his teachers and fellow-students. They had read the Quran together every day and held long discussions that lasted late into the night.

'I was not involved in politics or anything,' he said, 'and I didn't join any groups or societies. But I learnt to recognize what is wrong and what is true. I don't know how to explain these things to you: you don't understand matters like these.'

'Why did you shave your beard off?' I asked.

His fingers slid over his freshly shaven chin in a slow, exploratory movement. 'My family wanted me to,' he said.

'Especially my mother.'

'Why?'

'They were afraid,' he said. 'There's been trouble between the government and certain Islamic groups, and they were worried that something might happen to me—even though I don't belong to any group or party.'

He shook his head and let out an ironic snort of laughter. 'This is a Muslim country,' he said. 'And it isn't safe to look like a Muslim.'

Then, abruptly, he dropped the subject and began asking me why I had not written for so long and what I had been doing since I left Egypt. My recital was a long one, and towards the end of it he grew pensive and began to ask detailed questions—about how much I had paid to fly to Egypt and the current exchange rates of the Indian rupee, the American dollar and the Egyptian pound.

'I may have to buy an air-ticket soon,' he said, at length. 'I've been trying to get a job outside. I worked in Iraq while I was in college, and if God wills I shall go there again.'

The first time he went, he said, was after his second year in college. One of his cousins, who was a foreman on a construction site in Baghdad, had taken him there so he could earn some money during his summer vacation. He had had to get a special kind of passport, because as a rule the Egyptian government did not allow its citizens to go abroad until they had completed their time in the army. Getting the passport hadn't been easy, but it had proved to be well worth it, in the end. He had earned so much money that his father was able to add a new room to their house.

He showed me a few photographs taken in Iraq, and I immediately recognized several other faces, besides his—friends and cousins of his, whom I'd known in Lataifa or Nashawy. The pictures were mostly taken in markets and parks in Baghdad, on holidays—I could almost see them myself, setting off in their best clothes, their faces alight with the pleasurable apprehension of being on their own in a faraway city, with their pockets full of money, well out of the reach of their parents and elders.

'What was it like there?' I asked.

'I was young then,' Jabir said, 'and I was sometimes a little scared.'

The Iraqis were very rough in their ways, he explained. He and his cousins and friends wouldn't usually go out at nights; they would stay in their rooms, all of them together, and cook and watch television. But despite all that, Iraq was better than some other places; from what he had heard, the Gulf Emirates were much worse. At least in Iraq everyone got paid properly. As far as he was concerned, he didn't care how the Iraqis behaved —all he wanted was to go back, after finishing with college and the army.

For a while it had looked as though things would go exactly as he had planned. His time in the army had passed quickly and without hardship, for his college degree had earned him a comfortable bookkeeping job in his unit.

'I was near Alexandria and it was nice,' he said. 'The officers treated me differently, not like the other soldiers, because I'd been to college and everything. They treated me almost like I was one of them.'

He had applied for a passport as soon as he got out of the army, and wasted no time in writing letters to his friends and cousins in Iraq, asking them to look out for job openings. He had expected that he'd be able to find a job without difficulty, just as he had the last time. But soon he discovered that things had changed. Iraqi soldiers and reservists had begun to go back to work and there were fewer and fewer jobs for foreigners. Worse still, the Iraqi government had established strict new laws which made it hard for Egyptian workers to send money home. But dozens of his friends and relatives were still there, of course, and they were managing well enough—anything was better than sitting idly at home, after all. So he had written to them again and again, asking them to let him know as soon as they heard of a job—he didn't care what it was, he just wanted a job, somewhere 'outside', in Iraq or wherever.

In the meantime, he had come back to Lataifa to wait until he was notified about the government job to which he was entitled by virtue of his college degree. It was not much to look forward to, for the salary was a pittance, a fraction of what a construction worker could earn in Iraq. But still, it was something. He had waited for months to hear about the job, and when the notification still hadn't arrived, he had begun to work with a bricklayer, as an apprentice: there were many houses being built now, in Lataifa and Nashawy, with the money that people were receiving from 'outside'.

'It's just for the time being,' Jabir said quickly. 'Until I find a job outside. I'll leave as soon as I hear of something, insha'allah.'

Piling the photographs together, he put them away again, rearranging his suitcase in the process. I could tell from the way he did it that packing his suitcase had become a habit with him.

'I made a mistake,' he said at last, shutting the suitcase. 'I thought a degree would help me, so I went to college. It was an exciting time and I learnt so much, but at the end of it, look, what am I doing? I'm a construction worker. I wasted time by going to college; I missed the best opportunities.'

And as a measure of his folly, there was the example of his brother Mohammad, who had planned his future better.

Mohammad was a year younger than Jabir, but he looked older, being taller and more heavily built. Unlike Jabir, he had never taken an interest in his studies and had barely managed to get through school; the thought of going to college had never entered his mind. Instead, he did his National Service as soon as possible, and then apprenticed himself to a carpenter in a nearby village. After spending a few months in acquiring the rudiments of the trade, he got himself a job in Jordan—that was at a time when jobs were still easy to get. He'd been in Jordan ever since, making good money. Recently he had written to say that he was coming home for a while—there was a chance that he might be able to get a job in Italy soon and he wanted to make arrangements for his future.

Jabir broke off there, his lips tightly pursed. He wouldn't say any more but the rest was clear enough: Mohammad wanted to get married before going off again. He had probably saved enough money to buy a house or an apartment—in Damanhour perhaps, or somewhere else—so he was now in a position to make a good marriage and set up house. In all likelihood, the only reason he had waited so long was because Jabir was older, and therefore entitled, by custom, to marry first. But, of course, Jabir had no savings and no means of buying an apartment of his own. And without one he wouldn't be able to marry someone compatible, a girl with a college education—instead he would have to marry a cousin from Lataifa, and live with his family, with no place to call his own. That was why it was imperative for him to find a job as soon as possible; time was running out— Mohammad had waited long enough, and no one would blame him now if he went ahead and got married. He had more than done his duty by custom.

In some part of his mind, Jabir was probably entirely in

sympathy with his brother's predicament, yet if Mohammad were to be the first to marry, it would be a public announcement of his own failure. I had only to look at Jabir's face to know that if that happened he would be utterly crushed, destroyed.

Turning his back on me, Jabir busied himself with his suit-case, repacking it yet again, as though to satisfy a craving. 'I'll be going back to Iraq soon,' he said, in a voice that was barely audible.

I couldn't see his face but I knew he was near tears.

## 4

THE RETURN TO Aden, undertaken with such gladness of spirit, was to bring nothing but tragedy to Ben Yiju. Such were the misfortunes that befell him there that within three years or so he uprooted himself once again. It was to Egypt that he now moved, and shortly after his arrival there, he tried once more to establish direct communication with his brother Yusuf, in Sicily.

The letter he wrote on this occasion was a long one, like the last, but his mood and his circumstances were greatly changed and the nostalgic exuberance that had seized him upon his return to Aden had now yielded to a resigned and broken-hearted melancholy. Writing to his brother now, he felt compelled to provide him with an account of some of the events that had befallen him since he last wrote, in 1149.

'I wrote a letter to you a while ago,' Ben Yiju told Yusuf. 'It reached Mubashshir, but he did not care to deliver it to you: [instead] he arrived in Aden [himself].'

But Mubashshir's visit, so long awaited, had not turned out as Ben Yiju had expected: 'I did all that was in my power for him and more, but he dealt me a ruinous blow. The events would take too long to explain, O my brother...' A couple of lines scribbled in the margin provides a hint of what had passed between them. In the course of his stay in Aden, Mubashshir had defrauded his brother of a huge sum of money: 'As for Mubashshir, he is nothing but a lazy man; malevolent in spirit. I gave him whatever he asked for, and in return he dealt me a ruinous blow. The price of my deeds was a thousand dînârs...'

Yet, painful as it was, the discovery of his brother's dishonesty was a small matter compared to the weight of Ben Yiju's other misfortunes: in the meantime he had also suffered the loss of his first child, the son born of his union with Ashu, to whom he had given the joyful name Surur.

The surviving copy of the letter still contains a part of the passage in which Ben Yiju tells Yusuf of his son's death. He had once had, he writes, 'two children like sprigs of sweet basil...'— but here the sentence breaks off, for the letter has been badly damaged over the centuries. The little that remains of the passage is punctuated with a bizarrely expressive succession of silences, as though time had somehow contrived to provide the perfect parentheses for Ben Yiju's grief by changing the scansion of his prose. It reads:

And the elder [of the two children] died in Aden...
I do not know what to describe of it...
I have left a daughter, his sister...

It was partly because of this daughter, Sitt al-Dâr, that Ben Yiju was now writing to his brother; he had been separated from her for prolonged periods over the last several years, and her future was now his most pressing concern.

Soon after moving to Aden, Ben Yiju had transferred his base out of that city and into the highlands of the interior, to a city called Dhû Jibla, which served as one of the principal seats of the ruling Zuray'id dynasty. For about three years afterwards he had lived mostly in the Yemeni mountains while his daughter remained in Aden, in the custody of his old and faithful friend Khalaf ibn Ishaq, living in his house as a member of his family.

The reasons for Ben Yiju's move are not entirely clear, but the loss of his son must have played a part in inducing him to leave Aden. In any event, he was already living in the mountains when he received news of yet another loss, just a couple of years after his arrival in Aden.

In 1151 Ben Yiju's old friend and one-time mentor, Madmun ibn Bundar, died in Aden. Ben Yiju was to read of his death in a letter from a correspondent: 'The news reached your exalted honour's slave, of the death of the lord and owner Madmûn...the stalwart pillar, Nagîd of the land of Yemen, Prince of the communities, Crown of the Choirs...' To Ben Yiju the news of Madmun's death must have come as a terrible blow: among his few surviving pieces of verse is a Hebrew poem, composed in memory of his friend.

In some ways, however, Ben Yiju evidently found a good deal of fulfilment in his new home in the Yemeni highlands. Such documentation as there is on this period of his life suggests that he enjoyed a position of some prominence within the Jewish communities of the interior, and he may even have been appointed to serve as a judge. Yet there must also have been many anxieties attendant on living in that relatively inaccessible region: his correspondence shows that he was greatly concerned about the safety of the roadways, for instance, which is hardly surprising considering that he was separated from his only surviving child by a wide stretch of difficult terrain, in a divided and war-torn land.

An extraordinary dilemma was to result from Ben Yiju's long separation from his daughter. His friend Khalaf, whose house she was living in, eventually approached him with a proposal of marriage for her, on behalf of one of his sons. The documents provide no indication of what her wishes in the matter were, but it is more than likely of course that Khalaf was acting with her consent; it is even possible that it was the young couple themselves who had prevailed upon him to speak to Ben Yiju about a betrothal, expecting that the request could hardly be refused when it came from a friend of such long standing.

But close though Ben Yiju was to his friends in Aden, he stood apart from them in one respect: their family origins, unlike his own, lay in the region of Iraq. The matter need not have made a difference had Ben Yiju chosen to ignore it, for such marriages were commonplace within their circle. But in the event Ben Yiju chose to disregard his long-standing association with Khalaf and his family: almost as though he were seeking to disown a part of his own past, he now decided that he could not let his daughter marry a 'foreigner'. Instead, he began to dream again of reaffirming his bonds with his family in the accepted fashion of the Middle East, by marrying her to her cousin, his brother Yusuf's eldest son, Surur.

In his letter to his brother he explained the matter thus:

Shaikh Khalaf [ibn Ishaq] ibn Bundâr, in Aden, [asked her hand] for his son. She had lived 3 years in their house. But I refused him when I heard of your son Surûr. I said: the brother's son comes before foreign people. Then, when I

came with her to Egypt, many people sought her hand of
me. I write to you to tell you of this: to say less than this
would have been enough.

But in a culture where marital negotiations can cast the whole
weight of a family's honour upon the scales of public judgement,
the refusal of a proposal from an old friend, of distinguished
lineage, cannot have been a simple matter. It is probably not a
coincidence therefore that the Geniza contains no record of any
further communication between Ben Yiju and his friends in
Aden. His rejection of Khalaf's offer may well have led to an
irreversible break with him and his kinsmen, including Yusuf
ibn Abraham: indeed, it may even have been the immediate
cause of his departure.

Thus it was on a note of real urgency that Ben Yiju wrote to
his brother upon arriving in Egypt. He had been told, he said,
that Yusuf had a son, Surur, 'who is learned in the Torah', and if
he were to send him now to Egypt, to marry his daughter, he
would have all his goods—'and we will rejoice in her and in
him, and we will wed them…' For Ben Yiju everything now
hung on a quick response from his brother. 'Address your letters
to me in Egypt, insha'allâh,' he exhorted Yusuf, 'let there be a
letter in the hands of your son, Surûr.'

Indeed, beset by grief, disillusionment and misfortune, Ben
Yiju now had no recourse other than his brother and his
nephews. To the two couriers who were to carry his letter to
Sicily he entrusted a confession of quiet despair.

'Sulîmân and Abraham will tell you of the state I am in,' Ben
Yiju wrote. 'I am sick at heart.'

## 5

I COULD HAVE found Nabeel's house myself of course, but in the end I was grateful to the children who insisted on leading me there: on my own I would have been reluctant to knock on the doors of the structure that stood there now. The mud-walled rooms I so well remembered were gone and in their place stood the unfinished shell of a large new bungalow.

The door was opened by Nabeel's sister-in-law, Fawzia. She clapped her hands to her head, laughing, when she saw me outside. The first thing she said was: 'Nabeel's not here—he's not in the village, he's gone to Iraq.'

Then, collecting herself, she ushered me in and after putting a tea-kettle on the stove, she sat me down and told me the story of how Nabeel had left for Iraq. His father, old Idris the watchman, had died the year after I left, and his wife had not long outlived him. Nabeel had been away from the village on both occasions. He was in the army then, and he hadn't been able to return in time to see them before they died. On her deathbed his mother had called out for him, over and over again—he had always been her favourite and she had long dreamed of dancing at his wedding. On both occasions Nabeel had come down for a quick visit, to attend the ceremonies; he did not say much, either time, but it was easy to see that he had been profoundly affected.

His best friend, Fawzia's brother Isma'il, had long been urging him to apply for a passport so he could work in Iraq after finishing his National Service. Nabeel was not particularly receptive to the idea at first: he had always wanted a job in a government office, a respectable clerical job, and he knew that in Iraq he would probably end up doing manual labour of some kind. But the death of his parents changed his mind. He put in an application for a passport, and in 1986, soon after finishing his time in the army, he left for Iraq with Isma'il.

Things had turned out well for him in Iraq; within a few months he had found a job as an assistant in a photographer's shop in Baghdad. It didn't pay as much as Isma'il's job, in construction, but it was a fortune compared to what he would have earned in Egypt.

Besides it was exactly the kind of job that Nabeel wanted. 'You know him,' Fawzia said, laughing. 'He always wanted a job where he wouldn't have to get his hands dirty.'

There was a telephone where he worked, she said, and the man who owned the shop didn't mind him receiving calls every now and again. 'We'll give you the number,' she told me. "Ali's got it written down somewhere; he'll find it for you when he gets back.'

Once every couple of months or so the whole family—she, her husband 'Ali and his younger brothers—made the trip to Damanhour to telephone Nabeel in Baghdad. When it was Nabeel's turn to get in touch with them he simply spoke into a cassette-recorder and sent them the tape. In the beginning he had written letters, but everyone had agreed that it was nicer to hear his voice. He'd even sent money for a cassette-recorder, so they wouldn't have to take the tapes to their neighbours.

Later Nabeel had sent money for a television set and a washing-machine and then, one day, on one of his tapes he had talked about building a new house. Those tumbledown old rooms they'd always lived in wouldn't last much longer, he'd said. He would be glad to have a new house ready, when he came back to Egypt. He would be able to get married, and move in soon afterwards. His brothers were overjoyed at the suggestion: they called back immediately and within a month he had sent them the money to begin the construction.

'He sent a new tape a few days ago,' Fawzia said. 'We'll listen to it again, as soon as 'Ali gets back.'

After we had finished our tea Fawzia showed me proudly around the house: three or four rooms had already been completed on the ground floor, including a kitchen, a bathroom and a veranda. The wiring was not complete and the walls were still unpainted, but otherwise the house was perfectly habitable.

When the ground floor had received its finishing touches, Fawzia said, the builders would start on a second floor. After his marriage, Nabeel and his wife would live upstairs, they would have the whole floor to themselves. Their other brothers could build on top of that, if they wanted to, later; it all depended on whether they went away as Nabeel had, and earned money 'outside'.

'How different it is,' I said, when Fawzia took me into the new guest-room and showed me their television set and cassette-recorder. 'The first time I came here was at the time of your wedding, when you and 'Ali were sitting outside, with your chairs up against the mud wall.'

Fawzia smiled at the recollection. 'The saddest thing,' she said, 'is that their mother and father didn't live to see how things have changed for us.'

Her voice was soft and dreamlike, as though she were speaking of some immemorially distant epoch. I was not surprised; I knew that if my own memories had not been preserved in such artefacts as notes and diaries, the past would have had no purchase in my mind either. Even with those reminders, it was hard, looking around now, to believe how things had once stood for Nabeel and his family—indeed for all of Nashawy. It was not just that the lanes looked different; that so many of the old adobe houses had been torn down and replaced with red-brick bungalows—something more important had changed as well, the relations between different kinds of people in the village had been upturned and rearranged. Families who at that time had counted amongst the poorest in the community—Khamees's, 'Amm Taha's, Nabeel's—were now the very people who had new houses, bank accounts, gadgetry. I could not have begun to imagine a change on this scale when I left Nashawy in 1981; revisiting it now, a little less than eight years later, it looked as though the village had been drawn on to the fringes of a revolution—except that this one had happened in another country, far away.

Earlier that day, I had talked at length with Ustaz Sabry about the changes in Nashawy, the war between Iran and Iraq, and the men who'd left to go 'outside' (he was leaving himself soon, to take up a good job in a school in the Gulf).

'It's we who've been the real gainers in the war,' he told me. The rich Arab countries were paying the Iraqis to break the back of the Islamic Revolution in Iran. For them it was a matter of survival, of keeping themselves in power. And in the meantime, while others were taking advantage of the war to make money, it was the Iraqis who were dying on the front.

'But it won't last,' he had said, 'it's tainted, "forbidden" money, and its price will be paid later, some day.'

It had occurred to me then that Jabir, in his exclusion, was already paying a price of one kind; now looking around the house Nabeel had built, I began to wonder whether he was paying another, living in Iraq.

'What are things like in Iraq?' I asked Fawzia. 'Does Nabeel like it there?'

321

She nodded cheerfully. He was very happy, she said; in his tapes he always said he was doing well and that everything was fine.

'You can hear him yourself when 'Ali comes home,' she said. 'We'll listen to his tape on the recorder.'

There was a shock in store for me when 'Ali returned: he had one of his younger brothers with him, Hussein, who I remembered as a shy, reticent youngster, no more than twelve or thirteen years old. But now Hussein was studying in college, and he had grown to resemble Nabeel so closely in manner and bearing that I all but greeted him by that name. Later, noticing how often Nabeel's name featured in his conversation, I realized that the resemblance was not accidental: he clearly worshipped his elder brother and had modelled himself upon him.

We listened to the tape after dinner: at first Nabeel's voice sounded very stiff and solemn and, to my astonishment, he spoke like a townsman, as though he had forgotten the village dialect. But Fawzia was quick to come to his defence when I remarked on this. It was only on the tapes that he spoke like that, she said. On the telephone he still sounded exactly the same.

Nabeel said very little about himself and his life in Iraq; just that he was well and that his salary had recently been increased. He listed in detail the names of all the people he wanted his brothers to convey his greetings to, and he told them about various friends from Nashawy who were also in Iraq—that so and so was well, that someone had moved to another city, that someone else was about to come home and so on. Then he went through a set of instructions for his brothers, on how they were to use the money he was sending them, the additions they were to make to the house and exactly how much they were to spend. Everyone in the room listened to him rapt, all the way to the final farewells, though they had clearly heard the tape through several times before.

Later, Fawzia got Hussein to write down Nabeel's address, and the telephone number of his shop, on a slip of paper. 'The owner will probably answer the phone,' she said, handing it to me. 'You have to tell him that you want to talk to Nabeel Idris Badawy, the Egyptian. It costs a lot, but you can hear him like he was in the next room.'

Hussein took hold of my elbow and gave it a shake. 'You must telephone him,' he said emphatically. 'He'll be so pleased. Do you know, he's kept all your letters, wrapped in a plastic bag? He still talks of you a lot. Tell me, didn't you once say to him…'

And then, almost word for word, he recounted a conversation I had once had with Nabeel. It was about a trivial matter, something to do with my university in Delhi, but for some reason I had written it down in my diary at the end of the day, and so I knew that Hussein had repeated it, or at least a part of it, almost verbatim. I was left dumbfounded when he finished; it seemed to me that I had witnessed an impossible, deeply moving, defiance of time and the laws of hearsay.

'You can be sure that I will telephone him,' I said to Hussein. I explained that I was travelling to America soon, in connection with the research for the book I was writing, and I promised to call Nabeel as soon as I arrived.

'You must tell him that we are well,' said Hussein, 'and that he should send another cassette.'

'He'll be really surprised!' said Fawzia. 'He'll think someone's playing a joke on him.'

'We'll write and tell him,' said 'Ali. 'We'll write tomorrow so he won't be surprised. We'll tell him that you're going to phone him from America.'

For a while we talked of other things, of the state of politics in India and the Middle East and what it was like to watch the World Cup on television. It was only when it was time for me to leave that I got to ask 'Ali whether Nabeel liked living in Iraq.

'Ali shrugged. As far as he knew, he said, Nabeel was well enough. That was what he always said at any rate. The fact was, he didn't know; he had never been there himself.

'God knows,' he added, 'people say life is hard out there.'

It was dark outside now and I couldn't stay any longer. After we had said our goodbyes, Hussein insisted that he would see me to the main road. On the way, we stopped at his cousins' house and took one of Isma'il's younger brothers along with us. It turned out that they, like Nabeel and Isma'il before them, were best friends, and were studying at the same college as their brothers had.

It was eerie crossing the village with the two of them beside me. It was as though a moment in time had somehow escaped the hurricane of change that had swept Nabeel and Isma'il away to Iraq: the two cousins so much resembled their brothers that I could have been walking with ghosts.

# 6

BEN YIJU'S SECOND letter, unlike his first, did eventually reach his brother Yusuf and his family. They were then resident in a small town called Mazara (Mazara del Vallo), near the western tip of Sicily, not far from Palermo. Mazara had once been a busy port, serving ships from North Africa and the Levant, but the current hostilities between Sicily and Ifriqiya had affected its traffic badly and sent it into a sharp decline. In terms of material sustenance it had little to offer Yusuf and his family, who were reduced to extremely straitened circumstances while living there. But it had other compensations: through its long trade contacts with Ifriqiya, it had imbibed something of the cultural and educational ambience of that region, and Yusuf and his sons probably felt more at home there than they would have in other, more rudely prosperous parts of the island. Still, there can be no doubt that they felt themselves to be suffering the privations of exile in their new home: looking across the sea from the shores of that provincial town, the material and scholarly riches of Egypt must have shone like a beacon in the far distance.

It is easy to imagine, then, the great tumult of hope and enthusiasm that was provoked in this dispossessed and disheartened family by the arrival of Ben Yiju's letter. The young Surur for one clearly received his uncle's proposal of marriage with the greatest warmth: his immediate response was to set off for Egypt to claim his bride.

The preparations for Surur's voyage threw his whole family into convulsions of excitement. The elderly Yusuf and his wife launched upon a severe regimen of fasting and prayer to ensure his safe arrival, and Surur's brother Moshe went along to accompany him on the first leg of the journey.

To arrange Surur's passage to Egypt, the two brothers had first to proceed to a major port, since Mazara itself no longer served large eastbound ships. In the event they decided to go to Messina on the other end of the island rather than to nearby

Palermo—probably because they knew that that was where they would find the courier of their uncle's letter, Sulîmân ibn Ṣatrûn. They boarded a boat on a Friday night, having agreed upon a fare of three-eighths of a gold dinar, in exchange for being taken to a lighthouse adjoining Messina.

Arriving in Messina nine days later, they sought out their wayward uncle, Mubashshir, who was then living in that city. In this instance, Surur reported in a letter to his father, his uncle 'did not fall short [of his family duties],' and invited him and his brother to stay in his house. Later, the brothers sought out two friends of Ben Yiju's, one of whom was the courier Suliman ibn Satrun. Their efforts were immediately rewarded: 'I shall take care of your fare,' said Ibn Satrun to Surur, 'and you will go up [i.e. to Egypt] with me, if God wills.'

But now, seized by a yearning for travel, young Moshe too began to insist that he wanted to go on to Egypt with Surur. Ibn Satrun and their uncle Mubashshir both counselled against it—'they said: "There is nothing to be gained by it. He had better go back to his father"'—but Moshe was determined not to go back to Mazara 'empty-handed'. The matter was now for their father to decide, Surur wrote, and in the meanwhile they would stay in Messina to await his instructions.

Upon receiving the letter, Yusuf must have decided against allowing Moshe to go any further, for when Surur next wrote to his parents he was already in Egypt and his brother was back in Mazara. The letter he wrote on this occasion was a short one. 'I have sent you these few lines to tell you that I am well and at peace,' he wrote, and then went on to convey his greetings in turn to various friends at home as well as to his parents and his brothers, Moshe and Shamwal. But Surur had yet another reason for writing home at this time: he wanted a certain legal document from his father and in the course of his letter he asked him to send it on to Palermo, possibly with Moshe, so that it could be forwarded to him in Egypt.

As it happened, the letter rekindled Moshe's yearning for travel and prompted him to set out for Egypt himself. But the times were not propitious and the store of good fortune that had carried Surur safely to his destination ran out on his brother: Moshe's ship was attacked on the way and he was imprisoned in the Crusader-controlled city of Tyre.

Their parents, already prostrate with anxiety, were to learn of these developments in a letter from Surur. 'We were seized with grief when we read your letter,' Shamwal wrote back from Sicily, 'and we wept copiously. As for [our] father and mother *they could not speak*.' But their tears were soon stemmed: later in the same letter, they discovered that matters had already taken a happier turn. Moshe had since written to Surur from Tyre to let him know that he was now 'well and in good cheer.'

At home in Sicily meanwhile, things had got steadily worse. Food was short, the price of wheat had risen and the family had already spent most of its money. 'If you saw [our] father,' wrote Shamwal, 'you would not know him, for he weeps all day and night...As for [our] mother, if you saw her, you would not recognize her [so changed is she] by her longing for you, and by her grief. God knows what our state has been after you left...Know that all we have is emptiness since God emptied [our house]. Do not forget us, oh my brothers; to visit us and to write to us. You must know that those of your letters that reached us conjured up your two noble faces [for us]. Send us letters telling us your news, the least important and the most; do not scorn to tell us the smallest thing, till we know everything.'

But gradually things improved. The brothers were reunited in

Egypt, and Surur must have announced his wedding to his cousin shortly afterwards. His father, overwhelmed, wrote back to say: 'Come quickly home to us, you and your uncle's daughter...and [we shall] prepare a couple of rooms for her, and we shall celebrate [the wedding]...'

The marriage did indeed take place: a list recording Sitt al-Dar's wedding trousseau, now preserved in St. Petersburg, is proof that this child of a Nair woman from the Malabar was wedded in 1156 to her Sicilian cousin, in Fustat.

Both Surur and Moshe went on to become judges in rabbinical courts in Egypt, where they were probably later joined by their parents and Shamwal.

As for Ashu, neither Ben Yiju nor his nephews mention her in their letters. In all likelihood she never left India but remained in Mangalore after Ben Yiju's departure.

Ben Yiju himself disappears from the records after his daughter's marriage. His son-in-law and his other nephews do not mention him in their later correspondence, and nor, as far as I know, is his death referred to in any other document in the Cairo Geniza. There are many conceivable endings to Ben Yiju's story and if the most pleasing amongst them is one which has him returning to Ashu, in the Malabar, the most likely, on the other hand, is a version in which he dies in Egypt, soon after his daughter's wedding, and is buried somewhere in the vicinity of Fustat.

As for Bomma, there is no mention of him either, in Ben Yiju's correspondence with his brothers. But his story is not ended yet: one last journey remains.

# 7

MY RETURN TO Nashawy and Lataifa culminated in an unforeseen ending.

It so happened that my visit coincided with one of the region's annual events, a mowlid dedicated to the memory of a saintly figure known as Sidi Abu-Hasira, whose tomb lies on the outskirts of Damanhour.

As with all mowlids, a buzz of anticipation preceded the start of this one, and over a period of a few days I had the story of Sidi Abu-Hasira repeated to me over and over again. Except for a few unexpected twists, it was very similar to the legends that surrounded other local holy men such as those of Nashawy and Nakhlatain: like those other legends, it was set in a distant past, and it recounted the miracles wrought by a man of exemplary piety and goodness. The Sidi had been born into a Jewish family in the Maghreb, it was said, but he had transported himself to Egypt through a miracle that later found commemoration in his name: he had crossed the Mediterranean on a rush mat, which was why he was called 'Sîdî Abû-Ḥaṣîra', 'the Saint of the Mat'.

After arriving in Egypt, the story went, he had converted to Islam and had soon come to be recognized as a 'good man', endowed with the blessed and miraculous gift of 'baraka'. Eventually the Sidi had settled in Damanhour, where a large group of disciples and followers had gathered around him. Upon his death, they had built a tomb for him, on the outskirts of Damanhour, and it was there that his mowlid was now celebrated. Because of his Jewish origins, I was told, the Sidi still had many followers in Israel and ever since the opening of the borders they came to Damanhour in large numbers every year.

Indeed so many tourists came to attend the mowlid nowadays, and recently a large new memorial had been built on the site of Sidi Abu-Hasira's tomb.

I had missed the mowlid while living in Nashawy, because I had happened to be away in Cairo over the week when it was celebrated; now it seemed as though everyone I knew was determined to prevent my missing it again. The mowlid was a wonderful spectacle, I was told; there would be lights everywhere, stalls with pistols and airguns, swings and carousels; the streets would be lined with kebab-shops and vendors' carts and thronged with crowds of sightseers. The tourists alone were a good reason to go, they said, it was not often that one got to see foreigners in a place like Damanhour.

I was persuaded easily enough, but I had so much to catch up with in Lataifa and Nashawy after my long absence that I didn't have time to think of much else. The mowlid began towards the end of my visit, and my time seemed so pitifully short that I let it pass with no particular sense of regret. A couple of days before my departure I was told that the mowlid was over: that would have been the end of the story had it not been for Mohsin the taxi-driver.

Mohsin was from a hamlet near Nashawy, a corpulent youth in his mid-twenties or so. He had a little bristling moustache, and he always wore freshly laundered white jallabeyyas—great, dazzling garments that billowed around him like parachutes. Mohsin was a good talker, full of self-confidence, and amazingly knowledgeable about such things as the exchange rates of various kinds of dinars and the prices of Nikons and Seikos. He had acquired this stock of information while living in the Gulf where he had spent a couple of years working in construction. He hadn't cared much for his work however; climbing scaffolding didn't suit him. Eventually he had succeeded in persuading two of his brothers, who had jobs in Iraq, to join him in investing in a second-hand van, and for the last several months he had been ferrying passengers back and forth between the towns and villages of the district.

The day before my departure Mohsin drove me to the railway station in Damanhour to buy a ticket for Cairo, and on the way he explained that he was growing tired of spending his days on those dusty rural roads. Lately, seeing so many tourists coming into Damanhour for the mowlid, he had begun to think along a different track. It had occurred to him that it would be nice to have a permit that would let him take tourists back and forth from Alexandria and Cairo and places like that.

That was how the idea of our paying a visit to the tomb of Sidi Abu-Hasira came to be mooted. He had never been there himself, said Mohsin, but he had always wanted to go, and he would be glad to take me there next morning, on the way to the station. It was no matter that the mowlid was already over—the stalls and lights would probably be there still, and we would be able to get a good whiff of the atmosphere. And so it was agreed that we would stop by at the tomb when he picked me up at Lataifa next morning, to take me to the station.

I spent the rest of the day making a last round of Nashawy, saying good-bye to my friends and their families: to Khamees, now a prosperous landowner with two healthy children; to Busaina, who had recently bought a house with her own earnings, in the centre of the village; to their brother 'Eid, newly-returned from Saudi Arabia, and soon to be married to the girl to whom he had lost his heart, years ago; to Zaghloul, miraculously unaffected by the storm of change that was whirling through the village; to 'Amm Taha, whose business in eggs had now expanded into a minor industry and made him a man of considerable wealth; even, inadvertently, to Imam Ibrahim, who greeted me civilly enough, when we ran into each other in the village square. Finally I said goodbye to Fawzia, 'Ali and Hussein, who made me promise, once again, that I would soon telephone Nabeel in Iraq.

When Mohsin arrived in Lataifa next morning, I was taking my leave of Shaikh Musa, Jabir, and several others who had gathered in his guest-room. The leavetaking proved even harder than I had imagined and in one way or another my farewells lasted a great deal longer than I had expected.

In the meanwhile Mohsin had busied himself in preparing an appropriate accompaniment for the moment of my departure: a cassette of Umm Kolthum's had been cued and held ready, and the moment I climbed into the van a piercing lament filled the lanes of Lataifa. We began to roll forward in time with the tune, and after a final round of handshakes, Mohsin sounded a majestic blast on his horn. The younger boys ran along while the van picked up speed, and then suddenly Lataifa vanished behind us into a cloud of dust.

We stopped to ask directions on the borders of Damanhour, and then turned on to a narrow road that skirted around a crowded, working-class area. Nutshells and scraps of coloured papers lay scattered everywhere now, and it was easy to tell that the road had recently been teeming with festive crowds. Mohsin had never been to this part of the city before but he was confident that we were headed in the right direction. When next we stopped to ask for the tomb of Sidi Abu-Hasira, we were immediately pointed to a large structure half-hidden behind a row of date palms, a little further down the road.

I was taken by surprise at my first glimpse of the building; it looked nothing like the saints' tombs I had seen before. It was a sleek, concrete structure of a kind that one might expect to see in the newer and more expensive parts of Alexandria and Cairo: in that poor quarter of Damanhour, it was not merely incongruous—its presence seemed almost an act of defiance.

A long, narrow driveway led from the entrance of the compound to a covered porch adjoining the tomb. The grounds seemed deserted when we turned in at the gate, and it was not till we were halfway down the drive that we noticed a handful of men lounging around a desk, in the shade of the porch. One of them was dressed in a blue jallabeyya; the rest were armed and in uniform.

At the sight of those uniforms Mohsin suddenly became tense and apprehensive. Like me, he had expected to see a domed tomb, with some candles burning outside perhaps, and a few people gathered around a grave: the uniforms instantly aroused that deep mistrust of officialdom that had been bred into him by generations of fellah forefathers. I could tell that his every instinct was crying out to him to turn the van around and speed away. But it was already too late: the men were on their feet now, watching us, and some of them were fingering their guns.

The van was surrounded the moment we drew up under the porch. Reaching in through my window, a hand undid the lock and jerked the door open. I stepped out to find myself face to face with a ruddy, pink-cheeked man, dressed in a blue jallabeyya. He was holding the door open for me, and with a deep bow and a smile he gestured towards a police officer seated at the desk under the porch.

The officer was a young man, probably a recent graduate from training school. He watched with a puzzled and slightly annoyed expression as I walked over to his desk.

'What are you doing here?' he snapped at me, in the kind of tone he might have used towards a slow-witted subordinate.

'I came to look at the tomb,' I said. 'I heard there was a mowlid here recently.'

On hearing me speak he realized I was a foreigner and there was an instant change in his tone and manner. He looked me over, smiling, and a gleam of recognition came into his eyes.

'Israïli?' he said.

When I told him I was Indian, his smile vanished and was quickly replaced by a look of utter astonishment. Confirming what I had said with a glance at my passport, he turned to me in blank incomprehension. What was my business there, he wanted to know; what was I doing at that tomb?

My Arabic was becoming tangled now, but as best I could I explained that I had heard about the mowlid of Sidi Abu-Hasira and decided to pay the tomb a visit on my way to the station.

From his deepening frown, I knew that my answer had not been satisfactory. The mowlid was over, he said, the tourists were gone, and the tomb was closed. The time for sightseeing was now well past.

Opening my passport, he thumbed through it again, from back to front, coming to a stop at the page with my photograph.

'Are you Jewish?' he said.

'No.'

'Muslim?'

'No.'

'Christian?'

When I said no yet again he gave a snort of annoyance and slammed my passport on the desk. Turning to the others, he threw up his hands. Could they understand it? he asked. Neither Jewish, nor Muslim, nor Christian—there had to be something odd afoot.

I started to explain once more, but he had lost interest in me now. Rising to his feet, he turned towards Mohsin, who was waiting near the van. The man in the blue jallabeyya was standing beside him, and when the officer beckoned, he pushed Mohsin forward.

Mohsin was terrified now, and he would not look at me. His habitual confidence and good humour had ebbed away; he was cringing, his vast rotund form shaking with fear. Before the officer could speak, he began to blurt out an explanation. 'It's nothing to do with me, Your Excellency,' he cried, his voice rising in panic. 'I don't know who the foreigner is and I don't know what he's doing here. He was staying in a village next to ours, and he wanted to visit this tomb on the way to the station. I don't know anything more; I have nothing to do with him.'

The officer spun around to look at me. 'What were you doing in a village?' he snapped. 'What took you there? How long have you been travelling around the countryside without informing the proper authorities?'

I started to explain how I had first arrived in Lataifa as a student, years ago, but the officer was in no mood to listen: his mind could now barely keep pace with his racing suspicions. Without a pause he rattled off a series of questions, one after another.

Who had I been meeting in the villages? he asked. Were they from any particular organization? What had I talked about? Were there any other foreigners working with me?

My protests and explanations were brushed aside with an impatient gesture; the officer was now far too excited to listen. I would soon have an opportunity to explain to someone senior, he told me—this was too serious a matter for someone in his position to deal with.

Seating himself at his desk he quickly wrote out a note and handed it to the ruddy-faced man in the jallabeyya, along with my passport and Mohsin's papers.

'Go with him,' he told me. 'He will take you where you have to go.'

Mohsin and I found ourselves back on the van within moments, with the man in the jallabeyya sitting between us. He was holding Mohsin's papers and my passport firmly in his hands.

'Everything will soon be clear, sir,' he said, when I asked him where he was taking us. He was heavily-built, with a moustache that was almost blonde, and a clear-cut, angular profile that hinted at Macedonian or Albanian forbears somewhere in his ancestry.

He raised our papers reverentially to his forehead and bowed. 'I'm under your orders and at your command, taht amrak wa iznak…'

I noticed then that his speech, except for its elaborate unctuousness, was exactly that of a fellah, with only the faintest trace of a city accent. Dressed as he was, in his fellah's cap and jallabeyya, he would have been perfectly at home in the lanes of Nashawy and Lataifa.

Mohsin interrupted him, with a sudden show of anger, demanding to know what crime he had committed. He had regained his composure a little now that he was back in his van.

In reply the man began to thumb through Mohsin's licence and registration papers. Then, in a voice that was silky with feigned deference, he pointed out that the permit did not allow him to carry passengers.

Instantly Mohsin's shoulders sagged and his self-possession

evaporated: the man had taken his measure with practised accuracy. The papers had probably taken Mohsin months to acquire, maybe cost him a substantial sum of money, as well as innumerable hours spent standing at the desks of various government officials. The thought of losing them terrified him.

When Mohsin next spoke his voice was hoarse and charged with an almost hysterical urgency. 'You sound as though you're from the countryside around here, sir,' he said. 'Is your village in this area?'

The man in the jallabeyya nodded, smiling affably, and named a village not far from Damanhour. The name seemed to electrify Mohsin. 'Alhamdu'lillah!' he cried. 'God be praised! I know that village. I know it well. Why I've been there many times, many times.'

For the rest of the drive, in a desperate effort to invoke the protective bonds of neighbourhood and kinship, to tame the abstract, impersonal terror the situation had inspired in him, Mohsin mined every last vein of his memory for a name that would be familiar to his captor. The man humoured him, smiling, and deflected his questions with answers that were polite but offhand. Skilled in his craft, he knew perfectly well that there was no more effective way of striking terror into a village boy like Mohsin than by using his own dialect to decline his accustomed terms of communication—those immemorial courtesies of village life, by which people strove to discover mutual acquaintances and connections.

By the time we reached our destination, a high-walled, heavily-guarded building on a busy road, Mohsin was completely unnerved, drenched in sweat. He protested feebly as we were herded in past an armed sentry, but no one paid him any attention. He was marched quickly off towards a distant wing of the building while I, in turn, was led to a room at the end of a corridor and told to go in and wait.

The room was a pleasant one, in an old-fashioned way, large, airy and flooded with light from windows that looked directly out into a garden. From what I could see of it, the building seemed very much in the style of colonial offices in India with high ceilings and arched windows: it took no great prescience to tell that it had probably been initiated into its current uses during the British occupation of Egypt.

In a while the curtain at the door was pushed aside and a tall man in gold-rimmed aviator sunglasses stepped into the room. He was casually dressed, in a lightweight jacket and trousers, and there was a look of distinction about him, in the manner of a gracefully ageing sportsman.

Taking off his sunglasses, he seated himself behind the desk; he had a lean gunmetal face, with curly hair that was grizzled at the temples. He placed my passport and the note from the officer in front of him, and after he had looked them through he sat back in his chair, his eyes hard and unsmiling.

'What is the meaning of this?' he said.

I knew I had to choose my words with care, so speaking slowly, I told him that I had heard many people talking about the mowlid of Sidi Abu-Hasira over the last several days. They had said that many tourists came to Damanhour to visit the mowlid, so I had decided to do some sightseeing too, before catching the train to Cairo, later in the day.

He listened with close attention, and when I had finished, he said: 'How did you learn Arabic? And what were you doing travelling in the countryside?'

'I'd been here years ago,' I said, and I explained how, after learning Arabic in Tunisia, I had come to Egypt as a doctoral student and been brought to that district by Professor Aly Issa, one of the most eminent anthropologists in Egypt. Fortunately I had taken the precaution of carrying a copy of the permit I had been given when I first went to live in Lataifa and I handed it to him now as proof.

My interrogator examined the document and then, giving it back to me, he said: 'But this does not explain what you were doing at the tomb. What took you there?'

I had gone there out of mere curiosity, I told him. I had heard people talking about the mowlid of Sidi Abu-Hasira, just as they talked about other such events, and I had thought I would stop by to take a look, on the way to the station. I had had no idea that it would become a matter of such gravity, and I was at a loss to understand what had happened.

A gesture of dismissal indicated that my interrogator had no intention of offering me an explanation. 'What was it that interested you about that place?' he asked again. 'What exactly took you there?'

'I was just interested,' I said. 'That's all.'

'But you're not Jewish or Israeli,' he said. 'You're Indian— what connection could you have with the tomb of a Jewish holy man, here in Egypt?'

He was not trying to intimidate me; I could tell he was genuinely puzzled. He seemed so reasonable and intelligent, that for an instant I even thought of telling him the story of Bomma and Ben Yiju. But then it struck me, suddenly, that there was nothing I could point to within his world that might give credence to my story—the remains of those small, indistinguishable, intertwined histories, Indian and Egyptian, Muslim and Jewish, Hindu and Muslim, had been partitioned long ago. Nothing remained in Egypt now to effectively challenge his disbelief: not a single one, for instance, of the documents of the Geniza. It was then that I began to realize how much success the partitioning of the past had achieved; that I was sitting at that desk now because the mowlid of Sidi Abu-Hasira was an anomaly within the categories of knowledge represented by those divisions. I had been caught straddling a border, unaware that the writing of History had predicated its own self-fulfilment.

'I didn't know Sidi Abu-Hasira was a Jewish saint,' I said at last. 'In the countryside I heard that everyone went to visit the tomb.'

'You shouldn't have believed it,' he said. 'In the villages, as you must know, there is a lot of ignorance and superstition; the fellaheen talk about miracles for no reason at all. You're an educated man, you should know better than to believe the fellaheen on questions of religion.'

'But the fellaheen are very religious,' I said. 'Many amongst them are very strict in religious matters.'

'Is it religion to believe in saints and miracles?' he said scornfully. 'These beliefs have nothing to do with true religion. They are mere superstitions, contrary to Islam, and they will disappear with development and progress.'

He looked down at his papers, indicating that the subject was closed. After a moment's silence he scribbled a couple of sentences on a slip of paper and rose slowly to his feet.

'We have to be careful, you understand,' he said in a polite, but distant voice. 'We want to do everything we can to protect the tomb.'

He stood up, gave my hand a perfunctory shake and handed me my passport. 'I am going to instruct the man who brought you here to take you straight to the station,' he said. 'You should catch the first train to Cairo. It is better that you leave Damanhour at once.'

Leaving me sitting at his desk, he turned and left the room. I had to wait a while, and then a policeman came in and escorted me back to the van.

Mohsin was sitting inside, next to the man in the blue jallabeyya; he looked unharmed, but he was subdued and nervous, and would not look me in the eyes. The railway station was only a few minutes away, and we drove there in silence. When we got there, I went around to Mohsin's window, and after paying him the fare, I tried to apologise for the trouble the trip had caused. He took the money and put it away without a word, looking fixedly ahead all the while.

But the man in the jallabeyya had been listening with interest, and he now leant over and flashed me a smile. 'What about me, sir?' he said. 'Are you going to forget me and everything I did to look after you? Isn't there going to be anything for me?'

At the sight of his outstretched hand I lost control of myself. 'You son of a bitch,' I shouted. 'You son of a bitch—haven't you got any shame?'

I was cut short by a nudge from Mohsin's elbow. Suddenly I remembered that the man was still holding his papers in his hands. To keep myself from doing anything that might make matters worse for Mohsin, I went quickly into the station. When I looked back, they were still there; the man in the jallabeyya was waving Mohsin's papers in his face, haggling over their price.

I went down to the platform to wait for my train.

Over the next few months, in America, I learnt a new respect for the man who had interrogated me that morning in Damanhour: I discovered that his understanding of the map of modern knowledge was much more thorough than mine. Looking through libraries, in search of material on Sidi Abu-Hasira, I wasted a great deal of time in looking under subject headings such as 'religion' and 'Judaism'—but of course that tomb, and others like it, had long ago been wished away from those shelves, in the process of shaping them to suit the patterns of the Western academy. Then, recollecting what my interrogator had said about the difference between religion and superstition, it occurred to me to turn to the shelves marked 'anthropology' and 'folklore'. Sure enough, it was in those regions that my efforts met with their first rewards.

I discovered that the name Abu-Hasira, or Abou-Hadzeira, as it is spelt when transcribed from Hebrew, belongs to a famous line of zeddikim—the Jewish counterparts of Islamic marabouts and Sufi saints, many of whom had once been equally venerated by Jews and Muslims alike. Ya'akov Abou-Hadzeira of Damanhour, I discovered, was one of the most renowned of his line, a cabbalist and mystic, who had gained great fame for his miracles in his lifetime, and still had a large following among Jews of North African and Egyptian origin. 'The tomb of Rabbi Abû-Ḥaṣîra of Morocco [in Damanhour] attracted large numbers of pilgrims,' I learnt, 'both Jewish and non-Jewish, and the festivities marking the pilgrimage closely resembled the birthday of Muslim saints…'

It seemed uncanny that I had never known all those years that in defiance of the enforcers of History, a small remnant of Bomma's world had survived, not far from where I had been living.

# EPILOGUE

SOON AFTER I arrived in New York I tried to call Nabeel in Baghdad. It wasn't easy getting through. The directory listed a code for Iraq, but after days of trying all I got was a recorded message telling me that the number I had dialled didn't exist.

In the end I had to book a call with the operator. She took a while to put it through, but then the phone began to ring and a short while later I heard a voice at the other end, speaking in the blunt, rounded Arabic of Iraq.

'Ai-wah?' he said, stretching out the syllables. 'Yes? Who is it?'

I knew at once I was speaking to Nabeel's boss. I imagined him to be a big, paunchy man, sitting at the end of a counter, behind a cash-box, with the telephone beside him and a Kodacolor poster of a snow-clad mountain on the wall above. He was wearing a jallabeyya and a white lace cap; he had a pair of sunglasses in his breast pocket and a carefully trimmed moustache. The telephone beside him was of the old-fashioned kind, black and heavy, and it had a brass lock fastened in its dial. The boss kept the key, and Nabeel and the other assistants had to ask for it when they wanted to make a call.

It was late at night in New York so it had to be morning in

345

Baghdad. The shop must have just opened; they probably had no customers yet.

'Is Nabeel there?' I asked.

'Who?' said the voice.

'Nabeel Idris Badawy,' I said. 'The Egyptian.'

He grunted. 'And who're you?' he said. 'Wa mîn inta?'

'I'm a friend of his,' I said. 'Tell him it's his friend from India. He'll know.'

'What's that?' he said. 'From where?'

'From India, ya raiyis,' I said. 'Could you tell him? And quickly if you please, for I'm calling from America.'

'From America?' he shouted down the line. 'But you said you were Indian?'

'Yes, I am—I'm just in America on a visit. Nabeel quickly, if you please, ya raiyis…'

I heard him shout across the room: 'Ya Nabeel, somebody wants to talk to you, some Indian or something.'

I could tell from Nabeel's first words that my call had taken him completely by surprise. He was incredulous in the beginning, unwilling to believe that it was really me at the other end of the line, speaking from America. I was almost as amazed as he was: it would never have occurred to me, when I first knew him, that we would one day be able to speak to each other on the phone, thousands of miles apart.

I explained how I had recently been to Egypt and visited Nashawy, and how his family had given me his telephone number and told me to call him, in Baghdad. Suddenly, he gave a shout of recognition.

'Ya Amitab,' he cried. 'How are you? Zayyak? Where were you? Where have you been all these years?'

I gave him a quick report on how I had spent the last several years, and then it was my turn to ask: 'What about you? Zayyak inta?'

'Kullu 'âl,' he said, mouthing a customary response. Everything was well; he and his cousin Isma'il were managing fine, sharing rooms with friends from back home. Then he asked me about India, about each member of my family, my job, my books. When I had finished giving him my news, I told him about his own family in Nashawy, and about my visit to their new house. He was eager to hear about them, asking question after question, but in a voice that seemed to grow progressively more quiet.

'What about you, ya Nabeel?' I said at last. 'How do you like Iraq? What is the country like?'

'Kullu 'âl,' he said—everything was fine.

I wanted him to talk about Iraq, but of course he would not have been able to say much within earshot of his boss. Then I heard a noise down the line; it sounded as though someone was calling to him from across the room. He broke off to say, 'Coming, just one minute,' and I added hurriedly, 'I'm going back to India soon—I'll try to stop by and visit you on the way, in Baghdad.'

'We'll be expecting you,' he said. 'You must come.'

'I'll do my best,' I said.

'I'll tell Isma'il you're coming,' he said hurriedly. 'We'll wait for you.'

I heard his boss's voice again, shouting in the background. 'I'll come,' I promised. 'I'll certainly come.'

But as it turned out I was not able to keep my word: for a variety of reasons it proved impossible to stop in Baghdad on the way back to India. My breaking of that promise made me all the more determined to keep another: I resolved that I would do everything I could to return to Egypt in 1990, the following year. I had given my word to Shaikh Musa that I would.

I was certain that by then Nabeel would be back in Nashawy.

BOMMA'S STORY ENDS in Philadelphia.

At the corner of 4th and Walnut, in the heart of downtown Philadelphia, stands a sleek modern building, an imposing structure that could easily be mistaken for the headquarters of a great multinational corporation. In fact, it is the Annenberg Research Institute, a centre for social and historical research: it owes its creation to the vast fortune generated by the first and most popular of America's television magazines, 'TV Guide'.

Housed within the Institute's resplendent premises is a remarkable collection of Judaica, including manuscripts of many different kinds. Among them is a set of Geniza documents that was once in the possession of Philadelphia's Dropsie College.

The documents are kept in the Institute's rare book room, a great vault in the bowels of the building, steel-sealed and laser-beamed, equipped with alarms that need no more than seconds to mobilize whole fleets of helicopters and police cars. Within the sealed interior of this vault are two cabinets that rise out of the floor like catafalques. The documents lie inside them, encased in sheets of clear plastic, within exquisitely crafted covers.

Between the leaves of one of those volumes lies a torn sheet of paper covered with Ben Yiju's distinctive handwriting. The folio is a large one, much larger than any of Ben Yiju's other papers, but it is badly damaged and almost a quarter of the sheet is missing. The handwriting on the remaining parts of the fragment is unmistakably Ben Yiju's, but the characters are tiny and faint, as though formed by an unsteady and ageing hand.

The document is one of Ben Yiju's many sets of accounts, but the names of the people and the commodities that are mentioned in it are very different from those that figure in his earlier papers: they suggest that these accounts belong to the years he spent in Fustat, towards the end of his life.

The document mentions several people to whom Ben Yiju owed money for household purchases such as loaves of bread of various different kinds. Much of the document is indecipherable, but amongst the sentences that are clearly legible there is at least one that mentions a sum of money owed to Bomma.

It provides proof that Bomma was with Ben Yiju when he went back to settle in Egypt in the last years of his life.

In Philadelphia then, cared for by the spin-offs of 'Dallas' and 'Dynasty' and protected by the awful might of the American police, lies entombed the last testament to the life of Bomma, the toddy-loving fisherman from Tulunad.

Bomma, I cannot help feeling, would have been hugely amused.


AN ENTRY IN my passport records that I left Calcutta for Cairo on 20 August 1990, exactly three weeks after the Iraqi invasion of Kuwait. Newspapers were already talking of plans for the mobilization of hundreds of thousands of American and European troops: the greatest army ever assembled.

My most vivid memories of the journey are of reading about the vast flood of Egyptian workers that was now pouring out of Iraq, and of looking for Nabeel and Isma'il in the packed lounges of the airport at Amman, while changing planes.

In Egypt, everyone I talked to seemed to be in a state of confused apprehension: in the taxi from Cairo to Damanhour, the other passengers talked randomly of disaster, killing and vengeance. In the countryside the confusion was even worse than in the cities; Lataifa alone had five boys away in Iraq, and none of them had been heard from since the day of the invasion. Jabir, I discovered, was not amongst that five. He was still at home, in Lataifa, although he had been trying to leave for Iraq virtually until the day of the invasion. Shaikh Musa was well, but desperately worried: his nephew Mabrouk was one of the five who were away in Iraq.

Walking to Nashawy to inquire about Nabeel and Isma'il, my mind kept returning to that day, almost exactly a decade ago now, when Mabrouk had come running up to my room, and dragged me to his house to pronounce judgement on the 'Indian machine' his father had bought. And now, that very Mabrouk was in the immediate vicinity of chemical and nuclear weapons, within a few minutes' striking distance of the world's most advanced machinery; it would be he who paid the final price of those guns and tanks and bombs.

Fawzia was standing at the door of their family house; she saw me as I turned the corner. 'Nabeel's not back yet, ya Amitab,' she said the moment she saw me. 'He's still over there, in Iraq, and here we are, sitting and waiting.'

'Have you had any news from him? A letter?'

'No, nothing,' she said, leading me into their house. 'Nothing at all. The last time we had news of him was when Isma'il came back two months ago.'

'Isma'il's back?'

'Praise be to God,' she smiled. 'He's back in good health and everything.'

'Where is he?' I said, looking around. 'Can you send for him?'

'Of course,' she said. 'He's just around the corner, sitting at home. He hasn't found a job yet—does odd jobs here and there, but most of the time he has nothing to do. I'll send for him right now.'

Looking around me, I noticed that something seemed to have interrupted the work on their house. When I'd seen it last I had had the impression that it would be completed in a matter of months. But now, a year and a half later, the floor was still just a platform of packed earth and gravel. The tiles had not been laid yet, and nor had the walls been plastered or painted.

'Hamdu'lillah al-salâma.' Isma'il was at the door, laughing, his hand extended.

'Why didn't you come?' he said, once the greetings were over. 'You remember that day you called from America? Nabeel telephoned me soon after he'd spoken to you. He just picked up the phone and called me where I was working. He told me that you'd said that you were going to visit us. We expected you, for a long time. We made place in our room, and thought of all the places we'd show you. But you know, Nabeel's boss, the shop-owner? He got really upset—he didn't like it a bit that Nabeel had got a long-distance call from America.'

'Why didn't Nabeel come back with you? What news of him?'

'He wanted to come back. In fact he thought that he would. But then he decided to stay for a few more months, make a little more money, so that they could finish building this house. You see how it's still half-finished—all the money was used up. Prices have gone up this last year, everything costs more.'

'And besides,' said Fawzia, 'what would Nabeel do back here? Look at Isma'il—just sitting at home, no job, nothing to do...'

Isma'il shrugged. 'But still, he wanted to come back. He's been there three years. It's more than most, and it's aged him. You'd see what I mean if you saw him. He looks much older. Life's not easy out there.'

'What do you mean?'

'The Iraqis, you know,' he pulled a face. 'They're wild...they come back from the army for a few days at a time, and they go wild, fighting on the streets, drinking. Egyptians never go out on the streets there at night: if some drunken Iraqis came across you they would kill you, just like that, and nobody would even know, for they'd throw away your papers. It's happened, happens all the time. They blame us, you see, they say: "You've taken our jobs and our money and grown rich while we're fighting and dying."'

'What about Saddam Hussein?'

'Saddam Hussein!' he rolled his eyes. 'You have to be careful when you breathe that name out there—there are spies everywhere, at every corner, listening. One word about Saddam and you're gone, dead.'

Later Isma'il told me a story. Earlier in the year Egypt had played a football match with Algeria, to decide which team would play in the World Cup. Egypt had won and Egyptians everywhere had gone wild with joy. In Iraq the two or three million Egyptians who lived packed together, all of them young, all of them male, with no families, children, wives, nothing to do but stare at their newly bought television sets—they had exploded out of their rooms and into the streets in a delirium of joy. Their football team had restored to them that self-respect that their cassette-recorders and television sets had somehow failed to bring. To the Iraqis, who have never had anything like a normal political life, probably never seen crowds except at pilgrimages, the massed ranks of Egyptians must have seemed like the coming of Armageddon. They responded by attacking them on the streets, often with firearms—well-trained in war, they fell upon the jubilant, unarmed crowds of Egyptian workers.

'You can't imagine what it was like,' said Isma'il. He had tears in his eyes. 'It was then that I decided to leave. Nabeel decided to leave as well, but of course he always needed to think a long time about everything. But then at the last minute he thought he'd stay just a little bit longer...'

My mind went back to that evening when I first met Nabeel and Isma'il; how Nabeel had said: 'It must make you think of all the people you left at home when you put that kettle on the stove with just enough water for yourself.' It was hard to think of Nabeel alone, in a city headed for destruction.

A little later we went to Isma'il's house to watch the news on the colour TV he had brought back with him. It sat perched on its packing case, in the centre of the room, gleaming new, with chickens roosting on a nest of straw beside it. Soon the news started and we saw footage of the epic exodus: thousands and thousands of men, some in trousers, some in jallabeyyas, some carrying their TV sets on their backs, some crying out for a drink of water, stretching all the way from the horizon to the Red Sea, standing on the beach as though waiting for the water to part.

There were more than a dozen of us in the room now. We were crowded around the TV set, watching carefully, minutely, looking at every face we could see. There was nothing to be seen except crowds: Nabeel had vanished into the anonymity of History.

# NOTES

# Prologue

**13. The slave's first appearance:** E. Strauss (now Ashtor), 'Documents for the Economic and Social History of the Near East' (*Zion*, n.s. VII, Jerusalem, 1942).

**13. Khalif ibn Iṣḥaq:** The ṣ and the ḥ in the name Iṣḥaq are distinct consonants. The system of notation used here for transcriptions from Arabic is broadly similar to that of the *Encyclopaedia of Islam*. In general, I have tried to keep transcriptions to a minimum, usually indicating the spelling of a word or name only upon its first occurrence. As a rule I have included the symbol for the Arabic consonant *'ain* (') wherever it occurs, except in place names, where I have kept to standard usage. Specialists ought to be forewarned that if, in these pages, they seek consistency in the matter of transcription, they shall find only confusion—a result in part of the many different registers of Arabic that are invoked here. On the whole where the alternative presented itself, I have favoured the dialectical usage over the literary or the classical, a preference which may seem misleading to some since the rural dialects of the Delta differ markedly in certain respects from the urban dialect that is generally taken to represent colloquial Egyptian Arabic.

**14. A German army had arrived:** Ibn al-Qalânisî, *The Damascus Chronicle of the Crusades*, pp. 280, (ed. and trans. H. A. R. Gibb, Luzac & Co. Ltd., London, 1967).

**14. 'That year the German Franks':** The historian was the famous Ibn al-Athîr (quoted by Amin Maalouf in *The Crusades through Arab Eyes*, tr. Jon Rothschild, Al Saqi Books, London, 1984).

**14. Among the nobles:** See Steven Runciman, *History of the Crusades*, Vol. II, pp. 279–80, (Cambridge University Press, Cambridge, 1952).

**14. 'There was a divergence':** Ibn al-Qalanisi, *Damascus Chronicle*, p. 282.

**15. 'the German Franks returned':** Ibn al-Athir, quoted by Amin Maalouf in *The Crusades through Arab Eyes*. Ibn al-Qalanisi wrote a vivid description of this engagement in *The Damascus Chronicle*, pp. 281–4. See also Steven Runciman, *History of the Crusades*, Vol II, pp. 281–4; and Virginia G. Berry, 'The Second Crusade', in *A History of the Crusades*, Vol. I, pp. 508–10 (ed. K. M. Setton, University of Wisconsin Press, Madison, 1969). Hans Eberhard Mayer discusses the Crusaders' decision to attack Damascus in *The Crusades*, p. 103, (tr. John Gillingham, Oxford

University Press, Oxford, 1988).

16. **They were...quick to relay news:** One of the services that merchants rendered each other in this period was the supplying of information (see Norman Stillman's article, 'The Eleventh Century Merchant House of Ibn 'Awkal (A Geniza Study)', p. 24 (in *Journal of the Economic and Social History of the Orient*, XVI, pt. 1, 1973). Not long after Khalaf ibn Ishaq's lifetime an Arab scholar was to tell Sultan Salâḥ al-Dîn's (Saladin's) son, al-Malik al-Ẓâhir, that merchants were 'the scouts of the world'. (Cf. S. D. Goitein, 'Changes in the Middle East (950–1150), as illustrated by the documents of the Cairo Geniza', p. 19, in *Islamic Civilisation*, ed. P. Richards, Cassirer, Oxford, 1973).

16. **'things which have no price':** My translation is based on Strauss's transcription in 'Documents for Economic and Social History of the Middle East'. The line quoted here is line 17.

16. **'two jars of sugar':** Ibid., line 18.

16. **'plentiful greetings':** Ibid., line 23.

17. **The Slave's second appearance:** S. D. Goitein, *Letters of Medieval Jewish Traders*, Princeton University Press, Princeton, 1973 (henceforth *Letters*). The quotations from Khalaf ibn Ishaq's letter in the next four paragraphs are all taken from Goitein's translation in this volume (pp. 187–92).

17. **This is another eventful year:** Cf. Steven Runciman, *History of the Crusades*, Vol. II, p. 226. See also, H. A. R. Gibb, 'Zengi and the Fall of Edessa', in *A History of the Crusades*, Vol. I.

19. **I had...won a scholarship:** The body in question is the Inlaks Foundation, of London, and I would like to take this opportunity to thank them. I am grateful, in particular, to the foundation's director Count Nicoló Sella di Monteluce for his encouragement and support.

19. **At that moment, I...expected to do research:** I would like to add a tribute here to the late Dr Peter Lienhardt of the Institute of Social Anthropology, who supervised my D.Phil. at Oxford. I consider myself singularly fortunate in having had him as my supervisor: he was endlessly generous with encouragement, fearsome in his debunking of pretension, and tireless in the orchestration of logistical support. Yet if I think of him today as the best of supervisors, it is not for all those virtues, inestimable as they are, but one yet more valuable still, being the rarest of all in academics: that he did everything he could to make sure that I was left to myself to follow my interests as I chose. My gratitude to him is inexpressible.

**19. Laṭaîfa:** Neither this nor the names of any of the settlements around it are their actual names; nor are the names of those of their inhabitants who are referred to in the following pages.

# Laṭaîfa

**29. Being the kindest...of men:** I would like to acknowledge here my enormous debt to the late Professor Aly Issa of the Department of Anthropology, Faculty of Arts, Alexandria. Professor Issa cleared a path for me through all the official hurdles that surround the enterprise of 'fieldwork' and because of him I was able to move into Lataifa within a few weeks of arriving in Egypt. I remember him with the deepest respect and affection and it is a matter of profound regret to me that he is not alive today to see this book in print.

My thanks are due to many others in the Faculty of Arts, a place of which I have the warmest memories. Amongst others, Hisham Nofal, Mohammad Ghoneim, Moustafa Omar, Merwat al-Ashmawi Osman, Taysser Hassan Aly Gomaa and Moustafa Awad Ibrahim, who were research students in the Department of Anthropology at the time, did a great deal to make me feel welcome when I first arrived in Alexandria. I would like to thank them all for the hospitality and friendship which they showed me then, and with which they have enriched all my subsequent visits. I would also like to thank in particular Professor Ahmed Abu-Zeid of the Faculty of Arts.

**32. They are both...Maṣr:** The name is Miṣr, properly speaking.

**32. Like English, every major European language:** Albanian, which uses 'Misir' as well as 'Egjypt', is an exception—probably because of its large Muslim population.

**34. The fort has other names:** See Stanley Lane-Poole's *The Story of Cairo*, pp. 34–5 (J. M. Dent & Co., London, 1902); and Desmond Stewart's *Cairo, 5,500 years*, p. 28 (Thomas Y. Creswell & Co., New York, 1968). A. J. Butler also discusses the name of the fortress briefly in his monumental *Arab Conquest of Egypt* (Oxford University Press, Oxford, 1902), pp. 244–6.

**34. Babylon's principal embankment:** W. Kubiak points this out in his excellent monograph *Al-Fustat, Its Foundation and Early Urban*

*Development*, pp. 43–7 & 117–8 (American University in Cairo Press, Cairo, 1987). See also Oleg V. Volkoff's *Le Caire*, 969–1969, p. 7 (L'Institut Français d'Archéologie Orientale du Caire, 1971); and Janet L. Abu-Lughod's *Cairo, 1001 Years of the City Victorious*, pp. 4–5 (Princeton University Press, Princeton, 1971).

34. **In Ben Yiju's time:** See Nâṣir-e-Khosraw's *Safarnama* (Book of Travels), p. 55, (trans. W. M. Thackston Jr, Persian Heritage Series, ed. Ehsan Yarshater, No. 36, Persian Heritage Foundation, New York, 1986).

36. **'fossaton':** Cf. W. Kubiak, *Al-Fustat*, p. 11; Janet L. Abu-Lughod, *Cairo 1001 Years*, p. 13; and Desmond Stewart, *Cairo*, pp. 42–3.

36. **Their army routed the Egyptians:** Cf. Stanley Lane-Poole's *A History of Egypt in the Middle Ages*, p.102 (Frank Cass & Co. Ltd, London, new impression, 1968); and Oleg V. Volkoff's *Le Caire*, p. 44.

36. **In its original conception al-Qahira:** Volkoff, pointing out that it was not for nothing that the city was called al-Qâhira al-Maḥrûsa, 'the Guarded', compares it to Peking and Moscow (*Le Caire*, p. 49).

37. **Archæological excavations have shown:** The various different kinds of mud and earth that were used as building materials in medieval Fustat are discussed at length in Moshe Gil's article, 'Maintenance, Building Operations, and Repairs in the Houses of the Qodesh in Fusṭâṭ', p. 147–52 (*Journal of the Economic and Social History of the Orient*, XIV, part II, 1971). The terms used in Lataifa and Nashawy for the kinds of earth that serve as building materials are in many instances the same as those current in medieval Fustat (e.g. ṭîn aswad, ṭîn aṣfar, turâb).

37. **Possibly Fustat even had...look of an Egyptian village:** My speculations about the appearance of medieval Fustat are founded largely on Wladyslaw Kubiak's description of the archæological findings at the site (in his monograph *Al-Fustat*). I hasten to add that Kubiak does not himself suggest that the medieval city had a rustic appearance: however, the findings described in the monograph seem to me definitely to indicate that likelihood. See in particular the section on 'Streets', pp. 112–117. Some medieval travellers reported Fustat to be provincial in aspect but crowded and busy, while others spoke with admiration of large multi-storeyed buildings, suggesting that houses in some parts of Fustat were of imposing dimensions (Cf. Oleg V. Volkoff, *Le Caire*, p. 22; and S. D. Goitein, 'Urban Housing in Fatimid and Ayyubid Times', p. 14, *Studia Islamica*, 46–7, 1978). In all likelihood the township had a few

wealthy neighbourhoods which were built on a very different scale from the dwellings inhabited by the vast majority of the population. In many details the domestic architecture of medieval Fustat appears remarkably similar to that of rural (Lower) Egypt today. Indeed there was clearly a direct continuity between the living patterns of the surrounding countryside and those of the city of Fustat. Dwellings in medieval Fustat even made provision for cattle pens or zarîbas within the house (Cf. S. D. Goitein, 'A Mansion in Fustat: A twelfth-century Description of a Domestic compound in the Ancient Capital of Egypt', in *The Medieval City*, ed. H. A. Miskimin et. al., Yale University Press, New Haven, 1977). The word zarîba has of course passed into the English language as 'zareba'. A contemporary zarîba is soon to play a part in this narrative.

38. **The 'Palestinian' congregation:** The principal doctrinal division within the Jewish community of medieval Fustat lay between the Karaites and the other two groups, known collectively as the Rabbanites; the Karaites took the Bible as their sole sacred text while the others invested the Talmud and other later Rabbinical writings with the authority of Scripture as well, as do the majority of Jews today. Of the two Rabbanite groups, the 'Iraqis' consisted of Jews from the area of Mesopotamia, who followed the rites prescribed by the schools of that region, while the 'Palestinians' of course followed the rites of the school of Jerusalem. See S. D. Goitein's *A Mediterranean Society*, Vol. I, p. 18 (Univ. of California Press, Berkeley, 1967); and Norman Golb's article, 'Aspects of the Historical Background of Jewish Life in Medieval Egypt' (in *Jewish Medieval and Renaissance Studies*, ed. Alexander Altmann, Harvard University Press, Cambridge Mass., 1967).

39. **Incredible as it may seem, excavations:** See G. T. Scanlon's 'Egypt and China: Trade and Imitation', p. 88 (in *Islam and the Trade of Asia*, ed. D. S. Richards, Oxford and Philadelphia, 1971); and Ruth Barnes's article 'Indian Trade Cloth in Egypt: The Newberry Collection' (in the *Proceedings of the Textile Society of America*, 1990).

54. **For Ben Yiju the centre of Cairo:** It was once thought that the synagogue of Ben Ezra was originally a Coptic church, but that theory has long been discredited by S. D. Goitein, although it continues to be widely propagated. A church was indeed converted into a synagogue in Fustat, in the ninth century, but it probably belonged to a different congregation and stood upon another site. (Cf. *A Mediterranean Society*, Vol. I, p. 18; and Vol. II, p. 149, University of California Press, Berkeley, 1971).

Goitein has persuasively argued that the church which changed hands in the ninth century was bought by the 'Iraqi' congregation, which, being composed mainly of immigrants, probably needed a site for its synagogue. The site of the Synagogue of Ben Ezra on the other hand had probably belonged to the 'Palestinians' since antiquity.

54. **It is known to have had two entrances:** See S. D. Goitein's 'The Sexual Mores of the Common People', p. 47 (in *Society and the Sexes in Medieval Islam*, ed. A. L. al-Sayyid Marsot, Udena Publications, Malibu, 1979); and Vol. II of his *Mediterranean Society*, pp. 143–52.

55. **For the Synagogue…the influx of migrants:** Cf. S. D. Goitein, 'Changes in the Middle East (950–1150)', p. 25; and 'Mediterranean Trade in the Eleventh Century: Some Facts and Problems', p. 61, (in *Studies in the Economic History of the Middle East*, ed. M. A. Cook, Oxford University Press, London, 1970).

55. **The North Africans…affinity for the flourishing trade:** Jews and Muslims in North Africa and the Middle East may have turned increasingly to the India Trade after the tenth century because they had been squeezed out of the Mediterranean trade by the Christian states of the northern coast. (See, for example, S. D. Goitein's article 'Portrait of a Medieval India Trader; Three Letters from the Cairo Geniza', p. 449, *Bulletin of the School of Oriental and African Studies*, Vol. 50, part 3, 1987). After the twelfth century Jewish merchants appear to have been gradually pushed out of the eastern trade by the Muslim association of Kârimî merchants. (Cf. W. J. Fischel, 'The Spice Trade in Mamluk Egypt', pp. 166–7, *Journal of the Economic and Social History of the Orient*, Vol. I, part 2, E. J. Brill, London, 1958.)

56. **The vast majority…were traders:** See S. D. Goitein, *Studies in Islamic History and Institutions*, pp. 277–8 (Leiden, Brill, 1966). As Goitein points out elsewhere, the upper crust of the Jewish community in Fustat was formed largely by the members of the 'Iraqi' and Karaite congregations, not by the 'Palestinians': 'as a rule it was the middle and lower middle classes and not the economically and socially highest layer of Jewish society which have left us their day to day writings in the Geniza.' ('Changes in the Middle East [950–1150]' p. 18.) See also Goitein's article 'The Sexual Mores of the Common People', p. 50.

56. **Their doctors…studied Hippocrates:** Cf. S. D. Goitein, *A Mediterranean Society*, Vol. II, p. 249

56. **The chambers…known by the term 'Geniza':** Cf. S. D. Goitein, *A*

*Mediterranean Society*, Vol. I, p. 1.

**57. The Geniza...was added:** For the date of the construction of the Ben Ezra Geniza see S. D. Goitein, *A Mediterranean Society*, Vol. I, p. 18. On 31 December 1011, a Jewish funeral procession was attacked by Muslims, and twenty-three people were taken captive and threatened with death. They were saved at the last moment by the personal intervention of the Caliph. Goitein has suggested that this incident may have had a direct connection with the addition of the Geniza at the time of the synagogue's reconstruction in 1025. 'Recalling the terrifying events of December 1011, they must have mused: Corpses must be removed from the city notwithstanding the constant menace by the rabble. But why take the same risk with papers? Let's have a place in the synagogue roomy enough for storing discarded writings now and for ever. The idea was materialized and the result was the Cairo Geniza.' ('Urban Housing in Fatimid and Ayyubid Times', p. 6.) The Geniza does however contain several documents that predate the rebuilding of the Synagogue of Ben Ezra in the eleventh century. (See Simon Hopkins's article 'The Oldest Dated Document in the Geniza', in *Studies in Judaism and Islam*, ed. Shelomo Morag et al., Hebrew University, Jerusalem, 1981.)

**57. for some reason...was never cleared out:** The recent research of Mark R. Cohen and Yedida K. Stillman suggests that the practice of discarding manuscripts in a chamber within a synagogue and leaving them there permanently was common among Middle Eastern Jews well into this century. See their article 'The Cairo Geniza and the Custom of Geniza among Oriental Jewry: An Historical and Ethnographic Study', in the Hebrew journal *Pe'amin* (No. 24, 1985).

**57. The document...thought to be the last:** See S. D. Goitein, *A Mediterranean Society*, Vol. I, p. 9.

**81. From the late seventeenth century...Egyptomania:** See Erik Iversen's *The Myth of Egypt and its Hieroglyphs in European Tradition*, pp 88–123, (Geo Gad Publishers, Copenhagen, 1961).

**81. Concurrent with this...travellers undertook journeys:** Cf. Eric Iversen, *The Myth of Egypt*, pp 108–110.

**81. It was...the first report:** The Italian traveller, Obadiah of Be(a)artinoro had described the Synagogue of Ben Ezra in a letter to his father in 1488, but the Geniza does not figure in his account (Cf. Simon Hopkins, 'The Discovery of the Cairo Geniza', pp 144–6, *Bibliophilia Africana* IV, ed. C. Pama, Cape Town, 1981).

81. **The visit appears...unremarkable:** Cf. Norman Bentwich, *Solomon Schechter; A Biography*, p. 139, (Cambridge Univ. Press, Cambridge, 1938), and Simon Hopkins, 'The Discovery...', p. 147.

82. **In fact...Karl Leibniz:** See Erik Iversen's *The Myth of Egypt*, p. 125.

83. **'Can a man risk':** Simon Hopkins, 'The Discovery...', p. 149.

83. **'But who knows':** ibid., p. 150.

84. **The German scholar:** Paul Kahle, *The Cairo Geniza*, pp. 2–3, (Oxford University Press, London, 1947).

84. **He had obtained...documents:** Paul Kahle, for example, met Samaritan priests in Palestine who complained bitterly of how Firkowitch had swindled them of their manuscripts, paying them next to nothing (*The Cairo Geniza*, p. 4).

85. **'It is not often':** Elkan N. Adler, 'Notes of a Journey to the East', p. 6 (*Jewish Chronicle*, 7 December 1888).

85. **The Cattaouis:** See Gudrun Krämer's account of the history of the Cattaouis in *The Jews in Modern Egypt, 1914–1952*, pp. 88–98 (University of Washington Press, Seattle, 1989).

85. **By this time the indigenous Jews of Cairo:** Marion Woolfson, *Prophets in Babylon; Jews in the Arab World*, p. 102 (Faber and Faber, London 1980); and Gudrun Krämer and Alfred Morabia: 'Face à la Modernité: Les Juifs d'Egypte aux XIXe et XXe siècles', pp. 84–5, (in Jacques Hassoun ed. *Juifs du Nil*, Le Sycomore, Paris, 1981).

86. **Soon afterwards the British ambassador:** The Earl of Cromer, *Modern Egypt*, Vol. I, p. 336–41, (Macmillan, London, 1908).

86. **The Cattaouis...mansion:** Elkan N. Adler, 'Notes', p. 6 .

87. **The Bodleian Library...two members of its staff:** They were A. Cowley and A. Neubauer. Both Cowley and Neubauer were greatly excited by the newly discovered fragments and were desperately eager to lay their hands on more, but curiously enough, even as late as 1896 they do not appear to have had any idea of where the documents were coming from. (See A. Neubauer's article, 'Egyptian Fragments', *Jewish Quarterly Review*, pp. 541–561, Vol. VIII, 1895–6; and A. Cowley's article in the same issue, 'Some Remarks on Samaritan Literature and Religion', pp. 562–575. See also Mark R. Cohen's *Jewish Self-Government in Medieval Egypt*, p. 11, Princeton, 1980).

88. **He took with him letters...the Cattaoui family** E. N. Adler, 'An Eleventh Century Introduction to the Hebrew Bible' (*Jewish Quarterly Review*, p. 673, Vol. IX, pp. 669–716, Macmillan, London, 1896–7).

88. **Between them, they granted:** Ibid., p. 673.

89. **'Dear Mrs Lewis,':** A copy of the note is reprinted in Norman Bentwich's *Solomon Schechter,* opp. p. 111.

89. **'All students of the Bible':** *The Academy,* p. 405, No. 1254, 16 May 1896.

90. **'If it could be proved':** S. Schechter, 'A fragment of the Original Text of Ecclesiasticus', p. 1 (*Expositor,* Fifth Series, Vol. IV, London, 1896).

91. **So little did he think:** A. Lutfi al-Sayyid, *Egypt and Cromer: A Study in Anglo-Egyptian Relations,* p. 64 (John Murray, London, 1968).

91. **'We need not...inquire too closely':** Quoted in A. Lutfi al-Sayyid, *Egypt and Cromer,* p. 62.

91. **Schechter was fortunate...that Cromer:** See, for example, N. Bentwich's Introduction to *Solomon Schechter: Selected Writings,* (ed. N. Bentwich, East and West Library, Oxford, 1946). Bentwich writes: 'Lord Cromer, then the British Agent in Egypt, was interested in Schechter's exploration, and helped him to secure the removal of the treasure to Cambridge.' (p. 15).

91. **They decided to make...a present:** See S. D. Goitein, *A Mediterranean Society,* Vol. I, p. 5; and Paul Kahle, *The Cairo Geniza,* p. 7.

92. **It has sometimes been suggested:** Bentwich, for example, writes: 'It was fortunate that the Egyptian Jewish community regarded their archives at that time as little more than a rubbish heap, and were prepared to let him carry away the greater part of their collection to Cambridge...' (Introduction to *Solomon Schechter: Selected Writings*).

92. **In fact...lucrative trade:** Schechter himself was to comment later that the beadles of the Synagogue had 'some experience' in dealing with the documents. (S. Schechter, 'The Cairo Geniza', p. 102, in *Solomon Schechter: Selected Writings*).

92. **'I flirted with him':** Bentwich quotes these letters in his biography, *Solomon Schechter,* p. 129.

93. **'For weeks and weeks':** Ibid., p. 128.

93. **'The whole population':** *Solomon Schechter: Selected Writings,* pp. 102–3.

94. **'with the spoils':** E. N. Adler, 'An Eleventh Century Introduction', p. 673.

98. **So it happened:** My first explorations of Masr owed a great deal to the enthusiasm of Sudhir Vyas. I would like to thank him, and his colleague at the Indian Embassy Shri A. Gopinathan, for their hospitality. I would

also like to thank Shri K. P. S. Menon and Sm. Lalitha Menon for their interest in, and support of my work during their stay in Egypt. Later Laurent Ham's knowledge of the city was to prove invaluable to me: I am deeply grateful to him for his help and for innumerable kindnesses.

**99. Goitein...published in India:** Cf. S. D. Goitein, 'Letters and Documents on the India Trade in Medieval Times', (*Islamic Culture*, Vol. 37, pp. 188–205, 1963).

**99. The complete bibliography:** Robert Attal, *A Bibliography of the Writings of Professor Shelomo Dov Goitein*, Hebrew University, Jerusalem, 1975 (Supplement 1987).

**99. His interest in the Geniza:** See Mark R. Cohen's obituary 'Shelomo Dov Goitein (3 April 1900–6 February 1985)' in the American Philosophy Society *Year Book*, 1987.

**100. His monumental study:** The five volumes of S. D. Goitein's *A Mediterranean Society* were published in the following years, by the University of California Press: Vol. I, 1967; Vol. II, 1971; Vol. III, 1978; Vol. IV, 1983; Vol. V, 1988. The fifth volume appeared posthumously.

**100. Scanning Goitein's...oeuvre:** Goitein did however occasionally write biographical sketches. His posthumously published article 'Portrait of a Medieval India Trader: Three Letters from the Cairo Geniza' (*Bulletin of the School of Oriental and African Studies*, Vol. 50, part 3, pp. 449–64, 1987), for example, deals with the life of the trader 'Allân b. Ḥassûn.

**100. *The India Book*:** The catalogue numbers of the India Book documents were published in Shaul Shaked's *A Tentative Bibliography of Geniza Documents* (Mouton, Paris, 1964), which was published under the joint direction of D. H. Baneth and S. D. Goitein.

**101. Judæo-Arabic evolved:** This brief account is based largely upon the 'Introduction' in Joshua Blau's *Judæo-Arabic*, (Clarendon Press, Oxford, 1965), the standard work on the subject. Those who wish to learn more about this extraordinary and wonderful language are strongly recommended to consult Blau's excellent study.

**104. Mark Cohen's encouragement:** In case my debt to Mark Cohen is not apparent already, I would like to add a line of acknowledgement here. It was Mark Cohen who convinced me that I could indeed learn Judaeo-Arabic, and he has been very generous with constructive criticism as well as advice and encouragement ever since. My debt to him is incalculable.

**105. Over the next couple of years:** My Geniza research would not have been possible without the support of a great many people. To begin with, I would like to thank Dr A. Udovitch of the Department of Near Eastern Studies, Princeton and Dr Stefan C. Reif of the Taylor-Schechter Geniza Research Unit of the Cambridge University Library. To Dr Geoffrey Khan, also of the Taylor-Schechter Geniza Research Unit, Cambridge, I owe a very special debt—for guiding my first faltering steps in the field of Geniza studies, for giving me the benefit of his understanding of the material, and for his patience in answering my innumerable queries. Dr Menahem Ben Sasson also helped me a great deal in the early stages of my research and I would like to thank him for his advice, for many valuable suggestions and for checking several of my transcriptions. I need hardly add that neither he nor anyone else is in any way responsible for any of the views expressed here. Finally a tribute is due to the staff of the Manuscripts Reading Room of the Cambridge University Library for their efficiency and unfailing helpfulness.

# Nashâwy

**153. Since his friends...referred to him as al-Mahdawî:** Khalaf Ibn Ishaq for instance, addresses Ben Yiju as al-Mahdawî in his 1148 letter (National and University Library Jerusalem Geniza MS H.6, in Strauss, 'Documents').

**153. Mahdia...a major centre of Jewish culture:** See H. Z. Hirschberg's *A History of the Jews in North Africa*, Vol. I, pp. 339–41 (E. J. Brill, Leiden, 1974).

**153. 'altogether Mahdia offered':** Al-Sharîf al-Idrîsî, *Kitâb tazha al-mushtâq fi ihtirâq al-afâq*, p. 257 (Geographie d'Edrisi, ed. and trans. P. A. Jaubert, Vol. I, Paris, 1836).

**153. Of Ben Yiju's immediate family:** S. D. Goitein believed that Ben Yiju may have had another sister, Yumn (cf. *Letters*, pp. 204 fn).

**154. He was called Perahyâ:** The Jewish naming system in the medieval Arabic-speaking world was enormously complex being compounded out of two languages, Arabic and Hebrew. Most people had several names, each context-specific—tekonyms, nicknames, (both individual and collective), titles that were the equivalent of surnames, and so on. To simplify matters I have tried to refer to each individual by a single name throughout this narrative. As a rule (if a principle founded on indeterminacy can be called a rule) I have tried to use the name that is most commonly used for them in the documents themselves. I have also generally tried to transcribe the names as they occur in the documents, in the expectation that those spellings provide the nearest available approximation to the manner in which the names were actually pronounced, at the time, by the people who used them. But in such instances when those spellings produce results that are meaningless or absurd I have substituted the etymologically appropriate Hebrew equivalents. Thus I have generally used the Arabic 'Farhîa' instead of the Hebrew 'Peraḥyâ', taking at face value the following statement by Goitein: 'No such Heb. name (Peraḥyâ) exists in the Bible. This is one of the pseudo-biblical names invented during the Geniza period and I suspect that the verb contained in it was understood as Ar. faraḥ ("Joy in God") rather than Heb. peraḥ ("flower") which makes no sense.' (*Letters*, pp. 327). The relationship between the name and the Arabic root was evidently apparent to those who used it, since Farhia is usually twinned with the diminutive Surûr, which has a similar semantic value in Arabic. I have however used 'Berâkhâ' rather than 'Barkha' for example, (which is how the name is spelt by Ben Yiju, in his letter), since it has no Arabic equivalent or referent. I can only beg the indulgence of those who consider this method haphazard, or otherwise objectionable, while pointing out that when a naming system is intended to create multiple levels of identity, any procedure for privileging one name (or even one spelling) is bound to be arbitrary.

154. **and he was a Rabbi:** Khalaf ibn Ishaq once addressed Ben Yiju as the son of the '(R(abbi) Peraḥyâ, son of Yijû' (S. D. Goitein, *Letters*, pp. 192).

155. **Madmun ibn Bundar:** See S. D. Goitein, *Letters*, pp. 177; 181–82; and 'From Aden to India: Specimens of the Correspondence of India Traders of the Twelfth Century', p. 45, (in *Journal of the Economic and Social History of the Orient*, Vol. XXXIII, pts I and II, 1980). For the institution of the nagîd, see Goitein's articles, 'The Title and Office of the Nagid; a Re-examination' (*Jewish Quarterly Review*, pp. 93–119, LIII, 1962–3), and 'Mediterranean Trade in the Eleventh Century: Some Facts and Problems', p. 61 (in *Studies in the Economic History of the Middle East* ed. M. A. Cook, Oxford University Press, London, 1970). The Nagîdate and the interesting historiographical controversies surrounding it are also extensively discussed in Mark Cohen's *Jewish Self-Government in Medieval Egypt*.

156. **Madmun's earliest extant letters:** T–S 20.130. My assumption that this is the first item in Madmun's correspondence with Ben Yiju is based on a comment in the text (recto, lines 4–5) which seems to suggest that Ben Yiju had only recently made the journey to India.

156. **From the tone and content of those...letters:** Their business relations were patterned on a model of informal co-operation, widespread amongst Middle Eastern merchants, in which traders in different countries rendered each other mutual service. For more on the subject of co-operation amongst merchants see S. D. Goitein's article 'Mediterranean Trade in the Eleventh Century: Some Facts and Problems', p. 59; and Abraham L. Udovitch's 'Commercial Techniques in Early Medieval Islamic Trade', (in *Islam and the Trade of Asia*, ed. D. S. Richards).

156. **The letters are full of detailed instructions:** for example, one passage in a letter from Madmun to Ben Yiju in India reads: '...collect yourself all the letters for the people of Mangalore...and be careful with them because they contain things that I need urgently...deliver each one to the person to whom it is addressed, by hand, personally, for God's sake.' (T–S N.S. J 1, verso, lines 6–10). In a departure from the epistolary conventions of the time, Madmun used the second person pronoun, inta, a relatively familiar form, to address Ben Yiju: I have translated it as 'yourself' in this passage. It is a clear indication that there was a certain asymmetry in their relationship.

156. **The other was Khalaf ibn Ishaq:** Khalaf was a fine calligrapher and a prolific correspondent; many of his letters to various different correspondents have been preserved in the Geniza. See S. D. Goitein, 'Portrait of a Medieval India Trader', p. 453–54.

157. **Judah ha-Levi...composed poems in his honour:** See S. D. Goitein's article, 'The Biography of Rabbi Judah Ha-Levi in the Light of the Cairo Geniza Documents' (in *Essays in Medieval Jewish and Islamic Philosophy*, ed. Arthur Hyman, Ktav Publishing House, Inc., New York, 1977).

157. **Abû Sa'id Ḥalfon:** In a letter to Ben Yiju in Mangalore, Madmun refers to a certain 'Nâkhudha Abû Sa'îd' who might be Abu Sa'id Halfon (T–S MS Or 1081, J3, recto, line 3). Although to the best of my knowledge, no letters addressed directly from Ben Yiju to Abu Sa'id Halfon (or vice versa) have been preserved, several letters between others in the circle have survived (e.g. T–S MS Or. 1080 J 211 and T–S Box J 1 fol. 53 [Khalaf to Halfon]. Cf. Shaul Shaked, *Tentative Bibliography*, pp. 47, 150).

157. **The second of the great travellers:** Abû-Zikrî Sijilmâsî and Abu Sa'id Halfon were in fact partners in the Indian Trade, and several documents relating to their joint business dealings have been preserved in the Geniza (e.g. T–S 13 J 22, fol. 33, 'Memorandum to Ḥalfon b. Nethaneel, while on his way to India, from his partner Abû Zikrî' and T–S N.S. J 22, 'Deed of acquittance by Abû Zikrî to Ḥalfon b. Nathaneel in connection with their India business' (Shaul Shaked, *Tentative Bibliography*, pp. 132, 160).

158. **Chief Representative of Merchants:** See S. D. Goitein, *Letters.* p. 62; 'The Beginnings of the Kârim Merchants', pp. 176–7 (*Journal of the Economic and Social History of the Orient*, Vol. I, part 2, E. J. Brill, Leiden, 1958); and 'Bankers Accounts from the Eleventh Century AD', pp. 62–3 (*Journal of the Economic and Social History of the Orient*, IX, pt. I–II, 1966).

158. **References...a shipowner called Maḥrûz:** See T–S 8 J 7, fol. 23, recto, line 3; T–S N.S. J 10, verso 1st Account, line 9; and 2nd Account, line 1.

158. **So close were the...three:** See S. D. Goitein, *Letters*, pp. 62–5.

159. **At the time...gifted Hebrew poets:** Cf. Yosef Tobi, 'Poetry and Society in the works of Abraham ben Ḥalfon (Yemen, twelfth century)' (in *Biblical and Other Studies in Memory of S. D. Goetein*, ed. Reuben Ahroni, *Hebrew Annual Review*, Vol. IX, Dept. of Judaic and Near Eastern Languages and Literatures, Ohio State University, 1985).

159. **instances of Geniza traders living abroad:** See, for example, S. D. Goitein, 'Abraham Maimonides and his Pietist Circle', p. 157 (in *Jewish Medieval and Renaissance Studies*, ed. A. Altmann).

159. **The second reason...lies in a cryptic letter:** T–S MS Or. 1080 J 2 63, verso.

160. **Fortunately the scrap:** Ben Yiju was clearly the recipient of his letter, because the back of the letter is scribbled on in a handwriting which is unmistakably his. Professor Goitein included the catalogue number of this letter in Shaked's catalogue of Geniza documents, and he must have known of its contents for he described it there as the 'first part of a letter sent by Maḍmûn...of Aden to Ben Yijû in India,' (Shaul Shaked, *Tentative Bibliography*, p. 47). But he did not quote it in any of his published references to Ben Yiju and probably did not fully appreciate the implications it has for the story of Ben Yiju's life.

160. **'Concerning what he':** T–S MS Or. 1080 J 263, recto, lines 16–22.

The meaning of the second part of the last sentence is doubtful, and my reading of it must be taken as provisional at best. The reference to the 'court' may be to the council of foreign merchants (cf. M. N. Pearson, *Merchants and Rulers in Gujarat*, p. 17, University of California Press, Berkeley, 1976).

160. **'His servant spoke to [the king]'**: It is not quite clear who the reference is to. Aden in this period was controlled by the Zuray'ids, a dynasty of the Isma'îli sect, nominally linked to the Fatimids of Egypt. The dates and lines of succession within the dynasty are rather obscure, but it would appear that none of the Zuray'id rulers of this period bore the name Sa'id (cf. g. R. Smith, *The Ayyûbids and Early Rasûlids in the Yemen*, Vol. II, pp. 63–7, Luzac & Co. Ltd, London, 1978). However, the name could have been the popularly current name of the Zuray'î ruler of that time.

161. **The word is dhimma**: In Islamic law, members of tolerated religious groups are known as the dhimmi.

174. **In the twelfth century...Qus**: Cf. J-C. Garcin, 'Un centre musulman de la Haute-Égypte médiévale: Qûṣ' (Cairo, IFAO, 1976) and W. J. Fischel's 'The Spice Trade in Mamluk Egypt', pp. 162–4. The twelfth-century Arab geographer, Al-Idrisi wrote of Qus that it was a big mercantile city with many resources, but its air was unhealthy and few strangers escaped the insalubriousness of the climate (*Kitâb*, p. 127).

174. **'a station for the traveller'**: The quotation is from R. J. C. Broadhurst's translation of the *Raḥla* of Abû al-Ḥasan ibn Jubaîr (published as *The Travels of Ibn Jubaîr*, Jonathan Cape, London, 1952).

175. **Over the next seventeen days**: The crossing took Ibn Jubair only seventeen days, but Al-Idrisi asserts that it generally took at least twenty days (*Kitâb*, p. 132).

175. **Ibn Jubair remarked...'whoso deems it lawful'**: R. J. C. Broadhurst, *Travels*, p. 60.

176. **The area...inhabited by a tribe**: This was one of the Beja tribes of Sudan and southern Egypt who are referred to frequently by medieval Arab geographers and travellers (e.g. Al-Idrisi, *Kitâb*, p. 133). See also Paul Wheatley's article, 'Analecta Sino–Africana Recensa', p. 82 (in *East Africa and the Orient*, ed. H. Neville Chittick and R. I. Rotberg, Africana Publishing Co., New York and London, 1975).

176. **'Their men and'**: R. J. C. Broadhurst, *Travels*, p. 66.

176. **'A sojourn in'**: Ibid., p. 67.

176. 'It is one': Ibid., p. 63. for the maritime routes of the Red Sea, see G. R. Tibbetts, 'Arab Navigation in the Red Sea', pp. 322–4 (*Geographical Journal,* 127, 1961).

176. For about five hundred years Aidhab functioned: See, for example, H. A. R. Gibb's article on 'Aydhâb (in the *Encyclopaedia of Islam),* and G. W. Murray's article 'Aidhab' (in *The Geographical Journal,* 68, pp. 235–40, 1926).

176. In any case, all that remains: Cf. J-C. Garcin, 'Jean-Léon l'Africain et 'Aydab', p. 190 (*Annales Islamologiques,* XI, 1972).

177. 'The carrier of this letter': T-S N.S. J 1, recto, lines 13–16.

178. But the writing...is clear: Cf. Shaul Shaked, *Tentative Bibliography,* p. 134.

178. 'Shaikh Abraham Ibn Yijû bespoke': T-S 13 J 24, fol. 2, recto, lines 9–22 and margins.

178. 'For the affair of Shaikh Makhluf': T-S MS Ov. 1081 J 3, recto, margin.

227. The first...a legally attested deed: Cf. S. D. Goitein, *Letters,* p. 202.

227. The second...is a rough draft: T-S 12.458 verso, lines 5–13. I would like to thank Dr Geoffrey Khan for translating the Aramaic words in this document for me.

228. 'concubinage is permitted': Al-Idrisi, *Kitâb,* p. 179.

228. 'Let us thank God,': Cf. G. Ferrand, *Voyage du Marchand Arabe Sulayman en Inde et en Chine,* p. 124 (Paris, 1922).

228. 'Public women are everywhere': 'The Travels of Nicolo Conti in the East in the Early Part of the Fifteenth Century', p. 23 (translated from the original of Poggio Bracciolini by J. Winter Jones, in *India in the Fifteenth Century; Being a Collection of Narratives of Voyages to India,* ed. R. H. Major, Hakluyt Society, London, 1857).

228. 'Immediately after midday': 'Narrative of the Voyage of Abd-er-Razzak, Ambassador from Shah Rukh, A.H. 845, A.D. 1442', p. 29 (translated by R. H. Major from the French translation of the Persian by M. Quatremère, in *India in the Fifteenth Century,* ed. R. H. Major).

229. 'I have also sent': T–S N.S. J 1 recto, line 11.

229. The connection seems so obvious: S. D. Goitein, *Letters,* p. 202.

229. In a set of accounts...the name Naîr: T-S 20.137, verso, line 19 (account no.2). The word of Ben Yiju used was sahrî, 'brother-in-law' or male affine. It is worth noting that in Ben Yiju's circle this term was generally used in a specific sense, and not as a portmanteau kinship term

(for a case to point see p. 178 of S. D. Goitein's article 'The Beginnings of the Kârim Merchants').

229. **The lucky accident...links her...to the Nairs:** This squares well with what is known of the social composition of Mangalore at the time, for it is recorded in contemporary inscriptions that a community of Nairs was indeed resident in the area around that time. Accounts left by later travellers suggest that the Nairs of that region had developed particularly close links with foreign traders. See P. Gururaja Bhatt's *Studies in Tuḷuva History and Culture*, pp. 234–5 (Manipal, Karnataka, 1970).

230. **'And throughout the [land]':** Benjamin of Tudela, *The Itinerary*, pp. 120–1 (ed. Michael A. Signer, 1983).

# Mangalore

242. **When Ben Yiju arrived:** See Neville Chittick, 'East Africa and the Orient: Ports and Trade before the arrival of the Portuguese' (in *Historical Relations Across the Indian Ocean*, UNESCO, Paris, 1980).

242. **'living in a suburb':** See Ibn Battúta *Travels in Asia and Africa, 1325–1354*, p. 233 (trans. and selected by H. A. R. Gibb, Routledge & Sons, London, 1939).

243. **'China, Sumatra, Ceylon,':** Ibid, p. 234.

243. **'Arabs, Persians, Guzarates':** Duarte Barbosa, *A Description of the Coasts of East Africa and Malabar in the beginning of the sixteenth century*, p. 202 (trans. H. E. J. Stanley, The Hakluyt Society, London, 1856).

243. **'[They] possess...wives':** Ibid., p. 202.

243. **'They dress themselves':** 'Narrative of the Voyage of Abd-er-Razzak', p. 17 (in *India in the Fifteenth Century*, ed. R. H. Major).

244. **...the Arabic name 'Malabâr':** The name is spelt variously as Malâbâr and Malîbâr in the Geniza documents. It also sometimes occurs in plural forms, such as Malîbârât.

244. **The language of Mangalore:** See K. V. Ramesh, *A History of South Kanara*, xxiv–xxvi (Karnatak University Research Publications, Series 12, Dharwar, 1970); 'Geographical Factors in Tuluva History', p. 7 (*Academy Silver Jubilee Lecture*, Academy of General Education, Manipal, Karnataka, 1981); U. P. Upadhyaya & S. P. Upadhyaya (ed.), *Bhuta Worship: Aspects of a Ritualistic Theatre*, p. 1 (Regional Resources Centre

for Folk Performing Arts, M.G.M.College, Udupi, Karnataka, 1984); P. Claus, 'Mayndaḷa: A Legend and Possession Cult of Tuḷunâḍ', p. 96 (*Asian Folklore Studies*, Vol. 38:2, 1979); and G. R. Krishna, *Caste and Tribes of Fishermen*, pp. 103–11 (Discovery Publishing House, New Delhi, 1990).

244. **It is this language:** Tuḷu is spoken by 47 per cent of the population of South Kanara District—the area that was once known as Tuḷanâḍ (*Karnataka State Gazetteer [South Kanara District]*, p. 94, Govt. of Karnataka, Bangalore, 1973).

245. **Writing in Alexandria...Ptolemy:** The name of this dynasty is also spelt, in various inscriptions, as Aḷva, Aḷuka, Aḷupa and Aḷapa (Cf. K. V. Ramesh, *A History of South Kanara*, p. 30; and P. Gururaja Bhatt, *Studies*, p. 18).

245. **For several hundreds of years:** For detailed accounts of the history of the Aḷupas see K. V. Ramesh's *History of South Kanara;* P.Gururaja Bhatt's *Studies*, pp. 18–41; and B. A. Saletore's *Ancient Karnataka*, (*History of Tuluva*, Vol. I, Oriental Book Agency, Poona, 1936).

245. **it was in the reign of...:** Cf. K. V. Ramesh, *History of South Kanara*, p. 115. P.Gururaja Bhatt dates Kavi Aḷupendra's reign from 1115 to 1155 (*Studies* p. 23).

246. **I had been told:** I am indebted to a great many people for offering help, advice and criticism while I was working in Karnataka. I would particularly like to thank Dr C. Veeranna, Dr G. S. Sivarudrappa, Dr M. N. Srinivas, Sm. Tara N. Chandravarkar and Dr Vivek Dhareshwar of Bangalore; Dr Vijaya Dabbe of Mysore; and Dr K. S. Haridas Bhatt, Shri S. A. Krishnaiah, Dr Alphonsus D'Souza and Sm. L. Lobo-Prabhu of Mangalore. The late Shri K. S. Niranjana and Sm. Anupama Nivanjana were also very generous with their time and advice while I was in Bangalore; I would like to record my gratitude to them here.

247. **In the translated version of the letter:** S. D. Goitein, *Letters*, p. 191.

247. **Indeed...an accepted way of spelling the word:** The tenth-century Arab traveller and geographer Masûdî, for example, uses the word brâhma and various cognates frequently in his encyclopaedic compendium, *Murûj al-Dhahab (Les Prairies d'or)*, Vol. I, pp. 149, 154, & 157–8 (Arabic text and French Translation, C. Barbier de Meynard & Pavet de Courteille, Société Asiatique, Paris, 1861). The geographer Al-Idrisi, who happened to be a contemporary of Ben Yiju's, was perfectly familiar with the word although he never went anywhere near the Indian

Ocean. Al-Idrisi uses the word frequently but he sometimes uses it to mean Brahmin (as indeed does Mas'udi often).

248. **The slave-trade in Ben Yiju's time:** A Persian chronicler of the ninth century describes travelling merchants who took 'eunuchs, female slaves (and) boys' from 'the country of the Franks', in Europe, and traded them, in India and China, for 'musk, aloes, camphor and cinnamon', (Ibn Khurdâdhbih, quoted in Reinaud's introduction to Abû al-Fidâ's *Kitâb taqwîm al-buldân* (Géographie d'Aboulfélda), p. 58, Arabic text, ed. M. Reinaud & Baron MacGuckin de Slane, Paris, 1860). A century later, a geographer, Ibn Ḥauqâl, noted that Byzantine, Slavonic and Berber slaves were regularly traded in the cities of the east. (Cf. H. Z. Hirschberg, *Jews in North Africa*, p. 252). Edward H. Schafer deals briefly with the import of foreign slaves into China in *The Golden Peaches of Samarkand*, pp. 43–7 (University of California Press, Berkeley, 1963).

248. **Indeed, an obscure reference:** In one of his letters, Madmun, writing to Ben Yiju, remarks: 'This year the "traders" (jallâb) have not come here yet from Zabîd' (T-S 20.130, recto, lines 45–46). The word jallâb has the connotation of 'slave-traders'. The implication of the passage is that Ben Yiju had been expecting the arrival of a party of slave-traders in Mangalore. Al-Idrisi observes that Zabid was a major destination for Abyssinian slave-traders (*Kitâb*, Vol. I, p. 49).

248. **The slaves...traded in...Egypt:** See S. D. Goitein, 'Slaves and Slavegirls in the Cairo Geniza Records', (*Arabica*, Vol.9, 1–20, 1962); and *A Mediterranean Society*, Vol. I, pp. 130–147.

249. **But the slave's name:** Dr Geoffrey Khan has found the name Bâmah in a third-century AH Arabic papyrus, and he interprets it as a rendering of the Coptic name Pamei/Pame (personal communication). It is extremely unlikely however that the B-M-H of MS H.6 is intended to represent the same name, since it is spelt differently, not just once, but consistently through the whole range of Ben Yiju's correspondence.

249. **I discovered...Mâsaleya Bamma:** R. S. Panchamukhi (ed.), *Karnataka Inscriptions*, Vol. II., pp. 71–2 (Kannada Research Institute, Dharwar, 1951).

249. **Another...Seṭṭi Bamma:** Ibid., pp. 72–73.

250. **Over...but still preserved:** For example, one of the principal matrilineal clans of Tulunad bears the name 'Bommiya-baḷi'. There is also a Bommi-ṣeṭṭiya-baḷi among the many matrilineal baḷis mentioned in medieval inscriptions. See P. Gururaja Bhatt, *Studies*, pp. 243 & 250–1.

**251. But divided…the Tuluva:** Cf. P. Claus, 'Spirit Possession and Spirit Mediumship from the Perspective of Tulu Oral Traditions', (in *Culture, Medicine & Psychiatry*, 3:94–129, 1979). The distinctively Tuluva matrilineal system of law is known as Aliya-santâna law. By the rules of this system, men transmit their immoveable property, not to their own children, but matrilineally, to their sister's children. But it is important to note that among the Tuluva, as with most groups that are characterized as 'matrilineal', these rules apply only to certain categories of property. P. Claus in his article 'Terminological Aspects of Tulu Kinship: Kin Terms, Kin Sets, and Kin Groups of the Matrilineal Castes' (in *American Studies in the Anthropology of India*, 1981) has very rightly questioned the usefulness of labels such as 'matrilineal' and 'patrilineal' in these circumstances (p. 213). In his view some Tuluva institutions are suggestive of double unilineal descent (p. 234). Where I have used the term 'matrilineal' without qualification it is purely for convenience; these qualifications must be taken for granted.

**251. Equally, they shared in the worship of…Bhûtas:** See, for instance, the following articles: Heidrun Brückner, 'Bhûta-Worship in Coastal Karnâṭaka: An Oral Tuḷu myth and festival ritual of Jumâdi', p. 18 (*Studien zur Indologie und Iranistik*, 13/14, Reinbek, 1987); P. Claus, 'Possession, Protection and Punishment as Attributes of the Deities in a South Indian Village', p. 235 (*Man in India*, 53:231–242, 1973); and Mark Nichter, 'The Joga and Maya of Tuluva Buta', p. 140, (*Eastern Anthropologist*, 30:2).

**251. By tradition, each of the Tuluva castes:** Mark Nichter, 'The Joga and Maya of Tuluva Buta', p. 143.

**252. The cult was tied to the land:** Mark Nichter, 'Joga and Maya of Tuluva Buta', p. 139. It is also worth noting that Tuluva Brahmins follow patrilineal rules of succession. (See P. Claus, 'Terminological Aspects of Tulu Kinship: Kin Terms, Kin Sets, and Kin Groups of the Matrilineal Castes', p. 214).

**252. There was no contradiction:** See Mark Nichter's 'Joga and Maya' for a detailed account of the workings of this process.

**253. Koti and Chennaya:** Cf. G. R. Krishna, *Caste and Tribes*, p. 109.

**254. Later, he explained…Berme:** I am deeply grateful to Prof. B. A. Viveka Rai for this and many other comments and suggestions, for his unstinting generosity with his time and erudition, and for a great many other kindnesses. On the subject of Berme see H. Brückner, 'Bhûta-

Worship in Coastal Karnâtaka', p. 29; and P. Claus, 'Spirit Possession and Spirit Mediumship from the Perspective of Tulu Oral Traditions', p. 40. Bermeru, or the Tulu Brahma is always depicted as a figure seated on a horse with a sword in hand. Cf. plates 437–8 in P. Gururaja Bhatt, *Studies*, and U. P. Upadhyaya & S. P. Upadhyaya (ed.), *Bhuta Worship: Aspects of a Ritualistic Theatre*, plate 4.

**255. The letter in question:** T-S 20.137 recto. Ben Yiju used the reverse side of this fragment for jotting down certain invaluable notes and accounts.

**255. It is worth adding…this sum of money:** These figures are computed on the basis of E. Ashtor's statistics, pp. 200–201, (*A Social and Economic History of the Near East in the Middle Ages*, University of California Press, Berkeley, 1976.). The figures for mutton and olive oil are based on prices prevalent at the beginning of the eleventh century. There were however considerable differences in value between the Malikî dinars of Aden and Fatimid dinars, at various points in time. The reader is cautioned therefore, that these figures are, at best, very rough approximations.

**256. Alternatively,…three adult Spaniards:** Cf. S. D. Goitein, 'Changes in the Middle East (950–1150)'. The ransom for an adult person in Spain at that time was $33^1/3$ dinars (p. 21).

**256. …the wage of any artisan:** E. Ashtor, *Social and Economic History*, p. 200. Standard earnings were remarkably stable throughout the eleventh and twelfth centuries (cf. S. D. Goitein, 'Urban Housing in Fatimid Times', p. 9).

**256. Madmun's accounts show:** T-S 20.137, recto, line 36–7; T-S N.S. J 1, recto, line 5–6.

**256. enough to buy a…mansion in Fustat:** See E. Ashtor, *Histoire des prix et des salaires dans l'Orient médiéval*, p. 184, Paris, 1969.

**256. The expedition:** S. D. Goitein, 'Two Eye-Witness reports on an Expedition of the King of Kish (Qais) against Aden', (*Bulletin of the School of African and Oriental Studies*, XVI/2, pp. 247–57, London, 1956).

**257. The Amîrs of Kish…their depredations:** Cf. Al-Idrisi, *Kitâb*, pp. 59, 153 & 171.

**257. But…the pirates tried not to invite:** For the attempts of the Sung government to control piracy in Chinese waters see Jung-Pang Lo's article, 'Maritime Commerce and its relation to the Sung Navy', pp. 57–101 (*Journal of the Economic and Social History of the Orient*, XI, pt. III, 1968). Lo points out: 'the problem of piracy suppression was not just a simple matter of police action. Beside the unscrupulous merchants who were in league with the outlaws, there were respectable merchants who started out their career as pirates', (p.74).

257. **...ever tried to gain control of the seas:** The historian K. N. Chaudhuri, for instance remarks: 'Before the arrival of the Portuguese in the Indian Ocean in 1498 there had been no organised attempt by any political power to control the sea-lanes and the long distance trade of Asia...The Indian Ocean as a whole and its different seas were not dominated by any particular nations or empires.' (*Trade and Civilisation in the Indian Ocean*, p. 14, Cambridge University Press, Cambridge, 1985).

258. **Sirâf:** Sirâf was one of the most important ports of the Persian Gulf in the Middle Ages. See K. N. Chaudhuri's *Trade and Civilisation*, p. 48; and Rita Rose Di Meglio's article, 'Arab Trade with Indonesia and the Malay Peninsula from the eighth to the sixteenth century', p. 106 (in *Islam and the Trade of Asia*, ed. D. S. Richards).

258. **Ramisht of Siraf:** See S. M. Stern, 'Râmisht of Sîrâf, a Merchant Millionaire of the Twelfth Century', p. 10, (*Journal of the Royal Asiatic Society*, pp. 10–14, 1967).

258. **Ramisht's trading empire:** Cf. S. D. Goitein, *Letters*, p. 193.

258. **'Thus God did not':** S. D. Goitein, 'Two Eye-Witness Reports...', p. 256.

259. **'And after that':** T-S 20.137, recto, lines 1–5.

259. **entirely different from...'slavery':** M. I. Finley, *Ancient Slavery and Modern Ideology*, pp. 58–62, (Chatto and Windus, London, 1990).

260. **Slavery...a kind of career opening:** S. D. Goitein began the section on slavery in *A Mediterranean Society* (Vol. I) with the observation: 'In order to be able to understand the economic role and the social position of slaves in the society reflected in the Geniza records, we must free ourselves entirely of the notions familiar to us from our readings about life on American plantations or in ancient Rome.' (p. 130). In the extensive anthropological literature on the subject it has of course, long been recognized that it is almost impossible to distinguish formally between slavery and certain other social estates.' (Cf. Claude Meillasoux, *L'esclavage en Afrique précoloniale*, Paris, 1975; and Jack Goody, 'Slavery in Time and Space', in James L. Watson ed. *Asian and African Systems of Slavery*, University of California Press, Berkeley, 1980).

260. **In the medieval world, slavery:** In various languages words that are

now translated as 'slave' actually had the sense of dependant. For a discussion of the meaning and etymology of Chinese slave-terms, see E. G. Pulleybank, 'The Origins and Nature of Chattel Slavery in China', pp. 193–204, *Journal of the Economic and Social History of the Orient*, Vol. I, pt. 2, (E. J. Brill, Leiden, 1958).

**261. In their poetry:** M. Chidanandamurthy, in his account of slavery in medieval Karnataka, in *Pâgaraṇa mattu itara samprabandhagaḷu* ('Pagarana and other research papers', Pustaka Chilume, Mysore, 1984) for instance, draws much of his material from the work of Basavaṇṇa and other Vachanakara saint-poets (I am grateful to Prof. B. A. Viveka Rai for translating portions of the relevant article for my benefit).

**261. Judaism...felt the influence of Sufism:** Cf. Paul Fenton's translation of 'Obadyâh Maimonides', (1228–1265), *Treatise of the Pool*, pp. 2–3 (Octagon Press, London, 1981). Fenton's introduction provides an outline of Sufi influences on Jewish mysticism.

**261. Egypt, in particular:** See for example S. D. Goitein's 'A Jewish Addict to Sufism in the time of the Nagid David II Maimonides', (*Jewish Quarterly Review*, Vol. 44, pp. 37–49 1953–54).

**262. 'worthier disciples':** S. D. Goitein, 'Abraham Maimonides and the Pietist Circle', p. 146, (in *Jewish Medieval and Renaissance Studies*, ed. Alexander Altmann).

**262. Their own conceptions:** See Annemarie Schimmel, *Mystical Dimensions of Islam*, p. 141–3 (University of North Carolina Press, Chapel Hill, 1975).

**262. For the Sufis...the notion of being held by bonds:** Forms of the Arabic root which expresses the idea 'to bind, tie up', r-b-ṭ, are threaded through Sufi discourse: they range from the brotherhoods called rabîta to the murâbiṭ (marabouts) of Morocco and rabita kurmak, the Turkish phrase which expresses the tie between the Sufi Shaikh and his disciples. (See Annemarie Schimmel, *Mystical Dimensions*, pp. 231 & 237).

**262. 'the slave of his slave':** Ibid., p. 292; see also Franz Rosenthal's *The Muslim Concept of Freedom Prior to the Nineteenth Century*, p. 93, (Leiden, E. J. Brill, 1960).

**263. Amongst the members of:** A large number of documents relating to such esoteric and magical cults, as well as protective talismans etc. have survived in the Geniza. See Norman Golb, 'Aspects of the Historical Background of Jewish Life in Medieval Egypt', pp. 12–16. The custom of visiting saint's graves was followed widely within the congregation of the

Synagogue of Ben Ezra in Fustat (see, for example, S. D. Goitein's article, 'The Sexual Mores of the Common People', p. 58). For the use of talismans in North African Jewish communities in modern times see Yedida Stillman, 'The Evil Eye in Morocco', (in *Folklore Research Centre Studies*, Vol. I, ed. Dov Noy, Issachar Ben-Ami, Hebrew University of Jerusalem, Jerusalem, 1970).

264. **it was...dismissed:** P. Gururaja Bhatt, for example, writes: 'devil-worship has been, for centuries, the core of the Tuḷuva cult among the non-Brahmins.' (*Studies*, p. 356).

265. **The spot was tended by a Pujari:** For the role of the Pujari in Bhûtaradhana see G. R. Krishna's *Caste and Tribes*, pp. 175–8.

266. **Over the years...Bomma's role:** See for example, S. D. Goitein, *Letters*, p. 191; E. Strauss, 'Documents', p. 149 (line 23 'to brother Bomma especially from me, plentiful greetings'); and T-S 18 J 4, fol. 18, recto, line 47, 'and special greetings to Shaikh Bomma'.

267. **Among the items he brought back:** T-S 20.137, recto, lines 46–48, & T-S N.S. J 1, recto, lines 8–11. Coral was an important product of the medieval Muslim west. It was obtained from the coasts of Spain and North Africa (Cf. Norman Stillman, 'The Merchant House of Ibn 'Awkal', p. 63). Soap was another luxury item exported by the Muslim west. Stillman writes: 'It was the Arabs who first discovered that soap could be made from olive oil instead of foul-smelling animal fats. The Arabs often perfumed their soap, and in Europe soap from the Arab countries was considered an article of luxury.' (p. 66, ibid.). Ben Yiju frequently imported soap from Aden to Mangalore.

267. **'They wear only bandages':** R. H. Major, *India in the Fifteenth Century*, p. 17. 'Abd al-Razzaq notes that this apparel was common to 'the king and to the beggar'. See Goitein's discussion of attitudes towards clothing as they are represented in the Geniza documents (*A Mediterranean Society*, Vol. IV, pp. 153–159, 1983).

267. **Several...mention imported Egyptian robes:** These garments were referred to as fûṭa and maqṭaʿ. See, for example, T-S 1080 J 95, recto, lines 8–9; T-S 10 J 9, fol. 24, lines 14–15; T-S 20.137, recto, line 48; and T-S 10 J 12, fol. 5, verso, line 9, & T-S 10 J 9, fol. 24, recto, lines 14–15 (maqṭaʿ iskandarânî). For cloths that he may have used as turbans, see T-S 8 J 7, fol. 23, recto margin.

268. **'I have also...sent for you':** T-S 18 J 2, fol. 7, recto, lines 15–18.

268. **In the Middle East...paper:** For treatments of the medieval paper

industry in the Middle East, see S. D. Goitein, 'The Main Industries of the Mediterranean Area as Reflected in the Records of the Cairo Geniza', pp. 189–193 (*Journal of the Economic and Social History of the Orient,* Vol. IV, 1961); and E. Ashtor, 'Levantine Sugar Industry in the Later Middle Ages—An Example of Technological Decline', pp. 266–73, (*Israel Oriental Studies,* VII, Tel Aviv University, 1977). For the role of paper in medieval Muslim culture, see Qazi Ahmadmian Akhtar, 'The Art of Waraqat', (*Islamic Culture,* pp. 131–45, Jan. 1935); and 'Bibliophilism in Medieval Islam', (*Islamic Culture,* pp. 155–169, April 1938). There is of course an extensive literature on the manufacture of books in the Islamic world in the Middle Ages. See for example, T.W. Arnold & A. Grohmann, *The Islamic Book,* (Paris, Pegasus Press, 1929).

**268. 'the best available':** T-S K 25. 252, verso, lines 14–15.

**268. 'no one has its like':** T-S 18 J 2, fol. 7, recto, lines 19–20. For some other references to paper (waraq) in Ben Yiju's correspondence see T-S 8 J 7, fol. 23, verso, line 1 (waraq maṣrî); T-S 18 J 4, fol. 18, recto, line 42; T-S Misc. Box 25, fragm. 103, recto, line 48; & T-S N.S. J 1, recto, line 9.

**269. Much of his kitchenware:** For mention of 'iron frying-pans' (maqlâ ḥadîd) see T-S 20.137, recto, line 47; for glasses (zajjâj), 20.137, recto, line 45; T-S MS Or. 1081 J 3, recto, lines 7; and for soap (ṣâbûn), T-S 10 J 9, fol. 24, recto, line 16; T-S 8 J 7, fol. 23, recto margin, and T-S 20.137, recto, line 48.

**269. For his mats:** For references to mats from Berbera (ḥuṣar barbarî) see T-S 18 J 2, fol. 7, recto, line 12; T-S 20.137, recto, line 46; and T-S K 25.252, recto, line 21. For mention of a 'Barûjî ṭanfasa' see T-S K 25.252, recto, line 23.

**269. His friends…sent him raisins':** For references to sugar (sukkar in Ben Yiju's correspondence) see, T-S 10 J 12, fol. 5, recto, line 22; T-S 10 J 9, fol. 24, recto, line 16; T-S K 25.252, verso, line 13; T-S 18 J 2, fol. 7, recto, line 22; T-S Misc. Box 25. 103, recto, line 43; T-S N.S. J 1, recto, line 9; and (National and University Library, Jerusalem) Geniza MS H.6, line 18 (E. Strauss, 'Documents…'). For raisins (zabîb) see T-S 18 J 5, fol. 1, recto, line 23; T-S N.S. J 1, recto, line 9; T-S K 25.252, verso, line 13; T-S 10 J 9, fol. 24, recto, line 16; T-S 18 J 2, fol. 7, recto, line 22; T-S Misc. Box 25, fragm. 103, recto, line 43; T-S 8 J 7, fol. 23, recto margin; and (National and University Library, Jerusalem) Geniza MS H.6, line 19 (E. Strauss, 'Documents…').

**269. The various kinds of palm-sugar:** Failing to find sugar in Aden once,

Khalaf ibn Ishaq commented 'Your servant looked for sugar, but there is none to be had this year,' as though in apology for the deprivation he was inflicting on his friend (T-S 18 J 5, fol. 1, recto, margin).

269. **If it seems curious:** Ben Yiju's imports of sugar offer a sidelight on the history of that commodity in India. Sugar cane is, of course, native to India and is even mentioned in the Vedas. In his article, 'Sugar-Making in Ancient India' (*Journal of the Economic and Social History of the Orient*, VII, pt. 1, 1964, pp. 57–72) Lallanji Gopal points out that processes for the manufacturing of refined sugar are mentioned in the Jatakas and were evidently well-known in India since antiquity. Yet, the travellers who visited the Malabar in the later Middle Ages (such as Marco Polo), generally refer to sugar made from palm products, not cane-sugar (p. 68, fn.). This must mean either that cane-sugar was not manufactured in India on a commercial scale or that the process was not widely in use on the Malabar coast. At any rate, the fact that Ben Yiju imported sugar from the Middle East indicates clearly that refined sugar was not generally available in the Malabar coast, and was probably not commercially produced in India at the time. By the sixteenth century, however, sugar had become a major export in Bengal (cf. Archibald Lewis, 'Maritime Skills in the Indian Ocean', *Journal of the Economic and Social History of the Orient*, XVI, pts. II–III, 1973). This means that processes of sugar manufacturing had been widely adopted in India in the intervening centuries—possibly from the Middle East. This may be the reason why the names of certain sugar products in India still invoke Middle Eastern origins.

269. **In the Middle Ages, it was Egypt:** The reader is referred to E. Ashtor's excellent article 'The Levantine Sugar Industry in the Later Middle Ages—An Example of Technological Decline', (*Israel Oriental Studies*, VII, Tel Aviv Univ., 1977). See also Norman Stillman's 'The Merchant House of Ibn 'Awkal', p. 47.

270. **As fishermen...free of restrictions:** However, it is worth noting that the origins and nature of the prohibition on sea travel for Hindus ('crossing the black water') of which so much was made in the nineteenth century, are extremely obscure. The indications are that the privileging of restrictions on sea-travel amongst Hindus was a relatively late, possibly post-colonial development. For a useful discussion of this question the reader is referred to M. N. Pearson's excellent article 'Indian Seafarers in the Sixteenth Century', p. 132, (in M. N. Pearson, *Coastal Western India*,

# Notes

*Studies from the Portuguese Records,* Concept Publishing Co., New Delhi, 1981).

271. **Soon after I reached Mangalore...Bobbariya-bhuta:** See U. P. Upadhyaya & S. P. Upadhyaya, *Bhuta Worship,* p. 60; B. A. Saletore, *Ancient Karnataka,* p. 461, (Oriental Book Agency, Poona, 1936); and K.Sanjiva Prabhu, *Special Study Report on Bhuta Cult in South Kanara District,* pp. 143–4, (*Census of India,* Series 14, Mysore, 1971). The legends and rituals associated with the Bobbariya-Bhuta are discussed at some length in G. R. Krishna's *Caste and Tribes,* (pp. 180–5), which is a detailed study of the Magavira caste.

271. **No Magavira settlement...without its Bobbariya shrine:** U. P. Upadhyaya & S. P. Upadhyaya, *Bhuta Worship,* p. 60.

275. 'With a whole temple': Allama Prabhu, trans. A. K. Ramanujan, *Speaking of Siva,* p. 153 (Penguin Books, London, 1987).

275. 'The kâ[r]dâr': T-S 20.137, verso, 2–4. In this account Ben Yiju misspells the word 'kârdâr' as kâdâr.

276. 'You my master': S. D. Goitein, *Letters,* p. 193. I have substituted the words 'disgrace' and 'censure' for the words 'excommunicate' and 'excommunication'. The words used in the manuscript (T-S 12.320 recto) are two forms of the Arabic root 'sh-m-t'. I am informed by Dr Geoffrey Khan that this is not the root that is normally used to designate excommunication in the Geniza documents; it should be read instead as 'the metathesized form of sh-t-m (to insult, defame), which is used in Maghrebî Arabic...' The letter would, therefore, be referring to some form of public defamation, or 'rogues gallery' (personal communication). Prof. Goitein probably used the term 'excommunicate' on the assumption that the 'kârdâl' was Jewish. The evidence, as we shall see, suggests otherwise.

276. kârdâl: The word must have been unfamiliar to Yûsuf ibn Abraham for he misspelled it as 'kârdâl'.

276. 'As for the delay': T-S 18 J 4, fol. 18, recto, lines 25–28. It is worth noting that among Khalaf and his friends 'reminding a person of a debt was almost an insult', (S. D. Goitein, 'Portrait of a Medieval India Trader', p. 452).

276. **He and Yusuf continued:** For a somewhat fuller version of the affair of the kârdâr's cardamom see my article, 'The Slave of MS H.6', (in *Subaltern Studies,* Vol. VII, Oxford University Press, New Delhi, 1992). I would like to take this opportunity to thank the faculty of the Centre for

Studies in Social Sciences, Calcutta (where this book was mainly written) for their comments and criticisms of an earlier version of that article. I also wish to thank Professor Asok Sen, Ranabir Samaddar, Tapati Guha Thakurta, Anjan Ghosh, Pradip Bose and Tapti Roy for the many discussions and arguments with which they have enriched my thinking. Partha Chatterjee has been a constant (if laconic) source of support and encouragement for many years and his comments and suggestions on this manuscript have been invaluable to me. To thank him would be an impertinence.

**276. The clue lies...in a throwaway scrap:** The sentence goes thus: 'Remaining (with me) for Nâîr, the brother of the kârdâr, 3 fîlî dirham-s.' T-S N.S. J 10, verso, margin.

**278. Long active...Gujarati merchants:** Cf. M. N. Pearson, *Merchants and Rulers in Gujarat*, pp. 7–12 (University of California Press, Berkeley, 1976). The Vanias were usually referred to as a single group in Ben Yiju's papers—Baniyân—but they were actually composed of many different sub-castes (see Pearson's *Merchants and Rulers*, p. 26). For the transoceanic dispersal of Gujarati traders in the Middle Ages, see Paul Wheatley's *The Golden Khersonese*, p. 312 (University of Malaya Press, Kuala Lumpur, 1961). Wheatley quotes an observation by Tomé Pires, the sixteenth-century Portuguese chronicler, that of the 4,000 foreign merchants resident in Malacca in 1509, 1,000 were Gujaratis. See also R. B. Serjeant, *The Portuguese off the South Arabian Coast*, p. 10 (Clarendon Press, Oxford, 1963); M. N. Pearson's article, 'Indian Seafarers in the Sixteenth Century', p. 132; and Archibald Lewis's article, 'Maritime Skills in the Indian Ocean', pp. 243–4.

**278. Madmun, for one:** In one of his letters Madmun asked Ben Yiju to inform his Gujarati contacts about the probable behaviour of the prices of pepper and iron in the Middle East in the coming year (T-S 18 J 2, fol. 7, verso, lines 3–6). See also S. D. Goitein's article, 'From Aden to India', p.53.

**278. Ben Yiju...served as a courier:** Cf. T-S N.S. J 1, verso, line 4–10.

**278. Madmun...proposed a joint venture:** T-S 18 J 2, fol. 7, verso, lines 1–2. Curiously Ishaq is referred to as 'the Bâniyân'. The names of the others are spelt: Kanâbtî and Sûs Sîtî respectively. I am grateful to Prof. B. A. Viveka Rai for the suggestion that the latter could be 'Sesu Shetty'. Cf. also Goitein, ibid.

**278. Equally, the ships:** S. D. Goitein thought it possible that the name of the powerful Kârimî merchants association was derived from the Tamil word kâryam, 'which, among other things, means "business, affairs"' ('The Beginnings of the Kârim Merchants', p. 183).

**278. Among the...nâkhudas:** For 'Pattani-svâmi' see Goitein, *Letters*, p. 188, fn. One NMBRNI is mentioned as a shipowner by Madmun (T-S K 25.252 recto, line 13). For a discussion of the meaning of the term nâkhuda (which is spelt in various different ways in Ben Yiju's documents), see M. N. Pearson's 'Indian Seafarers in the 16th. century', p. 118.

**279. 'between him and me':** Goitein, *Letters*, p. 64. The letter was addressed to Abu Zikri Sijilmasi, who was in Gujarat.

**279. In addition, Ben Yiju...connected with...metalworkers:** Bronze objects and utensils that Ben Yiju shipped to his friends are referred to repeatedly in the documents. See, for example, T-S K 25.252, verso, line 11; T-S Misc. Box 24, fragm. 103, recto, line 34; ; T-S 18 J 5, fol. 1, line 13; T-S 18 J 4, fol. 18, recto, line 35; & T-S 8 J 7, fol. 23 recto, line 4. Locks are referred to it the following documents, T-S K 25.252, verso, line 11 & T-S 18 J 2, fol. 7, recto, line 7. See also S. D. Goitein, *Letters*, p. 192–5.

**279. The names of these craftsmen:** The workmen's names, spelt 'Iyârî and LNGY appear to be variants of the Tamil Brahmin name Ayyar and the name-element Linga. Imports of copper, lead and bronze for the workshop are frequently alluded to in his papers. See for example, T-S K 25.252, recto, lines 6 & 28; & T-S 8 J 7, fol. 23, verso, line 6. See also S. D. Goitein, *Letters*, pp. 192–194.

**279. Membership...involved binding understandings:** The economy of Fatimid Egypt was, to use Goitein's words, largely a 'paper economy'— that is payments were generally made not in cash, but by debt transfers, letters of credit and orders of payment. Cf. S. D. Goitein, 'Changes in the Middle East (950–1150)', p. 19; 'Bankers Accounts from the Eleventh Century AD', pp. 28–68; and *A Mediterranean Society*, Vol. I, pp. 241–62. See also W. J. Fischel, 'The Spice Trade in Mamluk Egypt', p. 170; and A. L. Udovitch, 'Commercial Techniques', p.53–61. Ben Yiju's papers and accounts suggest that this paper economy was not localized in Egypt or the Middle East. There are several references in Ben Yiu's papers to credit arrangements between himself, his friends in Aden and Indian merchants.

**280. Common sense suggests...the language:** The cultural and linguistic diversity of the regions surrounding the Indian Ocean were represented in microcosm in all its major ports. A Portuguese observer, Tomé Pires, who spent two and a half years in Malacca at the beginning of the sixteenth century, reported that eighty-four languages could be heard in the streets of that city—Babel realized! (Cf. Paul Wheatley, *The Golden Khersonese*, p. 312). Taken at face value, that figure would suggest that communication had effectively ceased in Malacca—or that it was possible only within tiny speech communities.

**281. Given what we know:** See Kees Versteegh, *Pidginization and Creolization: The Case of Arabic*, p. 114 (*Current Issues in Linguistic Theory: 33*, Amsterdam, 1984); and Keith Whinnom, 'Lingue France: Historical Problems', p. 296 (in A.Valdman (ed.) *Pidgin and Creole Linguistics*, Indiana University Press, Bloomington, 1977).

**281. The Arab geographer Mas'udi:** S. Muhammad Husayn Nainar, *The Knowledge of India Possessed by Arab Geographers down to the 14th. century AD with special reference to Southern India*, p. 95 (Madras University Islamic Series, University of Madras, 1942).

**282. Ben Yiju's usage:** See for example, Mas'udi, *Murûj*, Vol. I, p. 163, and Al-Idrisi, *Kitâb*, Vol. I, pp. 162–183. The names 'Şîn' and 'China' may of course derive from Sanskrit and Prakrit words (see the article 'The Name China' by Berthold Laufer in *T'oung Pao*, II/13, pp. 719–26, 1912, and Paul Pelliot's article 'L'Origine du nom de <Chine>', in the same issue (pp. 727–742).

**282. India,…as the Arab geographers well knew:** G. Ferrand, V*oyage du Marchand Arabe Sulayman*, p. 48; and Mas'udi, *Murûj*, p. 162.

**282. For several centuries…a king called the Ballahrâ:** Several medieval Arab geographers and travel writers asserted that the 'Ballahrâ' was India's 'king of kings', the pre-eminent ruler in the land. Thus, Ibn Khurdadhbih, writing in the ninth century remarked 'the greatest king of India is the Ballahrâ or king of kings,' while one of his contemporaries noted: "The Ballahrâ is the most noble of the princes of India; the Indians recognise his superiority.' (Gabriel Ferrand, *Relations de Voyages et Textes Géographiques, Arabes, Persanes et Turks, Relatifs à l'Extrème-Orient du VIIIe au XVIIIe Siècles*, Vol. I, pp. 22 & 42, Ernest Leroux, Paris, 1913). Mas'udi, writing in the tenth century, observed: 'The most powerful of the kings of India is the Ballahra, the lord of the city of Mankir. Most Indian chiefs turn towards him when they say their prayers.' (*Murûj*, Vol. I, p. 177). Al-Idrisi was to add his considerable authority to these statements a couple of centuries later (see *Kitâb*, p. 47, and G. Ferrand, *Relations*, p. 196). See also André Miquel, *La Géographie humaine du Monde Musulman jusqu'au milieu du 11e siècle*, Vol. II, p. 84 (Mouton, Paris, 1975).

282. **An eminent scholar:** S. M. H. Nainar, *The Knowledge of India*, pp. 138–140.

283. **…small kingdoms and principalities:** As Ibn Battuta put it: 'In (the Malabar) there are twelve infidel sultans, some of them strong with armies numbering fifty thousand men, and others weak with armies of three thousand. Yet there is no discord whatever between them, and the strong does not desire to seize the possessions of the weak.' (*Travels*, p. 232).

284. **The place…known as 'Jurbattan':** S. M. H. Nainar, *The Knowledge of India*, p. 41.

284. **After about two days…'Budfattan':** S. M. H. Nainar, *The Knowledge of India*, pp. 29–30. The town is also known as Valarapattanam.

285. **For much of the distance:** Ibn Battuta, *Travels*, p. 232.

285. **'Dahfattan'…lies:** S. M. H. Nainar, *The Knowledge of India*, p. 32. The town is also known as Dharmapattanam.

285. **A little further…Pantalayini Kollam:** S. M. H. Nainar, *The Knowledge of India*, p. 35.

286. **Cabral delivered a letter:** Cf. K. N. Chaudhuri, *Trade and Civilisation*, p. 68.

286. **The Portuguese fleet sailed:** Cf. R. S. Whiteway, *The Rise of Portuguese Power in India 1497–1550*, pp. 86–7.

286. **A year…later…da Gama returned:** Cf. George D. Winius, 'From Discovery to Conquest', p. 224, (in *Foundations of the Portuguese Empire, 1415–1580*, by Bailey W. Diffie and George D. Winius, University of Minnesota Press, Minneapolis, 1977).

287. **'The heathen [of Gujarat]':** Quoted by M. N. Pearson, in 'Indian Seafarers in the Sixteenth Century', p. 121.

288. **'between resistance and submission':** M. N. Pearson, *Merchants and Rulers*, p. 69. See also C. R. Boxer, *The Portuguese Seaborne Empire, 1415–1825*, p. 46 (A. A. Knopf, New York, 1969).

288. **As far as the Portuguese were concerned:** In 1595 Philip II of Spain took matters a step farther and 'decreed that no non-Christian resident in Western India could trade, either directly or through an intermediary, to places other than those on the Western India coast.' (M. N. Pearson, *Merchants and Rulers*, p. 53).

288. **In 1509AD:** See M. N. Pearson, *Merchants and Rulers*, p. 31; George

D. Winius, p. 240–1 (in *Foundations of the Portuguese Empire*) and S. A. I. Tirmizi, 'Portuguese problems under the Muzaffarids' (in *Some Aspects of Medieval Gujarat*, Munshiram Manoharlal, Delhi, 1968).

# Going Back

**299. The news...from Ifriqiya:** H. Wieruszowski, 'The Norman Kingdom of Sicily and the Crusades', p. 22.

**299. 'Shaikh Abû Isḥâq':** T-S 18 J 4, fol. 18, recto, lines 33–5.

**300. 'Concerning the news':** T-S Misc. Box 25, fragm. 103, recto, lines 27–9.

**300. 'My master [Ben Yiju]':** T-S 13 J 7, fol. 27, recto, lines 15–18. Altogether, five of Ben Yiju's letters, three from Khalaf ibn Ishaq and two from Yusuf ibn Abraham, refer to Mubashshir. These letters appear to have been written over a relatively short period of time. The last in the sequence is probably the letter of MS H.6 (from Khalaf ibn Ishaq) which has been dated by Strauss as having been written in 1148AD. Another letter from Khalaf, (T-S Misc. Box 24, fragm. 103) has been dated to 1147 by S. D. Goitein (cf. S. Shaked, *Tentative Bibliography*, pp. 147). Since Mubashshir's stay in Egypt was probably not a very long one, it seems likely that the others were written in the couple of years immediately preceding 1147. The five letters are: T-S 12.235 (from Yusuf ibn Abraham); T-S 13 J 7, fol. 27 (from Yusuf ibn Abraham);T-S 18 J 4, fol. 18, (from Khalaf ibn Ishaq); T-S Misc. Box 25, fragm. 103, (from Khalaf ibn Ishaq); MS H.6, E. Strauss, 'Documents', (from Khalaf ibn Ishaq).

**300. 'As for the news':** T-S 13 J 7, fol. 27, recto, lines 18–19;

**300. Disease and famine had followed:** Cf. H. Wieruszowski, 'The Norman Kingdom of Sicily and the Crusades', p. 23.

**300. In western Europe:** Cf. Virginia G. Berry, 'The Second Crusade', p. 463–512, in K. M. Setton (Gen. ed.) *A History of the Crusades*, Vol. I, University of Wisconsin Press, Madison, 1969.

**301. 'Behold the days of reckoning':** *The Jews and the Crusaders (The Hebrew Chronicles of the First and Second Crusades)*, p. 123, (translated and edited by Shlomo Eidelberg, University of Wisconsin Press, Madison, 1977).

**301. They were relatively lucky:** H. Z. Hirschberg, *History of the Jews in*

*North Africa*, p. 128, and 'The Almohade Persecutions and the India Trade', in *Yitzhak F. Baer Jubilee Volume* (ed. S. W. Baeon et. al., History Society of Israel, Jerusalem, 1960).

**301. The letter...by Abu Zikri's son:** H. Z. Hirschberg, 'The Almohade Persecutions and the India Trade'. This letter contains an extraordinary usage: the writer uses the Arabic word fataḥ (victory, lit. 'opening'), which has the sense of 'liberated', to describe the Almohad entry into Tlemcen—an event that he clearly regarded as a disaster. It is a striking instance of the ironies that Judæo-Arabic sometimes imposed on its users (line 41, p. 142).

**301. Not long before:** Cf. S. D. Goitein, *Letters*, pp. 62–65.

**301. On that occasion, Ben Yiju:** The nakhuda Mahruz frequently acted as a courier for Ben Yiju and his friends and is mentioned several times in their letters (Cf. T-S 8 J 7, fol. 23, recto, line 3; T-S N.S. J 10, verso, 1st. Account, line 9, 2nd. Account, line 1. See also S. D. Goitein, *Letters*, pp. 62–5. Goitein notes there that Mahruz's sister was married to Judah b. Joseph ha-Kohen (Abu Zikri Sijilmasi).

**302. 'I asked [some people]':** Cf. E. Strauss, 'Documents', p. 149 (lines 10–14, MS H.6).

**302. 'Every year you speak':** Cf. E. Strauss, 'Documents' p. 149 (lines 23–4, MS H.6).

**302. 'I do not know':** The catalogue number of this document is T-S 10 J 10, fol. 15. This letter was first transcribed and published by J. Braslawsky in *Zion*, (7, pp. 135–139) in 1942. Goitein also published an English translation of it in 1973 (*Letters*, pp. 201–6). All except one of the following quotations from this document are taken from Goitein's translation.

**303. '[Therefore], I ask you':** I have made the word 'brother' plural here to preserve the implied sense of the passage.

**303. 'I heard of what happened':** I have translated this passage directly from Braslawsky's transcription (Cf. *Zion*, 7, p. 138), (T-S 10 J 10, fol. 15, lines 41–44 [verso 5–8]).

**304. 'I wished to ask':** Bod. Lib. Ox. MS Hebr., d. 66, fol. 139, recto, lines 6–12.

**313. Such were the misfortunes:** The chronology of this period of Ben Yiju's life is not easy to establish. The document T-S 12.337 appears to have been written some three years or so after T-S 10 J 10, fol. 15, which Goitein has dated as being written on 11 September 1149 (*Letters*, p.

201). This plus the sequence of documents and events that follow upon it, suggest that T-S 12.337 was written in 1152–3 or thereabouts.

**313.** 'I wrote a letter to you': T-S 12.337, recto, lines 4–6.)

**314.** 'I did all...in my power': T-S 12.337, recto, lines 6–8.)

**314.** 'As for Mubashir':T-S 12.337, recto margin.

**314.** ...the joyful name Surûr: 'Surur' was of course, the diminutive for Farhia (Perahyâ), and both names derive from roots that have the connotation of 'joyfulness' (cf. Goitein, *Letters*, p. 327, fn.). Farhia was also Ben Yiju's father's name which was why both he and his brother Yusuf named their first-born sons Farhia (Surur). Ben Yiju was in fact sometimes addressed by the tekonym 'Abû Surûr' or 'father of Surur'

**314.** 'two children like sprigs': T-S 12.337, recto, line 13.

**314.** 'And the elder': T-S 12.337, recto, lines 14–16.,

**315.** Dhû Jibla: G. R. Smith, *Ayyûbids and Early Rasûlids*, p. 66.

**315.** 'The news reached your...slave: T-S 10 J 13, fol. 6, lines 13–17. The second part of the quotation (lines 14–17) are in Hebrew, and were kindly translated for me by Dr Geoffrey Khan. See also S. Shaked's *Tentative Bibliography*, p. 102.

**315.** Ben Yiju...a Hebrew poem: T-S 8 J 16, fol. 23. Cf. S. Shaked's *Tentative Bibliography*, p. 86.

**315. Such documentation as there is:** Such was his position that one of his correspondents of that time used phrases such as 'the gracious sage', 'the head of the community' and other such honorifics to address him. Cf. T-S 10 J 13, fol. 6, lines 5 and 7 (I am grateful to Dr Geoffrey Khan for translating these honorifics for me). A document containing parts of three legal opinions written by Ben Yiju, suggest that he had some judicial functions within the community. They are written on the reverse side of a letter that Yusuf ibn Abraham had sent to him in Mangalore (T-S 10 J 9, fol. 24), but Goitein was of the opinion that the drafts were written after Ben Yiju's departure from India, 'probably in Yemen' (S. Shaked, *Tentative Bibliography*, p. 100).

**315. Yet there must...have been anxieties:** The letter in question is Bod. Lib. Ox. MS Hebr. d. 66 (Catalogue n. 2878), fol. 61. Lines 10–15 deal with the safety of the roads and were evidently written in answer to a query from Ben Yiju. The Yemen in this period was riven by struggles between the Mahdids and the Najâhids (see G. R. Smith, *Ayyûbids and Early Rasûlids*, p. 58).

**316.** ...such marriages were commonplace: Khalaf's relative Madmun for example, was married to the sister of Abu Zikri Sijilmasi, who was, of course, originally from the Maghreb (see S. D. Goitein, *Letters*, p. 62).

316. **Instead, he began to dream:** For a brief review of the literature on cousin marriage in the Middle East see J. M. B. Keyser's article, 'The Middle Eastern Case: Is There a Marriage Rule?', (*Ethnology*, 13, pp. 293–309).

316. **'Shaikh Khalaf [ibn Ishaq]':** T-S 12.337, recto, lines 20–25.

317. **'and we will rejoice':** T-S 12.337, recto, line 19.

317. **'Address your letters to me':** T-S 12.337, recto, lines 30–32.

317. **'Suliman and Abraham':** T-S 12.337, recto, line 34 & margin.

325. **But it had other compensations:** At this time, and until well afterwards, the Jews of Sicily looked to North Africa in matters of liturgy and religion (see David S. H. Abulafia, 'The End of Muslim Sicily', in *Muslims Under Latin Rule*, ed. James M. Boswell, Princeton University Press, Princeton, 1990).

325. **The young Surur:** My description of Surur's voyage to Messina is based on S. D. Goitein's translation of the letter he wrote home after reaching that city (Letters, pp. 327–330).

326 **Sulîmân ibn Ṣaṭrûn:** Mentioned in Ben Yiju's second letter to Yusuf (T-S 12.337, recto, lines 25–6)

326. **In this instance,...in a letter:** In his letter home Surur evidently spelt this name as 'Ben Siṭlûn'. Goitein points out in his translation of this letter, that the name is identical with 'Ibn Ṣaṭrûn' and it seems almost certain the individual in question was the same person that Ben Yiju referred to in his letter to his brother Yusuf (T-S 12.337, lines 25–26.)

326. **The letter...was a short one:** The letter contains a reference to one 'Abû'l Fakhr al-Amshâṭî' who was a family friend, and Surur's contact in Fustat.

326. **But Surur had...another reason:** T-S 8 J 36, fol. ´3, recto, lines 4–6.

327. **Their parents, already prostrate:** Surur's letter home has not survived, but the letter his brother Shamwal wrote back in reply has. Its catalogue number is Bod. Lib. Ox. MS Hebr., b. 11 (Cat. no. 2874), fol. 15 (S. Shaked, *Tentative Bibliography*, p. 207).

327. **'We were seized with grief':** Bod. Lib. Ox. MS Hebr., b. 11 (Cat. no. 2874), fol. 15, recto, lines 8–9. I would like to thank Dr Geofrrey Khan for translating the Hebrew phrase in this passage (in italics).

327. **'well and in good cheer':** T-S 13 J 20, fol. 7, recto, lines 22–23.

327. **Food was short:** Bod. Lib. Ox. MS Hebr., b. 11 (Cat. no. 2874), fol.

15, recto, lines 34–35 & 36–37.

327. 'If you saw [our] father': Bod. Lib. Ox. MS Hebr., b. 11 (Cat. no. 2874), fol. 15, lines (recto) 45—(verso) 4 & (verso) 8–13.

328. 'Come quickly home': T-S 16.288, recto, lines 10–11.

328. The marriage did indeed take place: S. D. Goitein, *Letters*, pp. 202.

328. Both Surur and Moshe: Ibid., pp. 186 & 328.

342. I discovered that the name Abu-Hasira: The most important scholarly work on the cult of saints amongst North African Jews is that of the eminent Israeli folklorist, Issachar Ben-Ami. See, for example, his article 'Folk Veneration of Saints among Moroccan Jews', (in *Studies in Judaism and Islam*, ed. Shelomo Morag et al., Hebrew University, Jerusalem, 1981). In the course of their fieldwork amongst Moroccan Jews Ben Ami and his associates compiled a list of 571 saints, twenty-one of whom were women. The French scholar, L. Voinot, estimated in 1948 that forty-five Jewish saints in Morocco were revered by Muslims and Jews alike while thirty-one were claimed by both Jews and Muslims as their own (quoted by Ben-Ami in 'Folk Veneration of Saints', p. 283).

342. 'The tomb of Rabbi': See Alex Weingrod's article, 'Saints and Shrines, politics and culture: a Morocco-Israel comparison', pp. 228 (in *Muslim Travellers*, ed. Dale F. Eickelman and James Piscatori, University of California Press, Berkeley, 1990); Gudrun Krämer, *The Jews in Modern Egypt*, 1914–1952, pp. 114. University of Washington Press, Seattle, 1989; Issachar Ben-Ami, 'Folk Veneration of Saints', pp. 324–328; and Baba Sali, His Life, Piety, Teachings and Miracles (Rav Yisrael Abuchatzeirah), by Rav Eliyahu Alfasi & Rav Yechiel Torgeman, written and edited by C. T. Bari, trans. Leah Doniger (Judaica Press Inc., New York, 1986).

# Epilogue

349. The document is one of Ben Yiju's sets of accounts: Dropsie 472. The following are the other Geniza documents I have used in reconstructing Bomma and Ben Yiju's lives. This list includes only those documents with which I have worked principally or in part from my own transcriptions, made directly from the manuscripts (in such instances where I have worked with published transcriptions or translations, the

references are provided in the endnotes). I would like to thank the Syndics of the University Library, Cambridge, for giving me permission to use and quote from these documents. I would also like to thank the Bodleian Library, Oxford, and the Annenberg Research Centre, Philadelphia, for allowing me to consult their Geniza collections.

1. T-S 12.235
2. T-S 12.337
3. T-S 16.288
4. T-S 20.130
5. T-S 20.137
6. T-S N.S. J 1
7. T-S N.S. J 5
8. T-S N.S. J 10
9. T-S K 25.252
10. T-S MS Or. 1080 J 95
11. T-S MS Or. 1080 J 263
12. T-S MS Or. 1081 J 3
13. T-S Misc. Box. 25, fragm. 103
14. T-S 6 J 4, fol. 14
15. T-S 8 J 7, fol. 23
16. T-S 8 J 36, fol. 3
17. T-S 10 J 9, fol. 24
18. T-S 10 J 10, fol. 15
19. T-S 10 J 12, fol. 5
20. T-S 10 J 13, fol. 6
21. T-S 13 J 7, fol. 13
22. T-S 13 J 7, fol. 27
23. T-S 13 J 20, fol. 7
24. T-S 13 J 24, fol. 2
25. T-S 18 J 2, fol. 7
26. T-S 18 J 4, fol. 18
27. T-S 18 J 5, fol. 1
28. Bod. Lib. Ox. MS Hebr., b. 11, fol. 15
29. Bod. Lib. Ox. MS Hebr., d. 66, fol. 61
30. Bod. Lib. Ox. MS Hebr., d. 66, fol. 139

# VINTAGE DEPARTURES

## PECKED TO DEATH BY DUCKS
### by Tim Cahill

In his latest grand tour of the earth's remote, exotic, and dismal places, Tim Cahill sleeps with a grizzly bear, witnesses demonic possession in Bali, assesses the cuteness quotient of giant clams in the South Pacific, and survives a run-in with something called the Throne of Doom in Guatemala. The resulting travel pieces are at once vivid, nerve-wracking, and outrageously funny.

"Tim Cahill [has] the what-the-hell adventuresomeness of a T. E. Lawrence and the humor of a P. J. O'Rourke." —*Condé Nast Traveler*

Travel/Adventure/0-679-74929-2

## FALLING OFF THE MAP
### SOME LONELY PLACES OF THE WORLD
### by Pico Iyer

Pico Iyer voyages from the nostalgic elegance of Argentina to the raffish nonchalance of Australia, documents the cruising rites of Icelandic teenagers, gets interrogated by tipsy Cuban police, and attends a screening of Bhutan's first feature film. Throughout, he remains both uncannily observant and hilarious.

"[Iyer is the] rightful heir to Jan Morris [and] Paul Theroux.... He writes the kind of lyrical, flowing prose that could make Des Moines sound beguiling."
—*Los Angeles Times Book Review*

Travel/Adventure/0-679-74612-9

## RIDING THE WHITE HORSE HOME
### A WESTERN FAMILY ALBUM
### by Teresa Jordan

The daughter and granddaughter of Wyoming ranchers tells the stories of her forebears—men who saw broken bones as professional credentials and women who coped with physical hardship and killing loneliness. She acquaints us with the lore and science of ranching, and does so with a breathtaking immediacy that recalls the best writing of Wallace Stegner and Gretel Ehrlich.

"A haunting and elegant memoir." —Terry Tempest Williams, author of *Refuge*

Memoir/Travel/0-679-75135-1

## BALKAN GHOSTS
### A JOURNEY THROUGH HISTORY
### by Robert D. Kaplan

As Kaplan travels from the breakaway states of Yugoslavia to Romania, Bulgaria, and Greece, he reconstructs the Balkans' history as a time warp in which ancient passions and hatreds are continually resurrected.

"Powerfully argued...the most insightful and timely work on the Balkans to date."
—*Boston Globe*

History/Current Affairs/Travel/0-679-74981-0

## A YEAR IN PROVENCE
### by Peter Mayle

An "engaging, funny and richly appreciative" (*The New York Times Book Review*) account of an English couple's first year living in Provence, settling in amid the enchanting gardens and equally festive bistros of their new home.

"Stylish, witty, delightfully readable."  —*The Sunday Times* (London)

Travel/0-679-73114-8

## MAIDEN VOYAGES
### THE WRITINGS OF WOMEN TRAVELERS
*Edited and with an Introduction by Mary Morris*

In this delightful and generous anthology, women such as Beryl Markham, Willa Cather, Annie Dillard, and Joan Didion share their experiences traveling throughout the world. From the Rocky Mountains to a Marrakech palace, in voices wry, lyrical, and sometimes wistful, these women show as much of themselves as they do of the strange and wonderful places they visit.

A Vintage Original/Travel/Women's Studies/0-679-74030-9

## IRON & SILK
### by Mark Salzman

The critically acclaimed and bestselling adventures of a young American martial arts master in China.

"Dazzling...exhilarating...a joy to read from beginning to end."  —*People*

Travel/Adventure/0-394-75511-1

## RIGHT ON THE EDGE OF CRAZY
### ON TOUR WITH THE U.S. DOWNHILL SKI TEAM
### by Mike Wilson

Mike Wilson follows the underfunded, underreported athletes of the U.S. downhill ski team through a World Cup season that culminates at the 1992 Winter Olympics in France. Juxtaposing scenes of raw courage and gonzo excess, the result is authentic enough to leave the reader windburned.

"The best [book] ever written about ski-racing."  —*Denver Post*

Sports/Travel/0-679-74987-X

\_\_ *One Dry Season* by Caroline Alexander    $10.95    0-679-73189-X

\_\_ *The Emperor's Last Island* by Julia Blackburn    $12.00    0-679-73937-8

\_\_ *Among the Thugs* by Bill Buford    $12.00    0-679-74535-1

\_\_ *Pecked to Death by Ducks* by Tim Cahill    $12.00    0-679-74929-2

\_\_ *Road Fever* by Tim Cahill    $11.00    0-394-75837-4

\_\_ *A Wolverine Is Eating My Leg* by Tim Cahill    $12.00    0-679-72026-X

\_\_ *The Heart of the World* by Nik Cohn    $12.00    0-679-74437-1

\_\_ *Coyotes* by Ted Conover    $11.00    0-394-75518-9

\_\_ *Whiteout* by Ted Conover    $11.00    0-679-74178-X

\_\_ *The Road from Coorain* by Jill Ker Conway    $11.00    0-679-72436-2

\_\_ *In Xanadu* by William Dalrymple    $13.00    0-679-72853-8

\_\_ *Danziger's Travels* by Nick Danziger    $15.00    0-679-73994-7

\_\_ *The Good Rain* by Timothy Egan    $10.00    0-679-73485-6

\_\_ *The Elder Brothers* by Alan Ereira    $12.00    0-679-74336-7

\_\_ *Bad Trips*, edited by Keath Fraser    $12.00    0-679-72908-9

\_\_ *In An Antique Land* by Amitav Ghosh    $13.00    0-679-72783-3

\_\_ *Samba* by Alma Guillermoprieto    $11.00    0-679-73256-X

\_\_ *Motoring with Mohammed* by Eric Hansen    $10.00    0-679-73855-X

\_\_ *Native Stranger* by Eddy Harris    $12.00    0-679-74232-8

\_\_ *Falling Off the Map* by Pico Iyer    $10.00    0-679-74612-9

\_\_ *The Lady and the Monk* by Pico Iyer    $12.00    0-679-73834-7

\_\_ *Video Night in Kathmandu* by Pico Iyer    $13.00    0-679-72216-5

\_\_ *Shooting the Boh* by Tracy Johnston    $11.00    0-679-74010-4

\_\_ *Riding the White Horse Home*    $11.00    0-679-75135-1
     by Teresa Jordan

\_\_ *Running the Amazon* by Joe Kane    $9.95    0-679-72902-X

\_\_ *Balkan Ghosts* by Robert D. Kaplan    $12.00    0-679-74981-0

\_\_ *Making Hay* by Verlyn Klinkenborg    $9.00    0-394-75599-5

\_\_ *In Bolivia* by Eric Lawlor    $11.00    0-394-75836-6

\_\_ *Looking for Osman* by Eric Lawlor    $11.00    0-679-73822-3

\_\_ *The Other Side* by Rubén Martínez    $10.00    0-679-74591-2

\_\_ *Toujours Provence* by Peter Mayle    $10.00    0-679-73604-2

\_\_ *A Year in Provence* by Peter Mayle    $10.00    0-679-73114-8

# VINTAGE DEPARTURES

# Contents

Published by Methuen 2002
Methuen Publishing Ltd
215 Vauxhall Bridge Road,
London SW1V 1EJ

3 5 7 9 10 8 6 4 2

*Blithe Spirit* was first published in Great Britain in 1942
by Heinemann and republished in 1960 in Play Parade Vol. 5.
It is reprinted here by arrangement with William Heinemann Ltd

Methuen Publishing Limited Reg. No. 3543167

A CIP catalogue record for this book is available
from the British Library

ISBN 0 413 77197 0

Typeset by Deltatype Ltd, Birkenhead, Merseyside
Printed and bound in Great Britain by
Cox & Wyman Ltd, Reading, Berkshire

# Chronology

1899  16 December, Noël Pierce Coward born in Teddington, Middlesex, eldest surviving son of Arthur Coward, piano salesman and Violet (*née* Veitch). A 'brazen, odious little prodigy', his early circumstances were of refined suburban poverty.

1907  First public appearances in school and community concerts.

1908  Family moved to Battersea and took in lodgers.

1911  First professional appearance as Prince Mussel in *The Goldfish*, produced by Lila Field at the Little Theatre, and revived in same year at Crystal Palace and Royal Court Theatre. Cannard the page-boy, in *The Great Name* at the Prince of Wales Theatre, and William in *Where the Rainbow Ends* with Charles Hawtrey's Company at the Savoy Theatre.

1912  Directed *The Daisy Chain* and stage-managed *The Prince's Bride* at Savoy in series of matinées featuring the work of the children of the *Rainbow* cast. Mushroom in *An Autumn Idyll*, ballet, Savoy.

1913  An angel (Gertrude Lawrence was another) in Basil Dean's production of *Hannele*. Slightly in *Peter Pan*, Duke of York's.

1914  Toured in *Peter Pan*. Collaborated with fellow performer Esmé Wynne on songs, sketches, and short stories – 'beastly little whimsies'.

1915  Admitted to sanatorium for tuberculosis.

1916  Five-month tour as Charley in *Charley's Aunt*. Walk-on in *The Best of Luck*, Drury Lane. Wrote first full-length song, 'Forbidden Fruit'. Basil Pycroft in *The Light Blues*, produced by Robert Courtneidge, with daughter Cicely also in cast, Shaftesbury. Short spell as dancer at Elysée Restaurant (subsequently the Café de Paris). Jack Morrison in *The Happy Family*, Prince of Wales.

1917  'Boy pushing barrow' in D.W. Griffith's film *Hearts of the World*. Co-author with Esmé Wynne of one-acter

*Ida Collaborates*, Theatre Royal, Aldershot. Ripley Guildford in *The Saving Grace*, with Charles Hawtrey, 'who . . . taught me many points of comedy acting', Garrick. Family moved to Pimlico and re-opened boarding house.

1918  Called-up for army. Medical discharge after nine months. Wrote unpublished novels *Cats and Dogs* (loosely based on Shaw's *You Never Can Tell*) and the unfinished *Cherry Pan* ('dealing in a whimsical vein with the adventures of a daughter of Pan'), and lyrics for Darewski and Joel, including 'When You Come Home on Leave' and 'Peter Pan'. Also composed 'Tamarisk Town'. Sold short stories to magazines. Wrote plays *The Rat Trap*, *The Last Trick* (unproduced) and *The Impossible Wife* (unproduced). Courtenay Borner in *Scandal*, Strand. *Woman and Whiskey* (co-author Esmé Wynne) produced at Wimbledon Theatre.

1919  Ralph in *The Knight of the Burning Pestle*, Birmingham Repertory, played with 'a stubborn Mayfair distinction' demonstrating a 'total lack of understanding of the play'. Collaborated on *Crissa*, an opera, with Esmé Wynne and Max Darewski (unproduced). Wrote *I'll Leave It to You*.

1920  Bobbie Dermott in *I'll Leave It to You*, New Theatre. Wrote play *Barriers Down* (unproduced). *I'll Leave It to You* published, London.

1921  On holiday in Alassio, met Gladys Calthrop for the first time. Clay Collins in American farce *Polly with a Past*: during the run 'songs, sketches, and plays were bursting out of me'. Wrote *The Young Idea*, *Sirocco*, and *The Better Half*. First visit to New York, and sold parts of *A Withered Nosegay* to *Vanity Fair* and short-story adaptation of *I'll Leave It to You* to *Metropolitan*. House-guest of Laurette Taylor and Hartley Manners, whose family rows inspired the Bliss household in *Hay Fever*.

1922  *Bottles and Bones* (sketch) produced in benefit for Newspaper Press Fund, Drury Lane. *The Better Half*

produced in 'grand guignol' season, Little Theatre.
Started work on songs and sketches for *London
Calling!* Adapted Louise Verneuil's *Pour avoir Adrienne*
(unproduced). Wrote *The Queen Was in the Parlour* and
*Mild Oats*.

1923   Sholto Brent in *The Young Idea*, Savoy. Juvenile lead
in *London Calling!* Wrote *Weatherwise*, *Fallen Angels*, and
*The Vortex*.

1924   Wrote *Hay Fever* (which Marie Tempest at first
refused to do, feeling it was 'too light and plotless
and generally lacking in action') and *Easy Virtue*.
Nicky Lancaster in *The Vortex*, produced at Everyman
by Norman MacDermot.

1925   Established as a social and theatrical celebrity. Wrote
*On With the Dance* with London opening in spring
followed by *Fallen Angels* and *Hay Fever*. *Hay Fever* and
*Easy Virtue* produced, New York. Wrote silent screen
titles for Gainsborough Films.

1926   Toured USA in *The Vortex*. Wrote *This Was a Man*,
refused a licence by Lord Chamberlain but produced
in New York (1926), Berlin (1927), and Paris (1928).
*Easy Virtue*, *The Queen Was in the Parlour*, and *The Rat
Trap* produced, London. Played Lewis Dodd in *The
Constant Nymph*, directed by Basil Dean. Wrote *Semi-
Monde* and *The Marquise*. Bought Goldenhurst Farm,
Kent, as country home. Sailed for Hong Kong on
holiday but trip broken in Honolulu by nervous
breakdown.

1927   *The Marquise* opened in London while Coward was
still in Hawaii, and *The Marquise* and *Fallen Angels*
produced, New York. Finished writing *Home Chat*.
*Sirocco* revised after discussions with Basil Dean and
produced, London.

1928   Clark Storey in Behrman's *The Second Man*, directed
by Dean. Gainsborough Films productions of *The
Queen Was in the Parlour*, *The Vortex* (starring Ivor
Novello), and *Easy Virtue* (directed by Alfred
Hitchcock) released – but only the latter, freely
adapted, a success. *This Year of Grace!* produced,

London, and with Coward directing and in cast,
New York. Made first recording, featuring numbers
from this show. Wrote *Concerto* for Gainsborough
Films, intended for Ivor Novello, but never
produced. Started writing *Bitter-Sweet*.

1929   Played in *This Year of Grace!* (USA) until spring.
Directed *Bitter-Sweet*, London and New York. Set off
on travelling holiday in Far East.

1930   On travels wrote *Private Lives* (1929) and song 'Mad
Dogs and Englishmen', the latter on the road from
Hanoi to Saigon. In Singapore joined the Quaints,
company of strolling English players, as Stanhope for
three performances of *Journey's End*. On voyage home
wrote *Post-Mortem*, which was 'similar to my
performance as Stanhope: confused, under-rehearsed
and hysterical'. Directed and played Elyot Chase in
*Private Lives*, London, and Fred in *Some Other Private
Lives*. Started writing *Cavalcade* and unfinished novel
*Julian Kane*.

1931   Elyot Chase in New York production of *Private Lives*.
Directed *Cavalcade*, London. Film of *Private Lives*
produced by MGM. Set off on trip to South
America.

1932   On travels wrote *Design for Living* (hearing that Alfred
Lunt and Lynn Fontanne finally free to work with
him) and material for new revue including songs
'Mad about the Boy', 'Children of the Ritz' and
'The Party's Over Now'. Produced in London as
*Words and Music*, with book, music, and lyrics
exclusively by Coward and directed by him. The
short-lived Noël Coward Company, independent
company which enjoyed his support, toured UK with
*Private Lives*, *Hay Fever*, *Fallen Angels*, and *The Vortex*.

1933   Directed *Design for Living*, New York, and played Leo.
Films of *Cavalcade*, *To-Night Is Ours* (remake of *The
Queen Was in the Parlour*), and *Bitter-Sweet* released.
Directed London revival of *Hay Fever*. Wrote
*Conversation Piece* as vehicle for Yvonne Printemps,
and hit song 'Mrs Worthington'.

1934  Directed *Conversation Piece* in London and played
      Paul. Cut links with C. B. Cochran and formed own
      management in partnership with John C. Wilson.
      Appointed President of the Actors' Orphanage, in
      which he invested great personal commitment until
      resignation in 1956. Directed Kaufman and Ferber's
      *Theatre Royal*, Lyric, and Behrman's *Biography*, Globe.
      Film of *Design for Living* released, London. *Conversation
      Piece* opened, New York. Started writing
      autobiography, *Present Indicative*. Wrote *Point Valaine*.

1935  Directed *Point Valaine*, New York. Played lead in film
      *The Scoundrel* (Astoria Studios, New York). Wrote *To-
      Night at 8.30*.

1936  Directed and played in *To-Night at 8.30*, London and
      New York. Directed *Mademoiselle* by Jacques Deval,
      Wyndham's.

1937  Played in *To-Night at 8.30*, New York, until second
      breakdown in health in March. Directed (and
      subsequently disowned) Gerald Savory's *George and
      Margaret*, New York. Wrote *Operette*, with hit song
      'The Stately Homes of England'. *Present Indicative*
      published, London and New York.

1938  Directed *Operette*, London. *Words and Music* revised for
      American production as *Set to Music*. Appointed
      adviser to newly formed Royal Naval Film
      Corporation.

1939  Directed New York production of *Set to Music*.
      Visited Soviet Union and Scandinavia. Wrote *Present
      Laughter* and *This Happy Breed*: rehearsals stopped by
      declaration of war. Wrote for revue *All Clear*,
      London. Appointed to head Bureau of Propaganda
      in Paris, to liaise with French Ministry of
      Information, headed by Jean Giraudoux and André
      Maurois. This posting prompted speculative attacks
      in the press, prevented by wartime secrecy from
      getting a clear statement of the exact nature of his
      work (in fact unexceptional and routine). Troop
      concert in Arras with Maurice Chevalier. *To Step
      Aside* (short story collection) published.

1940    Increasingly 'oppressed and irritated by the Paris routine'. Visits USA to report on American isolationism and attitudes to war in Europe. Return to Paris prevented by German invasion. Returned to USA to do propaganda work for Ministry of Information. Propaganda tour of Australia and New Zealand, and fund-raising for war charities. Wrote play *Time Remembered* (unproduced).

1941    Mounting press attacks in England because of time spent allegedly avoiding danger and discomfort of Home Front. Wrote *Blithe Spirit*, produced in London (with Coward directing) and New York. MGM film of *Bitter-Sweet* (which Coward found 'vulgar' and 'lacking in taste') released, London. Wrote screenplay for *In Which We Serve*, based on the sinking of HMS *Kelly*. Wrote songs including 'London Pride', 'Could You Please Oblige Us with a Bren Gun?', and 'Imagine the Duchess's Feelings'.

1942    Produced and co-directed (with David Lean) *In Which We Serve*, and appeared as Captain Kinross (Coward considered the film 'an accurate and sincere tribute to the Royal Navy'). Played in countrywide tour of *Blithe Spirit*, *Present Laughter*, and *This Happy Breed*, and gave hospital and factory concerts. MGM film of *We Were Dancing* released.

1943    Played Garry Essendine in London production of *Present Laughter* and Frank Gibbons in *This Happy Breed*. Produced *This Happy Breed* for Two Cities Films. Wrote 'Don't Let's Be Beastly to the Germans', first sung on BBC Radio (then banned on grounds of lines 'that Goebbels might twist'). Four-month tour of Middle East to entertain troops.

1944    February–September, toured South Africa, Burma, India, and Ceylon. Troop concerts in France and 'Stage Door Canteen Concert' in London. Screenplay of *Still Life*, as *Brief Encounter*. *Middle East Diary*, an account of his 1943 tour, published, London and New York – where a reference to 'mournful little boys from Brooklyn' inspired formation of a lobby for the 'Prevention of Noël Coward Re-entering America'.

1945 *Sigh No More*, with hit song 'Matelot', completed and produced, London. Started work on *Pacific 1860*. Film of *Brief Encounter* released.

1946 Started writing '*Peace in Our Time*'. Directed *Pacific 1860*, London.

1947 Gary Essendine in London revival of *Present Laughter*. Supervised production of '*Peace in Our Time*'. *Point Valaine* produced, London. Directed American revival of *To-Night at 8.30*. Wrote *Long Island Sound* (unproduced).

1948 Replaced Graham Payn briefly in American tour of *To-Night at 8.30*, his last stage appearance with Gertrude Lawrence. Wrote screenplay for Gainsborough film of *The Astonished Heart*. Max Aramont in *Joyeux Chagrins* (French production of *Present Laughter*). Built house at Blue Harbour, Jamaica.

1949 Christian Faber in film of *The Astonished Heart*. Wrote *Ace of Clubs* and *Home and Colonial* (produced as *Island Fling* in USA and *South Sea Bubble* in UK).

1950 Directed *Ace of Clubs*, London. Wrote *Star Quality* (short stories) and *Relative Values*.

1951 Deaths of Ivor Novello and C. B. Cochran. Paintings included in charity exhibition in London. Wrote *Quadrille*. One-night concert at Theatre Royal, Brighton, followed by season at Café de Paris, London, and beginning of new career as leading cabaret entertainer. Directed *Relative Values*, London, which restored his reputation as a playwright after run of post-war flops. *Island Fling* produced, USA.

1952 Charity cabaret with Mary Martin at Café de Paris for Actors' Orphanage. June cabaret season at Café de Paris. Directed *Quadrille*, London. '*Red Peppers*', *Fumed Oak*, and *Ways and Means* (from *To-Night at 8.30*) filmed as *Meet Me To-Night*. September, death of Gertrude Lawrence: 'no one I have ever known, however brilliant . . . has contributed quite what she contributed to my work'.

1953   Completed second volume of autobiography, *Future Indefinite*. King Magnus in Shaw's *The Apple Cart*. Cabaret at Café de Paris, again 'a triumphant success'. Wrote *After the Ball*.

1954   *After the Ball* produced, UK. July, mother died. September, cabaret season at Café de Paris. November, Royal Command Performance, London Palladium. Wrote *Nude With Violin*.

1955   June, opened in cabaret for season at Desert Inn, Las Vegas, and enjoyed 'one of the most sensational successes of my career'. Played Hesketh-Baggott in film of *Around the World in Eighty Days*, for which he wrote own dialogue. October, directed and appeared with Mary Martin in TV spectacular *Together with Music* for CBS, New York. Revised *South Sea Bubble*.

1956   Charles Condomine in television production of *Blithe Spirit*, for CBS, Hollywood. For tax reasons took up Bermuda residency. Resigned from presidency of the Actors' Orphanage. *South Sea Bubble* produced, London. Directed and played part of Frank Gibbons in television production of *This Happy Breed* for CBS, New York. Co-directed *Nude With Violin* with John Gielgud (Eire and UK), opening to press attacks on Coward's decision to live abroad. Wrote play *Volcano* (unproduced).

1957   Directed and played Sebastien in *Nude With Violin*, New York. *Nude With Violin* published, London.

1958   Played Gary Essendine in *Present Laughter* alternating with *Nude With Violin* on US West Coast tour. Wrote ballet *London Morning* for London Festival Ballet. Wrote *Look After Lulu!*

1959   *Look After Lulu!* produced, New York, and by English Stage Company at Royal Court, London. Film roles of Hawthorne in *Our Man in Havana* and ex-King of Anatolia in *Surprise Package*. *London Morning* produced by London Festival Ballet. Sold home in Bermuda and took up Swiss residency. Wrote *Waiting in the Wings*.

1960   *Waiting in the Wings* produced, Eire and UK. *Pomp and*

*Circumstance* (novel) published, London and New York.

1961   Alec Harvey in television production of *Brief Encounter* for NBC, USA. Directed American production of *Sail Away*. *Waiting in the Wings* published, New York.

1962   Wrote music and lyrics for *The Girl Who Came to Supper* (adaptation of Rattigan's *The Sleeping Prince*, previously filmed as *The Prince and the Showgirl*). *Sail Away* produced, UK.

1963   *The Girl Who Came to Supper* produced, USA. Revival of *Private Lives* at Hampstead signals renewal of interest in his work.

1964   'Supervised' production of *High Spirits*, musical adaptation of *Blithe Spirit*, Savoy. Introduced Granada TV's 'A Choice of Coward' series, which included *Present Laughter*, *Blithe Spirit*, *The Vortex*, and *Design for Living*. Directed *Hay Fever* for National Theatre, first living playwright to direct his own work there. *Pretty Polly Barlow* (short story collection) published.

1965   Played the landlord in film, *Bunny Lake is Missing*. Wrote *Suite in Three Keys*. Badly weakened by attack of amoebic dysentry contracted in Seychelles.

1966   Played in *Suite in Three Keys*, London, which taxed his health further. Started adapting his short story *Star Quality* for the stage.

1967   Caesar in TV musical version of *Androcles and the Lion* (score by Richard Rodgers), New York. Witch of Capri in film *Broom*, adaptation of Tennessee Williams's play *The Milk Train Doesn't Stop Here Any More*. Lorn Loraine, Coward's manager, and friend for many years, died, London. Worked on new volume of autobiography, *Past Conditional*. *Bon Voyage* (short story collection) published.

1968   Played Mr Bridger, the criminal mastermind, in *The Italian Job*.

1970   Awarded knighthood in New Year's Honours List.

1971   Tony Award, USA, for Distinguished Achievement in the Theatre.

1973   26 March, died peacefully at his home in Blue Harbour, Jamaica. Buried on Firefly Hill.

# Blithe Spirit

*An Improbable Farce in Three Acts*

## Noël Coward

Methuen Drama

# Characters

**Edith**, *a maid*
**Ruth**
**Charles**
**Doctor Bradman**
**Mrs Bradman**
**Madame Arcati**
**Elvira**

The action of the play passes in the living-room of
**Charles Condomine**'s house in Kent.

**Act One**
Scene  I. Before dinner on a summer evening.
Scene II. After dinner.

**Act Two**
Scene  I. The next morning.
Scene II. Late the following afternoon.
Scene III. Early evening. A few days later.

**Act Three**
Scene  I. After dinner. A few days later.
Scene II. Several hours later.

# Act One

## Scene One

*The scene is the living-room of the* **Condomines**' *house in Kent.*

*The room is light, attractive and comfortably furnished. The arrangement of it may be left to the discretion of the producer. On the right there are french windows opening on to the garden. On the left there is an open fireplace. At the back, on the left, there are double doors leading into the dining-room. Up left, on an angle, there are double doors leading to the hall, the stairs, and the servants' quarters.*

*When the curtain rises it is about eight o'clock on a summer evening. There is a wood fire burning because it is an English summer evening.*

**Edith** *comes in from the hall carrying, rather uneasily, a large tray of cocktail things. Comes to centre table with tray of drinks. Sees there is not room so puts it on drinks table up stage right, with a sigh of relief.*

**Ruth** *comes in centre briskly. She is a smart-looking woman in the middle thirties. She is dressed for dinner but not elaborately.*

**Ruth**  That's right, Edith.

**Edith**  Yes'm.

**Ruth**  Now you'd better fetch the ice-bucket.

**Edith**  Yes'm.

**Ruth** (*arranges ornaments on piano*)  Did you manage to get the ice out of those little tin trays?

**Edith**  Yes'm – I 'ad a bit of a struggle though – but it's all right.

**Ruth**  And you filled the little trays up again with water?

**Edith**  Yes'm.

**Ruth** (*crosses to window and arranges curtains*)  Very good, Edith – you're making giant strides.

**Edith**   Yes'm.

**Ruth**   Madame Arcati, Mrs Bradman and I will have our coffee in here after dinner and Mr Condomine and Dr Bradman will have theirs in the dining-room – is that quite clear?

**Edith**   Yes'm.

**Ruth**   And when you're serving dinner, Edith, try to remember to do it calmly and methodically.

**Edith**   Yes'm.

**Ruth**   As you are not in the Navy it is unnecessary to do everything at the double.

**Edith**   Very good, 'm.

**Ruth**   Now go and get the ice.

**Edith** (*straining at the leash*)   Yes'm.

*She starts off at full speed.*

**Ruth**   *Not* at a run, Edith.

**Edith** (*slowing down*)   Yes'm.

**Edith** *goes.*

**Ruth** *crosses to fireplace, gives a comprehensive glance round the room.*

**Charles** *comes in centre to back of sofa. He is a nice-looking man of about forty wearing a loose-fitting velvet smoking-jacket.*

**Charles**   No sign of the advancing hordes?

**Ruth**   Not yet.

**Charles** (*going to the cocktail tray*)   No ice.

**Ruth**   It's coming. I've been trying to discourage Edith from being quite so fleet of foot. You mustn't mind if everything is a little slow motion to-night.

**Charles**   I shall welcome it. The last few days have been extremely agitating. What do you suppose induced Agnes to leave us and go and get married?

**Ruth**   The reason was becoming increasingly obvious, dear.

**Charles**   Yes, but in these days nobody thinks anything of that sort of thing – she could have popped into the cottage hospital, had it, and popped out again.

**Ruth**   Her social life would have been seriously undermined.

**Charles**   We must keep Edith in the house more.

**Edith** *comes in slowly with the ice-bucket.*

**Ruth**   That's right, Edith – put it down on the table.

**Edith** (*puts ice-bucket on drinks table – up stage right*)   Yes'm.

**Charles**   I left my cigarette-case on my dressing-table, Edith – would you get it for me?

**Edith**   Yes, sir.

*She runs out of the room.*

**Charles**   There now!

**Ruth**   You took her by surprise.

**Charles** (*at the cocktail table*)   A dry Martini, I think, don't you?

**Ruth** *takes a cigarette from box on mantelpiece and lights it, then crosses and sits in arm-chair.*

**Ruth**   Yes, darling – I expect Madame Arcati will want something sweeter.

**Charles**   We'll have this one for ourselves anyhow.

**Ruth** (*taking a cigarette and sitting down*)   Oh, dear!

**Charles**   What's the matter?

**Ruth**   I have a feeling that this evening's going to be awful.

**Charles**   It'll probably be funny, but not awful.

**Ruth**   You must promise not to catch my eye – if I giggle – and I'm very likely to – it will ruin everything.

**Charles**   You mustn't – you must be dead serious and if possible a little intense. We can't hurt the old girl's feelings, however funny she is.

**Ruth**   But why the Bradmans, darling? He's as sceptical as we are – he'll probably say the most dreadful things.

**Charles**   I've warned him. There must be more than three people and we couldn't have the vicar and his wife because (a) they're dreary, and (b) they probably wouldn't have approved at all. It had to be the Bradmans.

**Edith** *rushes into the room with* **Charles**'s *cigarette-case*.

**Charles** (*taking it*)   Thank you, Edith – steady does it.

**Edith** (*breathlessly*)   Yes, sir.

**Edith**, *with an obvious effort, goes out slowly*.

**Charles**   We might make her walk about with a book on her head like they do in deportment lessons.

**Charles** *comes to right of* **Ruth** *and gives her cocktail*.

**Charles**   Here, try this.

**Ruth** (*sipping it*)   Lovely – dry as a bone.

**Charles** (*raising his glass to her*)   To 'The Unseen'!

**Ruth**   I must say that's a wonderful title.

**Charles**   If this evening's a success I shall start on the first draft to-morrow.

**Ruth**   How extraordinary it is.

**Charles**   What?

**Ruth**   Oh, I don't know – being in right at the beginning of something – it gives one an odd feeling.

**Charles**   Do you remember how I got the idea for 'The

Light Goes Out'?

**Ruth** (*suddenly seeing that haggard, raddled woman in the hotel at Biarritz*) Of course I remember – we sat up half the night talking about it. . . .

**Charles** She certainly came in very handy – I wonder who she was.

**Ruth** And if she ever knew, I mean ever recognised, that description of herself – poor thing . . . here's to her, anyhow. . . . (*She finishes her drink.*)

**Charles** Have another.

**Ruth** Darling – it's most awfully strong.

**Charles** (*pouring it*) Never mind.

**Ruth** Used Elvira to be a help to you – when you were thinking something out, I mean?

**Charles** (*pouring out another cocktail for himself*) Every now and then – when she concentrated – but she didn't concentrate very often.

**Ruth** I do wish I'd known her.

**Charles** I wonder if you'd have liked her.

**Ruth** I'm sure I should – as you talk of her she sounds enchanting – yes, I'm sure I should have liked her because you know I have never for an instant felt in the least jealous of her – that's a good sign.

**Charles** Poor Elvira. (*Comes to left of* **Ruth** *and gives her cocktail.*)

**Ruth** Does it still hurt – when you think of her?

**Charles** No, not really – sometimes I almost wish it did – I feel rather guilty. . . .

**Ruth** I wonder if I died before you'd grown tired of me if you'd forget me so soon?

**Charles** What a horrible thing to say. . . .

**Ruth**   No – I think it's interesting.

**Charles**   Well, to begin with, I haven't forgotten Elvira – I remember her very distinctly indeed – I remember how fascinating she was, and how maddening – I remember how badly she played all games and how cross she got when she didn't win – I remember her gay charm when she had achieved her own way over something and her extreme acidity when she didn't – I remember her physical attractiveness, which was tremendous, and her spiritual integrity which was nil. . . .

**Ruth**   You can't remember something that was nil.

**Charles**   I remember how morally untidy she was. . . .

**Ruth**   Was she more physically attractive than I am?

**Charles**   That was a very tiresome question, dear, and fully deserves the wrong answer.

**Ruth**   You really are very sweet.

**Charles**   Thank you.

**Ruth**   And a little naïve, too.

**Charles**   Why?

**Ruth**   Because you imagine that I mind about Elvira being more physically attractive than I am.

**Charles**   I should have thought any woman would mind – if it were true. Or perhaps I'm old-fashioned in my view of female psychology. . . .

**Ruth**   Not exactly old-fashioned, darling, just a bit didactic.

**Charles**   How do you mean?

**Ruth**   It's didactic to attribute to one type the defects of another type – for instance, because you know perfectly well that Elvira would mind terribly if you found another woman more attractive physically than she was, it doesn't necessarily follow that I should. Elvira was a more physical person than I – I'm certain of that – it's all a question of degree.

**Charles** (*smiling*)  I love you, my love.

**Ruth**  I know you do – but not the wildest stretch of imagination could describe it as the first fine careless rapture.

**Charles**  Would you like it to be?

**Ruth**  Good God, no!

**Charles**  Wasn't that a shade too vehement?

**Ruth**  We're neither of us adolescent, Charles, we've neither of us led exactly prim lives, have we? And we've both been married before – careless rapture at this stage would be incongruous and embarrassing.

**Charles**  I hope I haven't been in any way a disappointment, dear.

**Ruth**  Don't be so idiotic.

**Charles**  After all your first husband was a great deal older than you, wasn't he? I shouldn't like you to think that you'd missed out all along the line.

**Ruth**  There are moments, Charles, when you go too far.

**Charles**  Sorry, darling.

**Ruth**  As far as waspish female psychology goes, there's a strong vein of it in you.

**Charles**  I've heard that said about Julius Caesar.

**Ruth**  Julius Caesar is neither here nor there.

**Charles**  He may be for all we know – we'll ask Madame Arcati.

**Ruth**  You're awfully irritating when you're determined to be witty at all costs – almost supercilious.

**Charles**  That's exactly what Elvira used to say.

**Ruth**   I'm not at all surprised – I never imagined – physically triumphant as she was – that she was entirely lacking in perception.

**Charles**   Darling Ruth!

**Ruth**   There you go again. . . .

**Charles** (*kissing her lightly*)   As I think I mentioned before I love you, my love.

**Ruth**   Poor Elvira.

**Charles**   Didn't that light, comradely kiss mollify you at all?

**Ruth**   You're very annoying, you know you are – when I said 'Poor Elvira' it came from the heart – you must have bewildered her so horribly.

**Charles**   Don't I ever bewilder you at all?

**Ruth**   Never for an instant – I know every trick.

**Charles**   Well, all I can say is that we'd better get a divorce immediately. . . .

**Ruth**   Put my glass down, there's a darling.

**Charles** (*taking it*)   She certainly had a great talent for living – it was a pity that she died so young.

**Ruth**   Poor Elvira.

**Charles**  – That remark is getting monotonous.

**Ruth** (*crosses up stage a pace*)   Poor Charles, then.

**Charles**   That's better.

**Ruth**   And later on, Poor Ruth, I expect.

**Charles**   You have no faith, Ruth. I really do think you should try to have a little faith.

**Ruth**   I shall strain every nerve.

**Charles**   Life without faith is an arid business.

**Ruth**  How beautifully you put things, dear.

**Charles**  I aim to please.

**Ruth**  If I died, I wonder how long it would be before you married again?

**Charles**  You won't die – you're not the dying sort.

**Ruth**  Neither was Elvira.

**Charles**  Oh yes, she was, now that I look back on it – she had a certain ethereal, not quite of this world quality – nobody could call you even remotely ethereal.

**Ruth**  Nonsense – she was of the earth earthy.

**Charles**  Well she is now, anyhow.

**Ruth**  You know that's the kind of observation that shocks people.

**Charles**  It's discouraging to think how many people are shocked by honesty and how few by deceit.

**Ruth**  Write that down, you might forget it.

**Charles**  You underrate me.

**Ruth**  Anyhow it was a question of bad taste more than honesty.

**Charles**  I was devoted to Elvira. We were married for five years. She died. I missed her very much. That was seven years ago. I have now – with your help, my love – risen above the whole thing.

**Ruth**  Admirable. But if tragedy should darken our lives – (*A bell rings.*) – I still say – with prophetic foreboding – poor Ruth!

**Charles**  That's probably the Bradmans.

**Ruth**  It might be Madame Arcati.

**Charles**  No, she'll come on her bicycle – she always goes everywhere on her bicycle.

**Ruth**   It really is very spirited of the old girl.

**Charles**   Shall I go, or shall we let Edith have her fling?

**Ruth**   Wait a minute and see what happens.

*There is a slight pause.*

**Charles**   Perhaps she didn't hear.

**Ruth**   She's probably on one knee in the pre-sprinting position waiting for cook to open the kitchen door.

*There is the sound of a door banging and* **Edith** *is seen scampering across the hall.*

**Charles**   Steady, Edith.

**Edith**   (*dropping to a walk*)   Yes, sir.

*After a moment,* **Dr** *and* **Mrs Bradman** *come into the room.* **Charles** *goes forward to meet them.* **Dr Bradman** *is a pleasant-looking middle-aged man.* **Mrs Bradman** *is fair and rather faded.* **Mrs Bradman** *comes to* **Ruth** *above sofa and shakes hands.* **Dr Bradman** *shakes hands with* **Charles***.*

**Edith**   Dr and Mrs Bradman.

**Dr Bradman**   We're not late, are we? I only got back from the hospital about half an hour ago.

**Charles**   Of course not – Madame Arcati isn't here yet.

**Mrs Bradman**   That must have been her we passed coming down the hill – I said I thought it was.

**Ruth**   Then she won't be long. I'm so glad you were able to come.

**Mrs Bradman**   We've been looking forward to it – I feel really quite excited. . . .

**Dr Bradman**   I guarantee that Violet will be good – I made her promise.

**Mrs Bradman**   There wasn't any need – I'm absolutely thrilled. I've only seen Madame Arcati two or three times in the village – I mean I've never seen her do anything at all peculiar, if you know what I mean?

**Charles** (*at cocktail table*) Dry Martini?

**Dr Bradman** By all means.

**Charles** (*mixing it*) She certainly is a strange woman. It was only a chance remark of the vicar's about seeing her up on the Knoll on Midsummer Eve dressed in sort of Indian robes that made me realise that she was psychic at all. Then I began to make enquiries – apparently she's been a professional in London for years.

**Mrs Bradman** It is funny, isn't it? I mean anybody doing it as a profession.

**Dr Bradman** I believe it's very lucrative.

**Mrs Bradman** Do you believe in it, Mrs Condomine – do you think there's anything really genuine about it at all?

**Ruth** I'm afraid not – but I do think it's interesting how easily people allow themselves to be deceived. . . .

**Mrs Bradman** But she must believe it herself, mustn't she – or is the whole business a fake?

**Charles** I suspect the worst. A real professional charlatan. That's what I am hoping for anyhow – the character I am planning for my book must be a complete impostor, that's one of the most important factors of the whole story.

**Dr Bradman** What exactly are you hoping to get from her?

**Charles** Jargon, principally – a few of the tricks of the trade – I haven't been to a séance for years. Ruth? I want to refresh my memory.

**Dr Bradman** Then it's not entirely new to you?

**Charles** (*hands drinks to* **Dr** *and* **Mrs Bradman**) Oh no – when I was a little boy an aunt of mine used to come and stay with us – she imagined that she was a medium and used to go off into the most elaborate trances after dinner.

My mother was fascinated by it.

**Mrs Bradman**   Was she convinced?

**Charles**   Good heavens, no – she just naturally disliked my aunt and loved making a fool of her. (*Gets cocktail for himself.*)

**Dr Bradman** (*laughing*)   I gather that there were never any tangible results?

**Charles**   Oh, sometimes she didn't do so badly. On one occasion when we were all sitting round in the pitch dark with my mother groping her way through Chaminade at the piano, my aunt suddenly gave a shrill scream and said that she saw a small black dog by my chair, then someone switched on the lights and sure enough there it was.

**Mrs Bradman**   But how extraordinary.

**Charles**   It was obviously a stray that had come in from the street. But I must say I took off my hat to Auntie for producing it, or rather for utilising it – even Mother was a bit shaken.

**Mrs Bradman**   What happened to it?

**Charles**   It lived with us for years.

**Ruth**   I sincerely hope Madame Arcati won't produce any livestock – we have so very little room in this house.

**Mrs Bradman**   Do you think she tells fortunes? I love having my fortune told.

**Charles**   I expect so—

**Ruth**   I was told once on the pier at Southsea that I was surrounded by lilies and a golden seven – it worried me for days.

*All laugh.*

**Charles**   We really must all be serious, you know, and pretend that we believe implicitly, otherwise she won't play.

**Ruth**   Also, she might really mind – it would be cruel to upset her.

**Dr Bradman**   I shall be as good as gold.

**Ruth**   Have you ever attended her, Doctor –
professionally, I mean?

**Dr Bradman**   Yes – she had influenza in January – she's
only been here just over a year, you know. I must say she
was singularly unpsychic then – I always understood that
she was an authoress.

**Charles**   Oh yes, we originally met as colleagues at one
of Mrs Wilmot's Sunday evenings in Sandgate. . . .

**Mrs Bradman**   What sort of books does she write?

**Charles**   Two sorts. Rather whimsical children's stories
about enchanted woods filled with highly conversational
flora and fauna, and enthusiastic biographies of minor
royalties, very sentimental, reverent and extremely funny.

*There is the sound of the front-door bell.*

**Ruth**   Here she is.

**Dr Bradman**   She knows, doesn't she, about to-night?
You're not going to spring it on her.

**Charles**   Of course – it was all arranged last week – I
told her how profoundly interested I was in anything to do
with the occult, and she blossomed like a rose.

**Ruth**   I really feel quite nervous – as though I were going
to make a speech.

**Edith** *is seen sedately going towards the door.*

**Charles**   You go and meet her, darling.

*Meanwhile* **Edith** *has opened the door, and* **Madame Arcati**'s
*voice, very high and clear, is heard.*

**Madame Arcati**   I've leant my bike up against that little
bush, it will be *perfectly* all right if no one touches it.

**Edith**   Madame Arcati.

**Ruth**   How nice of you to have come all this way.

**Madame Arcati** *enters. She is a striking woman, dressed not too extravagantly but with a decided bias towards the barbaric. She might be any age between forty-five and sixty-five.* **Ruth** *ushers her in.* **Ruth** *and* **Charles** *greet her simultaneously.*

**Charles** (*advancing*)   My dear Madame Arcati!

**Madame Arcati**   I'm afraid I'm rather late, but I had a sudden presentiment that I was going to have a puncture so I went back to fetch my pump (**Madame Arcati** *takes off cloak and hands it to* **Ruth** *who puts it on chair.*) and then of course I didn't have a puncture at all.

**Charles**   Perhaps you will on the way home.

**Madame Arcati** (*crosses to shake hands with* **Dr Bradman**. *Greeting him*)   Doctor Bradman – the man with the gentle hands!

**Dr Bradman**   I'm delighted to see you looking so well. This is my wife.

**Madame Arcati** *shakes hands with* **Mrs Bradman** *over back of sofa.*

**Madame Arcati**   We are old friends – we meet coming out of shops.

**Charles**   Would you like a cocktail?

**Madame Arcati** (*peeling off some rather strange-looking gloves*)   If it's a dry Martini, yes – if it's a concoction, no. Experience has taught me to be very wary of concoctions.

**Charles**   It is a dry Martini.

**Madame Arcati**   How delicious. It was wonderful cycling through the woods this evening – I was deafened with bird-song.

**Ruth**   It's been lovely all day.

**Madame Arcati**   But the evening's the time – mark my words. (*She takes the cocktail* **Charles** *gives her.*) Thank you.

Cheers! Cheers!

**Ruth**   Don't you find it very tiring bicycling everywhere?

**Madame Arcati**   On the contrary – it stimulates me – I was getting far too sedentary in London, that horrid little flat with the dim lights – they had to be dim, you know, the clients expect it.

**Mrs Bradman**   I must say I find bicycling very exhausting.

**Madame Arcati**   Steady rhythm – that's what counts. Once you get the knack of it you need never look back – on you get and away you go.

**Mrs Bradman**   But the hills, Madame Arcati – pushing up those awful hills—

**Madame Arcati**   Just knack again – down with your head, up with your heart, and you're over the top like a flash and skimming down the other side like a dragon-fly. This is the best dry Martini I've had for years.

**Charles**   Will you have another?

**Madame Arcati**   (*holding out her glass*)   Certainly. You're a very clever man. Anybody can write books, but it takes an artist to make a dry Martini that's dry enough.

**Ruth**   Are you writing anything nowadays, Madame Arcati?

**Madame Arcati**   Every morning regular as clockwork, seven till one.

**Charles** (*gives* **Madame Arcati** *a cocktail from above sofa*)   Is it a novel or a memoir?

**Madame Arcati**   It's a children's book – I have to finish it by the end of October to catch the Christmas sales. It's mostly about very small animals, the hero is a moss beetle.

**Mrs Bradman** *laughs nervously.*

**Madame Arcati**   I had to give up my memoir of

Princess Palliatani because she died in April – I talked to her about it the other day and she implored me to go on with it, but I really hadn't the heart.

**Mrs Bradman** (*incredulously*)   You *talked* to her about it the other day?

**Madame Arcati**   Yes, through my control, of course. She sounded very irritable.

**Mrs Bradman**   It's funny to think of people in the spirit world being irritable, isn't it? I mean, one can hardly imagine it, can one?

**Charles**   We have no reliable guarantee that the after life will be any less exasperating than this one, have we?

**Mrs Bradman** (*laughing*)   Oh, Mr Condomine, how *can* you?

**Ruth**   I expect it's dreadfully ignorant of me not to know – but who was Princess Palliatani?

**Madame Arcati**   She was originally a Jewess from Odessa of quite remarkable beauty. It was an accepted fact that people used to stand on the seats of railway stations to watch her whizz by.

**Charles**   She was a keen traveller?

**Madame Arcati**   In her younger days, yes – later on she married a Mr Clarke in the Consular Service and settled down for a while. . . .

**Ruth**   How did she become Princess Palliatani?

**Madame Arcati**   That was years later. Mr Clarke passed over and left her penniless with two strapping girls. . . .

**Ruth**   How unpleasant.

**Madame Arcati**   And so there was nothing for it but to obey the beckoning finger of adventure and take to the road again – so off she went, bag and baggage, to Vladivostock.

**Charles**  What an extraordinary place to go!

**Madame Arcati**  She had cousins there. Some years later she met old Palliatani who was returning from a secret mission in Japan. He was immediately staggered by her beauty and very shortly afterwards married her. From then on her life became really interesting.

**Dr Bradman**  I should hardly have described it as dull before.

**Ruth**  What happened to the girls?

**Madame Arcati**  She neither saw them nor spoke to them for twenty-three years.

**Mrs Bradman**  How extraordinary.

**Madame Arcati**  Not at all. She was always very erratic emotionally.

*The double doors of the dining-room open and* **Edith** *comes in.*

**Edith** (*nervously*)  Dinner is served, Mum.

**Ruth**  Thank you, Edith— Shall we—?

**Edith** *retires backwards into the dining-room.*

**All** *rise.*

**Madame Arcati**  No red meat, I hope?

**Ruth**  There's meat, but I don't think it will be very red – would you rather have an egg or something?

**Madame Arcati**  No, thank you – it's just that I make it a rule never to eat red meat before I work – it sometimes has an odd effect. . . .

**Charles**  What sort of effect?

**Madame Arcati**  Oh, nothing of the least importance – if it isn't very red it won't matter much – anyhow, we'll risk it.

**Madame Arcati** *goes out first with* **Ruth** *followed by* **Mrs Bradman**, **Dr Bradman** *and* **Charles**.

**Ruth**   Come along, then – Mrs Bradman – Madame Arcati – you're on Charles's right. . . .

*They all move into the dining-room as the lights fade on the scene.*

## Scene Two

*When the lights go up again, dinner is over, and* **Ruth, Mrs Bradman** *and* **Madame Arcati** *are sitting having their coffee;* **Mrs Bradman** *on pouffe down stage right.* **Madame Arcati** *on right end of sofa,* **Ruth** *on left end of sofa. All with coffee cups.*

**Madame Arcati**   . . . on her mother's side she went right back to the Borgias which I think accounted for a lot one way or another – even as a child she was given to the most violent destructive tempers – very inbred, you know.

**Mrs Bradman**   Yes, she must have been.

**Madame Arcati**   My control was quite scared the other day when we were talking – I could hear it in her voice – after all, she's only a child. . . .

**Ruth**   Do you always have a child as a control?

**Madame Arcati**   Yes, they're generally the best – some mediums prefer Indians, of course, but personally I've always found them unreliable.

**Ruth**   In what way unreliable?

**Madame Arcati**   Well, for one thing they're frightfully lazy and also, when faced with any sort of difficulty, they're rather apt to go off into their own tribal language which is naturally unintelligible – that generally spoils everything and wastes a great deal of time. No, children are undoubtedly more satisfactory, particularly when they get to know you and understand your ways. Daphne has worked with me for years.

**Mrs Bradman**   And she still goes on being a child – I mean, she doesn't show signs of growing any older?

**Madame Arcati** (*patiently*)   Time values on the 'Other Side' are utterly different from ours.

**Mrs Bradman**   Do you feel funny when you go off into a trance?

**Madame Arcati**   In what way funny?

**Ruth** (*hastily*)   Mrs Bradman doesn't mean funny in its comic implication, I think she meant odd or strange—

**Madame Arcati**   The word was an unfortunate choice.

**Mrs Bradman**   I'm sure I'm very sorry.

**Madame Arcati**   It doesn't matter in the least – please don't apologise.

**Ruth**   When did you first discover that you had these extraordinary powers?

**Madame Arcati**   When I was quite tiny. My mother was a medium before me, you know, and so I had every opportunity of starting on the ground floor as you might say. I had my first trance when I was four years old and my first ectoplasmic manifestation when I was five and a half – what an exciting day that was, I shall never forget it – of course the manifestation itself was quite small and of very short duration, but, for a child of my tender years, it was most gratifying.

**Mrs Bradman**   Your mother must have been so pleased.

**Madame Arcati** (*modestly*)   She was.

**Mrs Bradman**   Can you foretell the future?

**Madame Arcati**   Certainly not. I disapprove of fortune-tellers most strongly.

**Mrs Bradman** (*disappointed*)   Oh really – why?

**Madame Arcati**   Too much guesswork and fake mixed up with it – even when the gift is genuine – and it only very occasionally is – you can't count on it.

**Ruth**   Why not?

**Madame Arcati**  Time again – time is the reef upon which all our frail mystic ships are wrecked.

**Ruth**  You mean, because it has never yet been proved that the past and the present and the future are not one and the same thing.

**Madame Arcati**  I long ago came to the conclusion that nothing has ever been definitely proved about anything.

**Ruth**  How very wise.

**Madame Arcati** *hands her cup to* **Ruth**. **Mrs Bradman** *puts her cup behind her on small table down stage right.* **Edith** *comes in with a tray of drinks. She puts tray down on centre table by* **Ruth**. **Ruth** *moves a coffee cup and a vase to make room for it.* **Ruth** *takes off cigarette-box and ash-tray from table and gives them to* **Edith** *who puts them on drinks table.*

**Ruth**  I want you to leave the dining-room just as it is for to-night, Edith – you can clear the table in the morning.

**Edith**  Yes'm.

**Ruth**  And we don't want to be disturbed for the next hour or so for any reason whatsoever – is that clear?

**Edith**  Yes'm.

**Ruth**  And if anyone should telephone, just say we are out and take a message.

**Mrs Bradman**  Unless it's an urgent call for George.

**Ruth**  Unless it's an urgent call for Dr Bradman.

**Edith**  Yes'm.

**Edith** *goes out swiftly.*

**Ruth**  There's not likely to be one, is there?

**Mrs Bradman**  No, I don't think so.

**Madame Arcati**  Once I am off it won't matter, but an interruption during the preliminary stages might be disastrous.

**Mrs Bradman** I wish the men would hurry up – I'm terribly excited.

**Madame Arcati** Please don't be – it makes everything very much more difficult.

**Charles** *and* **Dr Bradman** *come out of the dining-room. They are smoking cigars.*

**Charles** (*cheerfully*) Well, Madame Arcati – the time is drawing near.

**Madame Arcati** Who knows? It may be receding!

**Charles** How very true.

**Dr Bradman** I hope you feel in the mood, Madame Arcati.

**Madame Arcati** It isn't a question of mood – it's a question of concentration.

**Ruth** You must forgive us being impatient. We can perfectly easily wait though, if you're not quite ready to start . . .

**Madame Arcati** Nonsense, my dear, I'm absolutely ready. (*She rises.*) Heigho, heigho, to work we go!

**Charles** Is there anything you'd like us to do?

**Madame Arcati** Do?

**Charles** Yes – hold hands or anything?

**Madame Arcati** All that will come later.

*She goes to window and opens it. The others rise.*

First a few deep, deep breaths of fresh air – (*Over her shoulder.*) You may talk if you wish, it will not disturb me in the least. (*She flings open the windows wide and inhales deeply and a trifle noisily.*)

**Ruth** (*with a quizzical glance at* **Charles**) Oh dear!

**Charles** (*putting his finger to his lips warningly*) An excellent dinner, darling – I congratulate you.

**Ruth**   The mousse wasn't quite right.

**Charles**   It looked a bit hysterical but it tasted delicious.

**Madame Arcati**   That cuckoo is very angry.

**Charles**   I beg your pardon?

**Madame Arcati**   I said that cuckoo is very angry . . .
listen. . . .

*They all listen obediently.*

**Charles**   How can you tell?

**Madame Arcati**   Timbre. . . . No moon – that's as well,
I think – there's mist rising from the marshes. . . . (*A thought
strikes her.*) There's no need for me to light my bicycle lamp,
is there? I mean, nobody is likely to fall over it?

**Ruth**   No, we're not expecting anybody else.

**Madame Arcati**   Good-night, you foolish bird. (*She closes
the windows.*) You have a table.

**Charles**   Yes. We thought that one would do.

**Madame Arcati** (*she puts her hands on the small table below
piano and then points to the centre table*)   I think the one that
has the drinks on it would be better.

**Dr Bradman**   Change over.

**Charles** (*to* **Ruth**)   You told Edith we didn't want to be
disturbed?

**Ruth**   Yes, darling.

**Madame Arcati** (*crosses down stage of séance table over to
mantelpiece. Walking about the room – twisting and untwisting her
hands*)   This is a moment I always hate.

**Ruth**   Are you nervous?

**Madame Arcati**   Yes. When I was a girl I always used
to be sick.

**Dr Bradman**   How fortunate that you grew out of it.

**Ruth**  Children are always much more prone to be sick than grown-ups, though, aren't they? I know I could never travel in a train with any degree of safety until I was fourteen.

**Mrs Bradman** *brings pouffe over to table.*

**Madame Arcati** (*still walking*)  Little Tommy Tucker sings for his supper, what shall he have but brown bread and butter? I despise that because it doesn't rhyme at all – but Daphne loves it.

**Dr Bradman**  Who's Daphne?

**Ruth**  Daphne is Madame Arcati's control – she's a little girl.

**Dr Bradman**  Oh, I see – yes, of course.

**Charles**  How old is she?

**Madame Arcati**  Rising seven when she died.

**Mrs Bradman**  And when was that?

**Madame Arcati**  February the sixth, 1884.

**Mrs Bradman**  Poor little thing.

**Dr Bradman**  She must be a bit long in the tooth by now, I should think.

**Madame Arcati** (*at fireplace. Stops walking and addresses* **Dr Bradman**)  You should think, Dr Bradman, but I fear you don't – at least, not profoundly enough.

**Mrs Bradman**  Do be quiet, George – you'll put Madame Arcati off.

**Madame Arcati**  Don't worry, my dear – I am quite used to sceptics – they generally turn out to be the most vulnerable and receptive in the long run.

**Ruth**  You'd better take that warning to heart, Dr Bradman.

**Dr Bradman**  Please forgive me, Madame Arcati – I

assure you I am most deeply interested.

**Madame Arcati**    It is of no consequence— Will you all sit round the table please, and place your hands downwards on it.

**Ruth**    Come, Mrs Bradman—

**Charles**    What about the lights?

**Madame Arcati**    All in good time, Mr Condomine, sit down, please.

*The four of them sit down at each side of a small square table.*
**Madame Arcati** *surveys them critically, her head on one side. She is whistling a little tune. Sings.*

The fingers should be touching ... that's right. ... I presume that that is the gramophone, Mr Condomine?

**Charles** (*half rising*)    Yes – would you like me to start it? It's an electric one.

**Madame Arcati**    Please stay where you are – I can manage. (*She goes over to the gramophone and looks over the records.*) Now let me see – what have we here – Brahms – oh, dear me, no – Rachmaninoff – too florid – where is the dance music?

**Ruth**    They're the loose ones on the left.

**Madame Arcati**    I see. (*She stoops down and produces a pile of dance records.*)

**Charles**    I'm afraid they're none of them very new.

**Madame Arcati**    Daphne is really more attached to Irving Berlin than anybody else – she likes a tune she can hum – ah, here's one – 'Always' ...

**Charles** (*half jumping up again*)    'Always'!

**Ruth**    Do sit down, Charles – what is the matter?

**Charles** (*subsiding*)    Nothing – nothing at all.

**Madame Arcati**    The light switch is by the door?

**Ruth**  Yes, all except the small one on the desk, and the gramophone.

**Madame Arcati**  Very well – I understand.

**Ruth**  Charles, do keep still.

**Mrs Bradman**  Fingers touching, George – remember what Madame Arcati said.

**Madame Arcati**  Now there are one or two things that I should like to explain, so will you all listen attentively.

**Ruth**  Of course.

**Madame Arcati**  Presently, when the music begins, I am going to switch out the lights. I may then either walk about the room for a little or lie down flat – in due course I shall draw up this dear little stool and join you at the table – I shall place myself between you and your wife, Mr Condomine, and rest my hands lightly upon yours – I must ask you not to address me or move or do anything in the least distracting – is that quite, quite clear?

**Charles**  Perfectly.

**Madame Arcati**  Of course, I cannot guarantee that anything will happen at all – Daphne may be unavailable – she had a head cold very recently, and was rather under the weather, poor child. On the other hand, a great many things might occur – one of you might have an emanation, for instance, or we might contact a poltergeist which would be extremely destructive and noisy. . . .

**Ruth** (*anxiously*)  In what way destructive?

**Madame Arcati**  They throw things, you know.

**Ruth**  I didn't know.

**Madame Arcati**  But we must cross that bridge when we come to it, mustn't we?

**Charles**  Certainly – by all means.

**Madame Arcati**  Fortunately an Elemental at this time

of the year is most unlikely. . . .

**Ruth**   What do Elementals do?

**Madame Arcati**   Oh, my dear, one can never tell –
they're dreadfully unpredictable . . . usually they take the
form of a very cold wind. . . .

**Mrs Bradman**   I don't think I shall like that—

**Madame Arcati**   Occasionally reaching almost hurricane
velocity—

**Ruth**   You don't think it would be a good idea to take
the more breakable ornaments off the mantelpiece before
we start?

**Madame Arcati** (*indulgently*)   That really is not necessary,
Mrs Condomine – I assure you I have my own methods of
dealing with Elementals.

**Ruth**   I'm so glad.

**Madame Arcati**   Now then – are you ready to empty
your minds?

**Dr Bradman**   Do you mean we're to try to think of
nothing?

**Madame Arcati**   Absolutely nothing, Dr Bradman.
Concentrate on a space or a nondescript colour, that's
really the best way. . . .

**Dr Bradman**   I'll do my damnedest.

**Madame Arcati**   Good work! I will now start the music.

*She goes to the gramophone, puts on the record of 'Always', and
begins to walk about the room; occasionally she moves into an abortive
little dance step, and once, on passing a mirror on the mantelpiece, she
surveys herself critically for a moment and adjusts her hair. Then with
sudden speed, she runs across the room and switches off the lights.*

**Mrs Bradman**   Oh, dear!

**Madame Arcati**   Quiet – please. . . .

*Presently in the gloom* **Madame Arcati**, *after wandering about a little, draws up a stool and sits at the table between* **Charles** *and* **Ruth**. *The gramophone record comes to an end. There is dead silence.*

Is there anyone there? ( *(A long pause.)* . . . Is there anyone there? . . . *(Another longer pause.)* . . . One rap for yes – two raps for no – now then – Is there anyone there? . . .

*After a shorter pause, the table gives a little bump.*

**Mrs Bradman** *(involuntarily)*   Oh!

**Madame Arcati**   Sshhh! . . . Is that you, Daphne? *(The table gives a louder bump.)* Is your cold better, dear? *(The table gives two loud bumps very quickly.)* Oh, I'm so sorry – are you doing anything for it? *(The table bumps several times.)* I'm afraid she's rather fretful. . . . *(There is a silence.)* Is there anyone there who wishes to speak to anyone here? *(After a pause the table gives one bump.)* Ah! Now we're getting somewhere. . . . No, Daphne, don't do that, dear, you're hurting me . . . Daphne, dear, please . . . Oh, oh, oh! . . . be good, there's a dear child. . . . You say there is someone there who wishes to speak to someone here? *(One bump.)* Is it me? *(Two sharp bumps.)* Is it Dr Bradman? *(Two bumps.)* Is it Mrs Bradman? *(Two bumps.)* Is it Mrs Condomine? *(Several loud bumps, which continue until* **Madame Arcati** *shouts it down.)* Stop it! Behave yourself! Is it Mr Condomine? *(There is dead silence for a moment, and then a very loud single bump.)* There's someone who wishes to speak to you, Mr Condomine. . . .

**Charles**   Tell them to leave a message.

*The table bangs about loudly.*

**Madame Arcati**   I really must ask you not to be flippant, Mr Condomine. . . .

**Ruth**   Charles, how can you be so idiotic – you'll spoil everything.

**Charles**   I'm sorry – it slipped out.

**Madame Arcati**   Do you know anybody who has passed over recently?

**Charles**   Not recently, except my cousin in the Civil Service, and he wouldn't be likely to want to communicate with me – we haven't spoken for years.

**Madame Arcati** (*hysterically*)   Are you Mr Condomine's cousin in the Civil Service? (*The table bumps violently several times.*) I'm afraid we've drawn a blank. . . . Can't you think of anyone else? Rack your brains. . . .

**Ruth** (*helpfully*)   It might be old Mrs Plummett, you know – she died on Whit Monday. . . .

**Charles**   I can't imagine why old Mrs Plummett should wish to talk to me – we had very little in common.

**Ruth**   It's worth trying, anyhow.

**Madame Arcati**   Are you old Mrs Plummett? (*The table remains still.*)

**Ruth**   She was very deaf – perhaps you'd better shout—

**Madame Arcati** (*shouting*)   Are you old Mrs Plummett? (*Nothing happens.*) There's nobody there at all.

**Mrs Bradman**   How disappointing – just as we were getting on so nicely.

**Dr Bradman**   Violet, be quiet.

**Madame Arcati** (*rises*)   Well, I'm afraid there's nothing for it but for me to go into a trance. I had hoped to avoid it because it's so exhausting – however, what must be must be. Excuse me a moment while I start the gramophone again. (*She comes to gramophone.*)

**Charles** (*in a strained voice*)   Not 'Always' – don't play 'Always'—

**Ruth**   Why ever not, Charles? Don't be absurd.

**Madame Arcati** (*gently*)   I'm afraid I must – it would be imprudent to change horses in midstream if you know what

I mean. . . . (*She re-starts the gramophone.*)

**Charles**   Have it your own way.

**Madame Arcati** *starts to moan and comes back slowly to stool and sits — then in the darkness a child's voice is heard reciting rather breathlessly:* 'Little Tommy Tucker'.

**Dr Bradman**   That would be Daphne — she ought to have had her adenoids out.

**Mrs Bradman**   George – please—

**Madame Arcati** *suddenly gives a loud scream and falls off the stool on to the floor.*

**Charles**   Good God!

**Ruth**   Keep still, Charles. . . .

**Charles** *subsides. Everyone sits in silence for a moment, then the table starts bouncing about.*

**Mrs Bradman**   It's trying to get away . . . I can't hold it. . . .

**Ruth**   Press down hard.

*The table falls over with a crash.*

There now!

**Mrs Bradman**   Ought we to pick it up or leave it where it is?

**Dr Bradman**   How the hell do I know?

**Mrs Bradman**   There's no need to snap at me.

*A perfectly strange and very charming voice says:* 'Leave it where it is.'

**Charles**   Who said that?

**Ruth**   Who said what?

**Charles**   Somebody said: 'Leave it where it is.'

**Ruth**   Nonsense, dear.

**Charles**  I heard it distinctly.

**Ruth**  Well, nobody else did – did they?

**Mrs Bradman**  I never heard a sound.

**Charles**  It was you, Ruth – you're playing tricks.

**Ruth**  I'm not doing anything of the sort. I haven't uttered.

*There is another pause, and then the voice says:* 'Good evening, Charles.'

**Charles** (*very agitated*)  Ventriloquism – that's what it is – ventriloquism. . . .

**Ruth** (*irritably*)  What is the matter with you?

**Charles**  You must have heard that – one of you must have heard that!

**Ruth**  Heard *what*?

**Charles**  You mean to sit there solemnly and tell me that none of you heard anything at all?

**Dr Bradman**  I certainly didn't.

**Mrs Bradman**  Neither did I – I wish I had. I should love to hear something.

**Ruth**  It's you who are playing the tricks, Charles – you're acting to try to frighten us . . .

**Charles** (*breathlessly*)  I'm not – I swear I'm not.

*The voice speaks again. It says:* 'It's difficult to think of what to say after seven years, but I suppose good evening is as good as anything else.'

**Charles** (*intensely*)  Who are you?

*The voice says:* 'Elvira, of course – don't be so silly.'

**Charles** *rises and goes to light-switch centre, then down stage right to fireplace. Others all rise.* **Madame Arcati** *on floor.*

**Charles**  I can't bear this for another minute. . . . (*He rises* *violently.*) Get up, everybody – the entertainment's over.

*He rushes across the room and switches on the lights.*

**Ruth**  Oh, Charles, how tiresome of you – just as we were beginning to enjoy ourselves.

**Charles**  Never again – that's all I can say. Never, never again as long as I live. . . .

**Ruth**  What on earth's the matter with you?

**Charles**  Nothing's the matter with me – I'm just sick of the whole business, that's all.

**Dr Bradman**  Did you hear anything that we didn't hear really?

**Charles** (*with a forced laugh*)  Of course not – I was only pretending . . .

**Ruth**  I know you were . . .

**Mrs Bradman**  Oh dear . . . look at Madame Arcati!

**Madame Arcati** *is lying on the floor with her feet up on the stool from which she fell. She is obviously quite unconscious.*

**Ruth**  What are we to do with her?

**Charles**  Bring her round – bring her round as soon as possible.

**Dr Bradman** (*going over and kneeling down beside her*)  I think we'd better leave her alone.

**Ruth**  But she might stay like that for hours.

**Dr Bradman**, *kneeling left of* **Madame Arcati**, **Ruth** *above her.* **Mrs Bradman**, *to left of* **Dr Bradman**, **Charles** *to right of* **Madame Arcati**, *below sofa.*

**Dr Bradman** (*after feeling her pulse and examining her eye*)  She's out all right.

**Charles** (*almost hysterically*)  Bring her round! It's dangerous to leave her like that. . . .

**Ruth**   Really, Charles, you are behaving most peculiarly.

**Charles** (*kneels right of* **Madame Arcati**, *shaking her violently*)   Wake up, Madame Arcati – wake up – it's time to go home.

**Dr Bradman**   Here – go easy, old man . . .

**Ruth** *goes to drinks table left pours brandy.* **Charles** *and* **Dr Bradman** *lift* **Madame Arcati** *and put her in arm-chair.* **Mrs Bradman** *takes stool from her feet and puts it back under piano.*

**Charles**   Get some brandy – give her some brandy – lift her into the chair – help me, Bradman . . .

**Ruth** *pours out some brandy while* **Charles** *and* **Dr Bradman** *lift* **Madame Arcati** *laboriously into an arm-chair.*

**Charles** (*leaning over her*)   Wake UP, Madame Arcati – Little Tommy Tucker, Madame Arcati!

**Ruth** *brings brandy to above arm-chair.* **Charles** *takes it and gives some to* **Madame Arcati** *on her right.* **Dr Bradman** *patting her hand on her left.* **Mrs Bradman** *above* **Dr Bradman**.

**Ruth**   Here's the brandy.

**Madame Arcati** *gives a slight moan and a shiver.*

**Charles** ( *forcing some brandy between her lips*)   Wake up!—

**Madame Arcati** *gives a prolonged shiver and chokes slightly over the brandy.*

**Mrs Bradman**   She's coming round.

**Ruth**   Be careful, Charles – you're spilling it all down her dress.

**Madame Arcati** (*opening her eyes*)   Well, that's that.

**Ruth** (*solicitously*)   Are you all right?

**Madame Arcati**   Certainly I am – never felt better in my life.

**Charles** Would you like some more brandy?

**Madame Arcati** So that's the funny taste in my mouth – well, really! Fancy allowing them to give me brandy, Doctor Bradman, you ought to have known better – brandy on top of a trance might have been catastrophic. Take it away, please – I probably shan't sleep a wink to-night as it is.

**Charles** I know I shan't.

**Ruth** Why on earth not?

**Charles** *crosses away to right to fireplace and takes cigarette.*

**Charles** The whole experience has unhinged me.

**Madame Arcati** Well, what happened – was it satisfactory?

**Ruth** Nothing much happened, Madame Arcati, after you went off.

**Madame Arcati** Something happened all right, I can feel it— (**Madame Arcati** *rises and crosses to fireplace – sniffs.*) No poltergeist, at any rate – that's a good thing. Any apparitions?

**Dr Bradman** Not a thing.

**Madame Arcati** No ectoplasm?

**Ruth** I'm not quite sure what it is, but I don't think so.

**Madame Arcati** Very curious. I feel as though something tremendous had taken place.

**Ruth** Charles pretended he heard a voice, in order to frighten us.

**Charles** It was only a joke.

**Madame Arcati** A very poor one, if I may say so— (*Round above sofa to right centre.*) Nevertheless, I am prepared to swear that there is someone else psychic in this room apart from myself.

**Ruth**   I don't see how there can be really, Madame
Arcati.

**Madame Arcati**   I do hope I haven't gone and released
something – however, we are bound to find out within a
day or two – if any manifestation should occur or you hear
any unexpected noises – you might let me know at once.

**Ruth**   Of course we will – we'll telephone immediately.

**Madame Arcati**   I think I really must be on my way
now.

**Ruth**   Wouldn't you like anything before you go?

**Madame Arcati**   No, thank you – I have some Ovaltine
all ready in a saucepan at home – it only needs hotting up.

**Dr Bradman**   Wouldn't you like to leave your bicycle
here and let us drive you?

**Mrs Bradman**   I honestly do think you should, Madame
Arcati, after that trance and everything – you can't be
feeling quite yourself.

**Madame Arcati**   Nonsense, my dear, I'm as fit as a
fiddle – always feel capital after a trance – rejuvenates me.
Good-night, Mrs Condomine.

**Ruth**   It was awfully sweet of you to take so much
trouble.

**Madame Arcati**   I'm so sorry so little occurred – it's that
cold of Daphne's, I expect – you know what children are
when they have anything wrong with them – we must try
again some other evening.

**Madame Arcati** *crosses above* **Ruth** *to right of* **Mrs
Bradman**.

**Ruth**   That would be lovely.

**Madame Arcati** (*shaking hands with* **Mrs
Bradman**)   Good-night, Mrs Bradman.

**Mrs Bradman**   It was thrilling, it really was – I felt the table absolutely shaking under my hands.

**Madame Arcati** *crosses above* **Mrs Bradman** *to* **Dr Bradman** *and shakes hands.*

**Madame Arcati** Good-night, Doctor.

**Dr Bradman** Congratulations, Madame Arcati.

**Madame Arcati** I am fully aware of the irony in your voice, Dr Bradman. As a matter of fact you'd be an admirable subject for telepathic hypnosis – a great chum of mine is an expert – I should like her to look you over.

**Dr Bradman** I'm sure I should be charmed.

**Madame Arcati** Good-night, everyone – next time we must really put our backs into it!

*With a comprehensive smile and a wave of the hand, she goes out, followed by* **Charles**.

**Ruth** *sinks down into sofa, laughing helplessly.*

**Mrs Bradman** *comes and sits left of arm-chair.* **Dr Bradman** *picks up séance table and puts desk chair back up stage right, then comes back and puts pouffe back in position down stage right. He then returns to left centre.*

**Ruth** Oh dear! . . . oh dear! . . .

**Mrs Bradman** (*beginning to laugh too*) Be careful, Mrs Condomine – she might hear you.

**Ruth** I can't help it – I really can't – I've been holding this in for ages.

**Mrs Bradman** She certainly put you in your place, George, and serve you right.

**Ruth** She's raving mad, of course – mad as a hatter.

**Mrs Bradman** But do you really think she *believes*?

**Dr Bradman** Of course not – the whole thing's a put up job – I must say, though, she shoots a more original line than they generally do.

**Ruth**   I should think that she's probably half convinced herself by now.

**Dr Bradman**   Possibly – the trance was genuine enough – but that, of course, is easily accounted for.

**Ruth**   Hysteria?

**Dr Bradman**   Yes – a form of hysteria, I should imagine.

**Mrs Bradman**   I do hope Mr Condomine got all the atmosphere he wanted for his book.

**Ruth**   He might have got a great deal more if he hadn't spoiled everything by showing off. . . . I'm really very cross with him.

*At this moment* **Elvira** *comes in through the closed french windows. She is charmingly dressed in a sort of negligee. Everything about her is grey; hair, skin, dress, hands, so we must accept the fact that she is not quite of this world. She passes between* **Dr** *and* **Mrs Bradman** *and* **Ruth** *while they are talking. None of them see her. She goes up stage and sits soundlessly on a chair. She regards them with interest, a slight smile on her face.*

**Ruth**   I suddenly felt a draught – there must be a window open.

**Dr Bradman** (*looking*)   No – they're shut.

**Mrs Bradman** (*laughing*)   Perhaps it was one of those what you may call 'ems that Madame Arcati was talking about.

**Dr Bradman**   Elementals.

**Ruth** (*also laughing again*)   Oh no, it couldn't be – she distinctly said that it was the wrong time of the year for Elementals.

**Charles** *comes in, to arm-chair centre.*

**Charles**   Well, the old girl's gone pedalling off down the drive at the hell of a speed – we had a bit of trouble lighting her lamp.

**Mrs Bradman**   Poor thing.

**Charles**   I've got a theory about her, you know – I believe she is completely sincere.

**Ruth**   Charles! How could she be?

**Charles**   Wouldn't it be possible, Doctor? Some form of self-hypnotism?

**Dr Bradman**   It might be . . . as I was explaining to your wife just now, there are certain types of hysterical subjects. . . .

**Mrs Bradman**   George dear – it's getting terribly late, we really must go home – you have to get up so early in the morning.

**Dr Bradman**   You see? The moment I begin to talk about anything that really interests me, my wife interrupts me. . . .

**Mrs Bradman**   You know I'm right, darling – it's past eleven.

**Dr Bradman**   (*crosses up stage to* **Charles** *centre*)   I'll do a little reading up on the whole business – just for the fun of it.

**Charles**   You must have a drink before you go.

**Dr Bradman**   No, really, thank you – Violet's quite right, I'm afraid. I have got to get up abominably early to-morrow – I have a patient being operated on in Canterbury.

**Mrs Bradman** *crosses to* **Ruth** *below sofa.* **Ruth** *rises.*

**Mrs Bradman**   It has been a thrilling evening – I shall never forget – it was sweet of you to include us.

**Dr Bradman**   Good-night, Mrs Condomine – thank you so much.

**Charles**   You're sure about the drink?

**Dr Bradman**   Quite sure, thanks.

**Ruth**   We'll let you know if we find any poltergeists whirling about.

**Dr Bradman**   I should never forgive you if you didn't.

**Mrs Bradman**   Come along, darling . . .

**Bradmans** *exit, followed by* **Charles**.

**Ruth** *crosses to piano, leans over* **Elvira** *and gets cigarette and lights it, then crosses back to fireplace.* **Charles** *comes back into the room.*

**Ruth**   Well, darling?

**Charles** (*to above left end of sofa. Absently*)   Well?

**Ruth**   Would you say the evening had been profitable?

**Charles**   Yes – I suppose so.

**Ruth**   I must say it was extremely funny at moments.

**Charles**   Yes – it certainly was.

**Ruth**   What's the matter?

**Charles**   The matter?

**Ruth**   Yes – you seem odd somehow – do you feel quite well?

**Charles**   Perfectly. I think I'll have a drink. (*Moves up stage to drinks table and pours whisky-and-soda.*) Do you want one?

**Ruth**   No, thank you, dear.

**Charles** (*pouring himself out a drink*)   It's rather chilly in this room.

**Ruth**   Come over by the fire.

**Charles**   I don't think I'll make any notes to-night – I'll start fresh in the morning.

**Charles** *turns with glass in hand, sees* **Elvira** *and drops his glass on the floor.*

**Charles**   My God!

**Ruth**  Charles!

**Elvira**  That was very clumsy, Charles dear.

**Charles**  Elvira! – then it's true – it was you!

**Elvira**  Of course it was.

**Ruth** (*starts to go to* **Charles**)  Charles – darling Charles – what are you talking about?

**Charles** (*to* **Elvira**)  Are you a ghost?

**Elvira** (*crosses below sofa to fire*)  I suppose I must be – it's all very confusing.

**Ruth** (*comes to right of* **Charles**, *becoming agitated*)  Charles – what do you keep looking over there for? Look at me – what's happened?

**Charles**  Don't you see?

**Ruth**  See what?

**Charles**  Elvira.

**Ruth** (*staring at him incredulously*)  Elvira!!

**Charles** (*with an effort at social grace*)  Yes – Elvira, dear, this is Ruth – Ruth, this is Elvira.

**Ruth** *tries to take his arm.* **Charles** *retreats down stage left.*

**Ruth** (*with forced calmness*)  Come and sit down, darling.

**Charles**  Do you mean to say you can't see her?

**Ruth**  Listen, Charles – you just sit down quietly by the fire and I'll mix you another drink. Don't worry about the mess on the carpet – Edith can clean it up in the morning. (*She takes him by the arm.*)

**Charles** (*breaking away*)  But you must be able to see her – she's there – look – right in front of you – there—

**Ruth**  Are you mad? What's happened to you?

**Charles**  You can't see her?

**Ruth**   If this is a joke, dear, it's gone quite far enough. Sit down for God's sake and don't be idiotic.

**Charles** (*clutching his head*)   What am I to do – what the hell am I to do!

**Elvira**   I think you might at least be a little more pleased to see me – after all, you conjured me up.

**Charles** (*above table left centre*)   I didn't do any such thing.

**Elvira**   Nonsense, of course you did. That awful child with the cold came and told me you wanted to see me urgently.

**Charles**   It was all a mistake – a horrible mistake.

**Ruth**   Stop talking like that, Charles – as I told you before, the joke's gone far enough.

**Charles**   I've gone mad, that's what it is – I've just gone raving mad.

**Ruth** (*pours out brandy and brings it to* **Charles** *below piano*)   Here – drink this.

**Charles** (*mechanically – taking it*)   This is appalling!

**Ruth**   Relax.

**Charles**   How can I relax? I shall never be able to relax again as long as I live.

**Ruth**   Drink some brandy.

**Charles** (*drinking it at a gulp*)   There, now – are you satisfied?

**Ruth**   Now sit down.

**Charles**   Why are you so anxious for me to sit down – what good will that do?

**Ruth**   I want you to relax – you can't relax standing up.

**Elvira**   African natives can – they can stand on one leg for hours.

**Charles**  I don't happen to be an African native.

**Ruth**  You don't happen to be a *what?*

**Charles** (*savagely*)  An African native!

**Ruth**  What's that got to do with it?

**Charles**  It doesn't matter, Ruth – really it doesn't matter – we'll say no more about it.

**Charles** *crosses to arm-chair and sits.* **Ruth** *comes up stage of him.*

**Charles**  See, I've sat down.

**Ruth**  Would you like some more brandy?

**Charles**  Yes, please.

**Ruth** *goes up to drinks table with glass.*

**Elvira**  Very unwise – you always had a weak head.

**Charles**  I could drink you under the table.

**Ruth**  There's no need to be aggressive, Charles – I'm doing my best to help you.

**Charles**  I'm sorry.

**Ruth** (*crosses to up stage of* **Charles** *with brandy*)  Here – drink this – and then we'll go to bed.

**Elvira**  Get rid of her, Charles – then we can talk in peace.

**Charles**  That's a thoroughly immoral suggestion, you ought to be ashamed of yourself.

**Ruth**  What is there immoral in that?

**Charles**  I wasn't talking to you.

**Ruth**  Who were you talking to, then?

**Charles**  Elvira, of course.

**Ruth**  To hell with Elvira!

**Elvira**  There now – she's getting cross.

**Charles**  I don't blame her.

**Ruth**  What don't you blame her for?

**Charles** (*rises and backs down stage left a pace*)  Oh, God!

**Ruth**  Now look here, Charles – I gather you've got some sort of plan behind all this. I'm not quite a fool. I suspected you when we were doing that idiotic séance . . .

**Charles**  Don't be so silly – what plan could I have?

**Ruth**  I don't know – it's probably something to do with the characters in your book – how they, or one of them would react to a certain situation – I refuse to be used as a guinea-pig unless I'm warned beforehand what it's all about.

**Charles** (*moves a couple of paces towards* **Ruth**)  Elvira is here, Ruth – she's standing a few yards away from you.

**Ruth** (*sarcastically*)  Yes, dear, I can see her distinctly – under the piano with a zebra!

**Charles**  But, Ruth . . .

**Ruth**  I am not going to stay here arguing any longer . . .

**Elvira**  Hurray!

**Charles**  Shut up!

**Ruth** (*incensed*)  How dare you speak to me like that!

**Charles**  Listen, Ruth – please listen—

**Ruth**  I will not listen to any more of this nonsense – I am going up to bed now, I'll leave you to turn out the lights. I shan't be asleep – I'm too upset. So you can come in and say good-night to me if you feel like it.

**Elvira**  That's big of her, I must say.

**Charles**  Be quiet – you're behaving like a gutter-snipe.

**Ruth** (*icily*)  That is all I have to say. Good-night, Charles.

**Ruth** *walks swiftly out of the room without looking at him again.*

**Charles** (*follows* **Ruth** *to door*)   Ruth . . .

**Elvira**   That was one of the most enjoyable half-hours I have ever spent.

**Charles** (*puts down glass on drinks table*)   Oh, Elvira – how could you!

**Elvira**   Poor Ruth!

**Charles** (*staring at her*)   This is obviously a hallucination, isn't it?

**Elvira**   I'm afraid I don't know the technical term for it.

**Charles** (*comes down stage to centre*)   What am I to do?

**Elvira**   What Ruth suggested – relax.

**Charles** (*crosses below chair to sofa*)   Where have you come from?

**Elvira**   Do you know, it's very peculiar, but I've sort of forgotten.

**Charles**   Are you to be here indefinitely?

**Elvira**   I don't know that either.

**Charles**   Oh, my God!

**Elvira**   Why, would you hate it so much if I was?

**Charles**   Well, you must admit it would be embarrassing?

**Elvira**   I don't see why, really – it's all a question of adjusting yourself – anyhow I think it's horrid of you to be so unwelcoming and disagreeable.

**Charles**   Now look here, Elvira . . .

**Elvira** (*near tears*)   I do – I think you're mean.

**Charles**   Try to see my point, dear – I've been married to Ruth for five years, and you've been dead for seven . . .

**Elvira**   Not dead, Charles – 'passed over'. It's considered vulgar to say 'dead' where I come from.

**Charles**   Passed over, then.

**Elvira**   At any rate now that I'm here, the least you can do is to make a pretence of being amiable about it . . .

**Charles**   Of course, my dear, I'm delighted in one way . . .

**Elvira**   I don't believe you love me any more.

**Charles**   I shall always love the memory of you.

**Elvira** (*crosses slowly down stage left above sofa by arm-chair*)   You mustn't think me unreasonable, but I really am a little hurt. You called me back – and at great inconvenience I came – and you've been thoroughly churlish ever since I arrived.

**Charles** (*gently*)   Believe me, Elvira, I most emphatically did not send for you – there's been some mistake.

**Elvira** (*irritably*)   Well, somebody did – and that child said it was you – I remember I was playing backgammon with a very sweet old Oriental gentleman – I think his name was Genghis Khan – and I'd just thrown double sixes, and then the child paged me and the next thing I knew I was in this room . . . perhaps it was your subconscious.

**Charles**   You must find out whether you are going to stay or not, and we can make arrangements accordingly.

**Elvira**   I don't see how I can.

**Charles**   Well, try to think – isn't there anyone that you know, that you can get in touch with over there – on the other side, or whatever it's called – who could advise you?

**Elvira**   I can't think – it seems so far away – as though I'd dreamed it . . .

**Charles**   You must know somebody else besides Genghis Khan.

**Elvira** (*to arm-chair a pace*)   Oh, Charles . . .

**Charles**   What is it?

**Elvira**   I want to cry, but I don't think I'm able to . . .

**Charles**   What do you want to cry for?

**Elvira**   It's seeing you again – and you being so irascible like you always used to be . . .

**Charles**   I don't mean to be irascible, Elvira . . .

**Elvira**   Darling – I don't mind really – I never did.

**Charles**   Is it cold – being a ghost?

**Elvira**   No – I don't think so.

**Charles**   What happens if I touch you?

**Elvira**   I doubt if you can. Do you want to?

**Charles** (*sits left end of sofa*)   Oh, Elvira. . . . (*He buries his face in his hands.*)

**Elvira** (*to left arm of sofa*)   What is it, darling?

**Charles**   I really do feel strange, seeing you again . . .

**Elvira** (*moves to right below sofa and round above it again to left arm*)   That's better.

**Charles** (*looking up*)   What's better?

**Elvira**   Your voice was kinder.

**Charles**   Was I ever unkind to you when you were alive?

**Elvira**   Often . . .

**Charles**   Oh, how can you! I'm sure that's an exaggeration.

**Elvira**   Not at all – you were an absolute pig that time we went to Cornwall and stayed in that awful hotel – you hit me with a billiard cue—

**Charles**   Only very, very gently. . . .

**Elvira**   I loved you very much.

**Charles**   I loved you too ... (*He puts out his hand to her and then draws it away.*) No, I can't touch you – isn't that horrible?

**Elvira**   Perhaps it's as well if I'm going to stay for any length of time ... (*Sits left arm of sofa.*)

**Charles**   I suppose I shall wake up eventually ... but I feel strangely peaceful now.

**Elvira**   That's right. Put your head back.

**Charles** (*doing so*)   Like that?

**Elvira** (*stroking his hair*)   Can you feel anything ... ?

**Charles**   Only a very little breeze through my hair ...

**Elvira**   Well, that's better than nothing.

**Charles** (*drowsily*)   I suppose if I'm really out of my mind they'll put me in an asylum.

**Elvira**   Don't worry about that – just relax—

**Charles** (*very drowsily indeed*)   Poor Ruth ...

**Elvira** (*gently and sweetly*)   To hell with Ruth.

*The curtain falls*

# Act Two

## Scene One

*It is about nine-thirty the next morning. The sun is pouring in through the open french windows.*

*Breakfast table set left centre below piano.* **Ruth** *sitting left of table back to window reading 'The Times'.* **Charles** *comes in and crosses to window – he kisses her.*

**Charles**   Good morning, darling.

**Ruth** (*with a certain stiffness*)   Good morning, Charles.

**Charles** (*going to the open window and taking a deep breath*)   It certainly is.

**Ruth**   What certainly is what?

**Charles**   A good morning – a tremendously good morning – there isn't a cloud in the sky and everything looks newly washed.

**Ruth** (*turning a page of 'The Times'*)   Edith's keeping your breakfast hot – you'd better ring.

**Charles** (*crosses to mantelpiece and rings bell up stage*)   Anything interesting in *The Times*?

**Ruth**   Don't be silly, Charles.

**Charles** (*sitting at the table and pouring himself out some coffee*)   I intend to work all day.

**Ruth**   Good.

**Charles** (*comes back to breakfast table*)   It's extraordinary about daylight, isn't it?

**Ruth**   How do you mean?

**Charles**   The way it reduces everything to normal.

**Ruth**   Does it?

**Charles** (*sits right of table opposite* **Ruth** *– firmly*)   Yes – it does.

**Ruth**   I'm sure I'm very glad to hear it.

**Charles**   You're very glacial this morning.

**Ruth**   Are you surprised?

**Charles**   Frankly – yes. I expected more of you.

**Ruth**   Well, really!

**Charles**   I've always looked upon you as a woman of perception and understanding.

**Ruth**   Perhaps this is one of my off days.

**Edith** *comes in with some bacon and eggs and toast – comes to above table between* **Charles** *and* **Ruth**.

**Charles** (*cheerfully*)   Good morning, Edith.

**Edith**   Good morning, sir.

**Charles**   Feeling fit?

**Edith**   Yes, sir – thank you, sir.

**Charles**   How's cook?

**Edith**   I don't know, sir – I haven't asked her.

**Charles**   You should. You should begin every day by asking everyone how they are – it oils the wheels.

**Edith**   Yes, sir.

**Charles**   Greet her from me, will you?

**Edith**   Yes, sir.

**Ruth**   That will be all for the moment, Edith.

**Edith**   Yes'm.

**Edith** *goes out.*

**Ruth**   I wish you wouldn't be facetious with the servants, Charles – it confuses them and undermines their morale.

**Charles**   I consider that point of view retrogressive, if not downright feudal.

**Ruth**   I don't care what you consider it, I have to run the house and you don't.

**Charles**   Are you implying that I couldn't?

**Ruth**   You're at liberty to try.

**Charles**   I take back what I said about it being a good morning – it's a horrid morning.

**Ruth**   You'd better eat your breakfast while it's hot.

**Charles**   It isn't.

**Ruth** (*putting down 'The Times'*)   Now look here, Charles – in your younger days this display of roguish flippancy might have been alluring – in a middle-aged novelist it's nauseating.

**Charles**   Would you like me to writhe at your feet in a frenzy of self-abasement.

**Ruth**   That would be equally nauseating but certainly more appropriate.

**Charles**   I really don't see what I've done that's so awful.

**Ruth**   You behaved abominably last night. You wounded me and insulted me.

**Charles**   I was the victim of an aberration.

**Ruth**   Nonsense – you were drunk.

**Charles**   Drunk?

**Ruth**   You had four strong dry Martinis before dinner – a great deal too much Burgundy at dinner – heaven knows how much Port and Kummel with Dr Bradman while I was doing my best to entertain that mad woman – and then two double brandies later – I gave them to you myself – of course you were drunk.

**Charles**   So that's your story, is it?

**Ruth**   You refused to come to bed and finally when I came down at three in the morning to see what had happened to you, I found you in an alcoholic coma on the sofa with the fire out and your hair all over your face.

**Charles**   I was not in the least drunk, Ruth. Something happened to me last night – something very peculiar happened to me.

**Ruth**   Nonsense.

**Charles**   It isn't nonsense – I know it looks like nonsense now in the clear remorseless light of day, but last night it was far from being nonsense – I honestly had some sort of hallucination . . .

**Ruth**   I would really rather not discuss it any further.

**Charles**   But you must discuss it – it's very disturbing.

**Ruth**   There I agree with you. It showed you up in a most unpleasant light – I find that extremely disturbing.

**Charles**   I swear to you that during the séance I was convinced that I heard Elvira's voice—

**Ruth**   Nobody else did.

**Charles**   I can't help that – I did.

**Ruth**   You couldn't have.

**Charles**   And later on I was equally convinced that she was in this room – I saw her distinctly and talked to her. After you'd gone up to bed we had quite a cosy little chat.

**Ruth**   And you seriously expect me to believe that you weren't drunk?

**Charles**   I *knew* I wasn't drunk. If I'd been all that drunk I should have a dreadful hangover now, shouldn't I?

**Ruth**   I'm not at all sure that you haven't.

**Charles**   I haven't got a trace of a headache – my tongue's not coated – look at it – (*He puts out his tongue.*)

**Ruth**   I've not the least desire to look at your tongue, kindly put it in again.

**Charles** (*rises, crosses to mantelpiece and lights cigarette*)   I know what it is – you're frightened.

**Ruth**   Frightened! Rubbish. What is there to be frightened of?

**Charles**   Elvira. You wouldn't have minded all that much even if I had been drunk – it's only because it was all mixed up with Elvira.

**Ruth**   I seem to remember last night before dinner telling you that your views of female psychology were rather didactic. I was right. I should have added that they were puerile.

**Charles**   That was when it all began.

**Ruth**   When what all began?

**Charles** (*moves up to above right end of sofa*)   We were talking too much about Elvira – it's dangerous to have somebody very strongly in your mind when you start dabbling with the occult.

**Ruth**   She certainly wasn't strongly in my mind.

**Charles**   She was in mine.

**Ruth**   Oh, she was, was she?

**Charles** (*crosses to face* **Ruth** *at breakfast table*)   You tried to make me say that she was more physically attractive than you, so that you could hold it over me.

**Ruth**   I did not. I don't give a hoot how physically attractive she was.

**Charles**   Oh yes, you do – your whole being is devoured with jealousy.

**Ruth** (*rises*)   This is too much!

**Charles** (*sits in arm-chair*)   Women! My God, what I think of women!

**Ruth**  Your view of women is academic to say the least of it – just because you've always been dominated by them it doesn't necessarily follow that you know anything about them.

**Charles**  I've never been dominated by anyone.

**Ruth**  (*crosses to below right breakfast chair*)  You were hag-ridden by your mother until you were twenty-three – then you got into the clutches of that awful Mrs Whatever her name was—

**Charles**  Mrs Winthrop-Llewelyn.

**Ruth**  (*clears plates on breakfast table and works round with her back to* **Charles** *to above table*)  I'm not interested. Then there was Elvira – she ruled you with a rod of iron.

**Charles**  Elvira never ruled anyone, she was much too elusive – that was one of her greatest charms. . . .

**Ruth**  Then there was Maud Charteris—

**Charles**  My affair with Maud Charteris lasted exactly seven and a half weeks and she cried all the time.

**Ruth**  The tyranny of tears – then there was—

**Charles**  If you wish to make an inventory of my sex life, dear, I think it only fair to tell you that you've missed out several episodes – I'll consult my diary and give you the complete list after lunch.

**Ruth**  It's no use trying to impress me with your routine amorous exploits. . . . (*Crosses up stage centre.*)

**Charles**  The only woman in my whole life who's ever attempted to dominate me is you – you've been at it for years.

**Ruth**  That is completely untrue.

**Charles**  Oh no, it isn't. You boss me and bully me and order me about – you won't even allow me to have an hallucination if I want to.

**Ruth** (*comes down stage to* **Charles** *above sofa*)  Charles,
alcohol will ruin your whole life if you allow it to get hold
of you, you know.

**Charles** (*rises and comes up stage above chair to face* **Ruth**)
Once and for all, Ruth, I would like you to understand
that what happened last night was nothing whatever to do
with alcohol. You've adroitly rationalised the whole affair to
your own satisfaction, but your deductions are based on
complete fallacy. I am willing to grant you that it was an
aberration, some sort of odd psychic delusion brought on
by suggestion or hypnosis – I was stone cold sober from
first to last and extremely upset into the bargain.

**Ruth**  *You* were upset indeed? What about me?

**Charles**  You behaved with a stolid, obtuse lack of
comprehension that frankly shocked me!

**Ruth**  I consider that I was remarkably patient. I shall
know better next time.

**Charles**  Instead of putting out a gentle comradely hand
to guide me – you shouted staccato orders at me like a
sergeant-major.

**Ruth**  You seem to forget that you gratuitously insulted
me.

**Charles**  I did not.

**Ruth**  You called me a guttersnipe – you told me to shut
up – and when I quietly suggested that we should go up to
bed you said, with the most disgusting leer, that it was an
immoral suggestion.

**Charles** (*exasperated*)  I was talking to Elvira!

**Ruth**  If you were I can only say that it conjures up a
fragrant picture of your first marriage.

**Charles**  My first marriage was perfectly charming and I
think it's in the worst possible taste for you to sneer at it.

**Ruth**  I am not nearly so interested in your first marriage

as you think I am. It's your second marriage that is
absorbing me at the moment – it seems to me to be on the
rocks.

**Charles**   Only because you persist in taking up this
ridiculous attitude.

**Ruth**   My attitude is that of any normal woman whose
husband gets drunk and hurls abuse at her.

**Charles** (*crosses to fireplace below sofa, shouting*)   I was not
drunk!

**Ruth**   Be quiet, they'll hear you in the kitchen.

**Charles**   I don't care if they hear me in the Folkestone
Town Hall – I was not drunk!

**Ruth**   Control yourself, Charles.

**Charles**   How can I control myself in the face of your
idiotic damned stubbornness? It's giving me claustrophobia.

**Ruth**   You'd better ring up Doctor Bradman.

**Edith** *comes in with a tray to clear away the breakfast things.*

**Edith**   Can I clear, please'm?

**Ruth**   Yes, Edith. (*Crosses to window.*)

**Edith**   Cook wants to know about lunch, mum.

**Ruth** (*coldly*)   Will you be in to lunch, Charles?

**Charles**   Please don't worry about me – I shall be
perfectly happy with a bottle of gin in my bedroom.

**Ruth**   Don't be silly, dear. (*To* **Edith**.) Tell cook we shall
both be in.

**Edith**   Yes'm.

**Ruth** (*conversationally – after a long pause*)   I'm going into
Hythe this morning – is there anything you want?

**Charles**   Yes, a great deal – but I doubt if you could get
it in Hythe.

**Ruth**    Tell cook to put Alka-Seltzer down on my list, will you, Edith.

**Edith**    Yes'm.

**Ruth**    (*at the window – after another long pause*)    It's clouding over.

**Charles**    You have a genius for understatement.

*In silence, but breathing heavily,* **Edith** *staggers out with the tray.*

**Ruth**    (*as she goes*)    Don't worry about the table, Edith – I'll put it away.

**Edith**    Yes'm.

*When* **Edith** *has gone* **Charles** *goes over to* **Ruth.**

**Charles**    (*coming over to breakfast table to* **Ruth** *who is folding cloth*)    Please, Ruth – be reasonable.

**Ruth**    I'm perfectly reasonable.

**Charles**    I wasn't pretending – I really did believe that I saw Elvira and when I heard her voice I was appalled.

**Ruth**    You put up with it for five years.

**Ruth** *puts chairs back up stage right and down left.* **Charles** *takes table off stage centre.*

**Charles**    When I saw her I had the shock of my life – that's why I dropped the glass.

**Ruth**    But you *couldn't* have seen her.

**Charles**    I know I couldn't have but I *did.*

**Ruth**    (*puts chair up right*)    I'm willing to concede then that you imagined you did.

**Charles**    That's what I've been trying to explain to you for hours. (*Crosses to mantelpiece.*)

**Ruth**    (*to centre below arm-chair*)    Well then, there's obviously something wrong with you.

**Charles**    (*sits on left arm of sofa*)    Exactly – there is something wrong with me – something fundamentally wrong with me – that's why I've been imploring your sympathy and all I got was a sterile temperance lecture.

**Ruth**   You had been drinking, Charles – there's no denying that.

**Charles**   No more than usual.

**Ruth**   Well, how do you account for it then?

**Charles** (*frantically*)   I can't account for it – that's what's so awful.

**Ruth** (*practically*)   Did you feel quite well yesterday – during the day I mean?

**Charles**   Of course I did.

**Ruth**   What did you have for lunch?

**Charles**   You ought to know, you had it with me.

**Ruth** (*thinking*)   Let me see now, there was lemon sole and that cheese thing—

**Charles**   Why should having a cheese thing for lunch make me see my deceased wife after dinner?

**Ruth**   You never know – it was rather rich.

**Charles**   Why didn't you see your dead husband then? You had just as much of it as I did.

**Ruth**   This is not getting us anywhere at all.

**Charles**   Of course it isn't, and it won't as long as you insist on ascribing supernatural phenomena to colonic irritation.

**Ruth**   Supernatural grandmother.

**Charles**   I admit she'd have been much less agitating.

**Ruth** (*standing at back of arm-chair*)   Perhaps you ought to see a nerve specialist.

**Charles**   I am not in the least neurotic and never have

been.

**Ruth**  A psycho-analyst then.

**Charles**  I refuse to endure months of expensive humiliation only to be told at the end of it that at the age of four I was in love with my rocking-horse.

**Ruth**  What do you suggest then?

**Charles**  I don't suggest anything – I'm profoundly uneasy.

**Ruth** (*sits in arm-chair*)  Perhaps there's something pressing on your brain.

**Charles**  If there were something pressing on my brain I should have violent headaches, shouldn't I?

**Ruth**  Not necessarily, an uncle of mine had a lump the size of a cricket ball pressing on his brain for years and he never felt a thing.

**Charles**  I know I should know if I had anything like that. (*Rises and goes over to fireplace.*)

**Ruth**  He didn't.

**Charles**  What happened to him?

**Ruth**  He had it taken out and he's been as bright as a button ever since.

**Charles**  Did he have any sort of delusions – did he think he saw things that weren't there?

**Ruth**  No, I don't think so.

**Charles**  Well, what the hell are we talking about him for then? It's sheer waste of valuable time.

**Ruth**  I only brought him up as an example.

**Charles**  I think I'm going mad.

**Ruth**  How do you feel now?

**Charles**  Physically, do you mean?

**Ruth**   Altogether.

**Charles** (*after due reflection*)   Apart from being worried I feel quite normal.

**Ruth**   Good. You're not hearing or seeing anything in the least unusual?

**Charles**   Not a thing.

**Elvira** *enters by windows carrying a bunch of grey roses. She crosses to writing-table up stage right and throws zinnias into waste-paper basket and puts her roses into the vase. The roses are as grey as the rest of her.*

**Elvira**   You've absolutely ruined that border by the sundial – it looks like a mixed salad.

**Charles**   Oh, my God!

**Ruth**   What's the matter now?

**Charles**   She's here again!

**Ruth**   What do you mean? – who's here again?

**Charles**   Elvira.

**Ruth**   Pull yourself together and don't be absurd.

**Elvira**   It's all those nasturtiums – they're so vulgar.

**Charles**   I like nasturtiums.

**Ruth**   You like what?

**Elvira** (*putting her grey roses into a vase*)   They're all right in moderation but in a mass like that they look beastly.

**Charles** (*crosses over to right of* **Ruth** *centre*)   Help me, Ruth – you've got to help me—

**Ruth** (*rises and retreats a pace to left*)   What did you mean about nasturtiums?

**Charles** (*takes* **Ruth**'s *hands and comes round to left of her*)   Never mind about that now – I tell you she's here again.

**Elvira** (*comes to above sofa*)  You have been having a nice scene, haven't you? I could hear you right down the garden.

**Charles**  Please mind your own business.

**Ruth**  If you behaving like a lunatic isn't my business nothing is.

**Elvira**  I expect it was about me, wasn't it? I know I ought to feel sorry but I'm not – I'm delighted.

**Charles**  How can you be so inconsiderate?

**Ruth** (*shrilly*)  Inconsiderate! – I like that I must say—

**Charles**  Ruth – darling – please . . .

**Ruth**  I've done everything I can to help – I've controlled myself admirably – and I should like to say here and now that I don't believe a word about your damned hallucination – you're up to something, Charles – there's been a certain furtiveness in your manner for weeks – why don't you be honest and tell me what it is?

**Charles**  You're wrong – you're dead wrong – I haven't been in the least furtive – I—

**Ruth**  You're trying to upset me— (*Breaks away from* **Charles** *to right centre.*) For some obscure reason you're trying to goad me into doing something that I might regret – I won't stand for it any more – you're making me utterly miserable. (*Crosses to sofa and falls into right end of it – she bursts into tears.*)

**Charles** (*crosses to* **Ruth** *right*)  Ruth – please . . .

**Ruth**  Don't come near me—

**Elvira**  Let her have a nice cry – it'll do her good. (*Saunters round to down stage left.*)

**Charles**  You're utterly heartless!

**Ruth**  Heartless!

**Charles** (*wildly*)  I was not talking to you – I was talking to Elvira.

**Ruth**   Go on talking to her then, talk to her until you're blue in the face but don't talk to me—

**Charles** (*crosses to* **Elvira** *down stage left*)   Help me, Elvira—

**Elvira**   How?

**Charles**   Make her see you or something.

**Elvira**   I'm afraid I couldn't manage that – it's technically the most difficult business – frightfully complicated, you know – it takes years of study—

**Charles**   You are here, aren't you? You're not an illusion?

**Elvira**   I may be an illusion but I'm most definitely here.

**Charles**   How did you get here?

**Elvira**   I told you last night – I don't exactly know—

**Charles**   Well you must make me a promise that in future you only come and talk to me when I'm alone—

**Elvira** (*pouting*)   How unkind you are – making me feel so unwanted – I've never been treated so rudely . . .

**Charles**   I don't mean to be rude, but you must see—

**Elvira**   It's all your own fault for having married a woman who is incapable of seeing beyond the nose on her face – if she had a grain of real sympathy or affection for you she'd believe what you tell her.

**Charles**   How could you expect anybody to believe this?

**Elvira**   You'd be surprised how gullible people are – we often laugh about it on the other side.

**Ruth**, *who has stopped crying and been staring at* **Charles** *in horror, suddenly gets up.*

**Ruth** *rises,* **Charles** *crosses to her down stage right.*

**Ruth** (*gently*)  Charles—

**Charles** (*surprised at her tone*)  Yes, dear—

**Ruth**  I'm awfully sorry I was cross—

**Charles**  But, my dear—

**Ruth**  I understand everything now – I do really—

**Charles**  You do?

**Ruth** (*patting his arm reassuringly*)  Of course I do.

**Elvira**  Look out – she's up to something—

**Charles**  Will you please be quiet.

**Ruth**  Of course, darling – we'll all be quiet, won't we? We'll be as quiet as little mice.

**Charles**  Ruth dear, listen—

**Ruth**  I want you to come upstairs with me and go to bed—

**Elvira**  The way that woman harps on bed is nothing short of erotic.

**Charles**  I'll deal with you later—

**Ruth**  Very well, darling – come along.

**Charles**  What are you up to?

**Ruth**  I'm not up to anything – I just want you to go quietly to bed and wait there until Doctor Bradman comes—

**Charles**  No, Ruth – you're wrong—

**Ruth** (*firmly*)  Come, dear—

**Elvira**  She'll have you in a strait-jacket before you know where you are—

**Charles** (*comes to* **Elvira** *– frantically*)  Help me – you must help me—

**Elvira** (*enjoying herself*)  My dear, I would with pleasure, but I can't think how—

**Charles**   I can. (*Back to* **Ruth**.) Listen, Ruth—

**Ruth**   Yes, dear?

**Charles**   If I promise to go to bed will you let me stay here for five minutes longer?

**Ruth**   I really think it would be better—

**Charles**   Bear with me – however mad it may seem – bear with me for just five minutes longer—

**Ruth**   (*leaving go of him*)   Very well – what is it?

**Charles**   Sit down.

**Ruth**   (*sitting down*)   All right – there.

**Charles**   Now listen – listen carefully—

**Elvira**   Have a cigarette, it will soothe your nerves.

**Charles**   I don't want a cigarette.

**Ruth**   (*indulgently*)   Then you shan't have one, darling.

**Charles**   Ruth, I want to explain to you clearly and without emotion that beyond any shadow of doubt, the ghost or shade or whatever you like to call it of my first wife Elvira, is in this room now.

**Ruth**   Yes, dear.

**Charles**   I know you don't believe it and are trying valiantly to humour me but I intend to prove it to you.

**Ruth**   Why not lie down and have a nice rest and you can prove anything you want to later on.

**Charles**   She may not be here later on.

**Elvira**   Don't worry – she will!

**Charles**   Oh God!

**Ruth**   Hush, dear.

**Charles** (*to* **Elvira**)   Promise you'll do what I ask?

**Elvira**   That all depends what it is.

**Charles** (*between them both, facing up stage*)   Ruth – you see that bowl of flowers on the piano?

**Ruth**   Yes, dear – I did it myself this morning.

**Elvira**   Very untidily if I may say so.

**Charles**   You may not.

**Ruth**   Very well – I never will again – I promise.

**Charles**   Elvira will now carry that bowl of flowers to the mantelpiece and back again. You will, Elvira, won't you – just to please me?

**Elvira**   I don't really see why I should – you've been quite insufferable to me ever since I materialised.

**Charles**   Please.

**Elvira**   All right, I will just this once – not that I approve of all these Maskelyne and Devant carryings on. (*She goes over to the piano.*)

**Charles** (*crosses to mantelpiece*)   Now, Ruth – watch carefully.

**Ruth** (*patiently*)   Very well, dear.

**Charles**   Go on, Elvira – take it to the mantelpiece and back again.

**Elvira** *takes bowl of pansies off piano – brings it slowly down stage below arm-chair to fire then suddenly pushes it towards* **Ruth***'s face, who jumps up.*

**Ruth** (*furiously*)   How dare you, Charles! You ought to be ashamed of yourself.

**Charles**   What on earth for?

**Ruth** (*hysterically*)   It's a trick – I know perfectly well it's a trick – you've been working up to this – it's all part of some horrible plan. . . .

**Charles**  It isn't – I swear it isn't – Elvira – do something else for God's sake—

**Elvira**  Certainly – anything to oblige.

**Ruth** (*becoming really frightened*)  You want to get rid of me – you're trying to drive me out of my mind—

**Charles**  Don't be so silly.

**Ruth**  You're cruel and sadistic and I'll never forgive you. . . .

**Elvira** *waltzes with chair from down stage left and puts it back and stands above window.*

*Making a dive for the door – crosses between arm-chair and sofa –* **Charles** *follows and catches her up stage left.*

**Ruth**  I'm not going to put up with this any more—

**Charles** (*holding her*)  You must believe it – you must—

**Ruth**  Let me go immediately . . .

**Charles**  That was Elvira – I swear it was—

**Ruth** (*struggling*)  Let me go . . .

**Charles**  Ruth – please—

**Ruth** *breaks away to windows.* **Elvira** *shuts them in her face and crosses quickly to mantelpiece.* **Ruth** *turns.*

**Ruth** (*looking at* **Charles** *with eyes of horror*)  Charles – this is madness – sheer madness – it's some sort of auto-suggestion, isn't it – some form of hypnotism, swear to me it's only that – (*Rushes to* **Charles** *centre.*) – swear to me it's only that.

**Elvira** (*taking an expensive vase from the mantelpiece and crashing it into the grate*)  Hypnotism my foot!

**Ruth** *gives a scream and goes into violent hysterics as the curtain falls.*

**Scene Two**

*The time is late on the following afternoon.*

*When the curtain rises* **Ruth** *is sitting alone at the tea-table, which is set in front of the fire. After a moment or two she gets up and, frowning thoughtfully, goes over to the mantelpiece and takes a cigarette out of a box.*

*As she returns to the table the front-door bell rings. She hears it and straightens herself as though preparing for a difficult interview.*

**Edith** *enters.*

**Edith**   Madame Arcati.

**Edith** *steps aside and* **Madame Arcati** *comes in.*

**Edith** *goes out.*

**Madame Arcati** *is wearing a tweed coat and skirt and a great many amber beads and, possibly, a beret.*

**Madame Arcati**   My dear Mrs Condomine – I came directly I got your message.

**Ruth**   That was very kind of you.

**Madame Arcati** (*briskly*)   Kind – nonsense – nothing kind about it – I look upon it as an outing.

**Ruth**   I'm so glad – will you have some tea?

**Madame Arcati**   China or Indian?

**Ruth**   China.

**Madame Arcati**   Good. I never touch Indian, it upsets my vibrations.

**Ruth**   Do sit down.

**Ruth** *sits left end of sofa and pours tea.*

**Madame Arcati** (*turning her head and sniffing*)   I find this room very interesting – very interesting indeed – I noticed it the other night.

**Ruth**   I'm not entirely surprised.

**Madame Arcati** (*sitting down and pulling off her gloves*)   Have you ever been to Cowden Manor?

**Ruth**   No, I'm afraid I haven't.

**Madame Arcati**   That's very interesting too – strikes you like a blow between the eyes the moment you walk into the drawing-room. Two lumps of sugar please and no milk at all.

**Ruth**   I am profoundly disturbed, Madame Arcati, and I want your help.

**Madame Arcati**   Aha! I thought as much. What's in these sandwiches?

**Ruth**   Cucumber.

**Madame Arcati**   Couldn't be better. (*She takes one.*) Fire away.

**Ruth**   It's most awfully difficult to explain—

**Madame Arcati**   Facts first – explanations afterwards.

**Ruth**   It's the facts that are difficult to explain – they're so fantastic—

**Madame Arcati**   Facts very often are. Take creative talent for instance, how do you account for that? Look at Shakespeare and Michael Angelo! Try to explain Mozart snatching sounds out of the air and putting them down on paper when he was practically a baby – facts – plain facts. I know it's the fashion nowadays to ascribe it all to glands but my reply to that is fiddlededee.

**Ruth**   Yes, I'm sure you're quite right.

**Madame Arcati**   There are more things in heaven and earth than are dreamt of in your philosophy, Mrs Condomine.

**Ruth**   There certainly are.

**Madame Arcati**   Come now – take the plunge – out

with it. You've heard strange noises in the night no doubt
– boards creaking – doors slamming – subdued moaning in
the passages – is that it?

**Ruth**    No – I'm afraid it isn't.

**Madame Arcati**    No sudden gusts of cold wind, I hope?

**Ruth**    No, it's worse than that.

**Madame Arcati**    I'm all attention.

**Ruth** (*with an effort*)    I know it sounds idiotic but the other
night – during the séance – something happened—

**Madame Arcati**    I knew it! Probably a poltergeist,
they're enormously cunning you know, they sometimes lie
doggo for days . . .

**Ruth**    You know that my husband was married before?

**Madame Arcati**    Yes – I have heard it mentioned.

**Ruth**    His first wife, Elvira, died comparatively young . . .

**Madame Arcati** (*sharply*)    Where?

**Ruth**    Here – in this house – in this very room.

**Madame Arcati** (*whistling*)    Whew! I'm beginning to see
daylight—

**Ruth**    She was convalescing after pneumonia and one
evening she started to laugh helplessly at one of the BBC
musical programmes and died of a heart attack.

**Madame Arcati**    And she materialised the other evening
– after I had gone?

**Ruth**    Not to me, but to my husband.

**Madame Arcati** *rises.*

**Madame Arcati** (*impulsively*)    Capital – capital – oh, but
that's splendid!

**Ruth** (*coldly*)    From your own professional standpoint I can
see that it might be regarded as a major achievement—

**Madame Arcati** (*delighted*)   A triumph, my dear! Nothing more or less than a triumph!

**Ruth**   But from my own personal point of view it is, to say the least of it, embarrassing.

**Madame Arcati** (*walking about the room*)   At last – at last – a genuine materialisation!

**Ruth**   Please sit down again, Madame Arcati . . .

**Madame Arcati**   How could anyone sit down at a moment like this – it's tremendous! I haven't had such a success since the Sudbury case . . .

**Ruth** (*sharply*)   Nevertheless I must insist upon you sitting down and controlling your natural exuberance. I appreciate fully your pride in your achievement but I would like to point out that it has made my position in this house untenable and that I hold you entirely responsible.

**Madame Arcati** (*comes to arm-chair and sits – contrite*) Forgive me, Mrs Condomine – I am being abominably selfish – how can I help you?

**Ruth**   How? By sending her back immediately to where she came from, of course.

**Madame Arcati**   I'm afraid that that is easier said than done.

**Ruth**   Do you mean to tell me that she is liable to stay here indefinitely?

**Madame Arcati**   It's difficult to say – I fear it depends largely on her.

**Ruth**   But my dear Madame Arcati. . . .

**Madame Arcati**   Where is she now?

**Ruth**   My husband has driven her into Folkestone – apparently she was anxious to see an old friend of hers who is staying at the Grand.

**Madame Arcati** *produces note-book from bag and takes notes* *through following speeches.*

**Madame Arcati**  Forgive this formality, but I shall have to make a report to the Psychical Research people . . .

**Ruth**  I would be very much obliged if there were no names mentioned.

**Madame Arcati**  The report will be confidential.

**Ruth**  This is a small village you know, and gossip would be most undesirable.

**Madame Arcati**  I quite understand. You say she is visible only to your husband?

**Ruth**  Yes.

**Madame Arcati**  Visible only to husband. Audible too – I presume?

**Ruth**  Extremely audible.

**Madame Arcati**  Extremely audible. Your husband was devoted to her?

**Ruth** (*with slight irritation*)  I believe so!

**Madame Arcati**  Husband devoted.

**Ruth**  It was apparently a reasonably happy marriage . . .

**Madame Arcati**  Oh, tut tut!

**Ruth**  I beg your pardon?

**Madame Arcati**  When did she pass over?

**Ruth**  Seven years ago.

**Madame Arcati**  Aha! That means she must have been on the waiting list.

**Ruth**  Waiting list?

**Madame Arcati**  Yes, otherwise she would have got beyond the materialisation stage by now. She must have marked herself down for a return visit and she'd never have been able to manage it unless there were a strong influence at work . . .

**Ruth**   Do you mean that Charles – my husband – wanted her back all that much?

**Madame Arcati**   Possibly, or it might have been her own determination. . . .

**Ruth**   That sounds much more likely.

**Madame Arcati**   Would you say that she was a woman of strong character?

**Ruth** (*with rising annoyance*)   I really don't know, Madame Arcati – I never met her. Nor am I particularly interested in how and why she got here, I am solely concerned with the question of how to get her away again as soon as possible.

**Madame Arcati**   I fully sympathise with you, Mrs Condomine, and I assure you I will do anything in my power to help – but at the moment I fear I cannot offer any great hopes.

**Ruth**   But I always understood that there was a way of exorcising ghosts – some sort of ritual?

**Madame Arcati**   You mean the old Bell and Book method?

**Ruth**   Yes – I suppose I do.

**Madame Arcati**   Poppycock, Mrs Condomine. It was quite effective in the old days of genuine religious belief but that's all changed now, I believe the decline of faith in the Spirit World has been causing grave concern. . . .

**Ruth** (*impatiently*)   Has it indeed?

**Madame Arcati**   There was a time of course when a drop of holy water could send even a poltergeist scampering for cover, but not any more – 'Ou sont les neiges d'antan?'

**Ruth**   Be that as it may, Madame Arcati, I must beg of you to do your utmost to dematerialise my husband's first wife as soon as possible.

**Madame Arcati**    The time has come for me to admit to you frankly, Mrs Condomine, that I haven't the faintest idea how to set about it.

**Ruth** (*rises*)    Do you mean to sit there and tell me that having mischievously conjured up this ghost or spirit or whatever she is and placed me in a hideous position you are unable to do anything about it at all?

**Madame Arcati**    Honesty is the best policy.

**Ruth**    But it's outrageous! I ought to hand you over to the police. (*Crosses to fireplace.*)

**Madame Arcati**    You go too far, Mrs Condomine.

**Ruth** (*furiously*)    I go too far indeed? Do you realise what your insane amateur muddling has done?

**Madame Arcati**    I have been a professional since I was a child, Mrs Condomine – 'Amateur' is a word I cannot tolerate.

**Ruth**    It seems to me to be the highest height of amateurishness to evoke malignant spirits and not be able to get rid of them again.

**Madame Arcati** (*with dignity*)    I was in a trance. Anything might happen when I am in a trance.

**Ruth**    Well all I can suggest is that you go into another one immediately and get this damned woman out of my house.

**Madame Arcati**    I can't go into trances at a moment's notice – it takes hours of preparation – in addition to which I have to be extremely careful of my diet for days beforehand. To-day, for instance, I happened to lunch with friends and had pigeon pie which, plus these cucumber sandwiches, would make a trance out of the question.

**Ruth**    Well, you'll have to do something.

**Madame Arcati**    I will report the whole matter to the

Society for Psychical Research at the earliest possible moment.

**Ruth**   Will they be able to do anything?

**Madame Arcati**   I doubt it. They'd send an investigation committee, I expect, and do a lot of questioning and wall tapping and mumbo jumbo and then they'd have a conference and you would probably have to go up to London to testify—

**Ruth** (*near tears*)   It's too humiliating – it really is.

**Madame Arcati** (*rises and goes to* **Ruth**)   Please try not to upset yourself – nothing can be achieved by upsetting yourself.

**Ruth**   It's all very fine for you to talk like that, Madame Arcati – you don't seem to have the faintest realisation of my position.

**Madame Arcati**   Try to look on the bright side.

**Ruth**   Bright side indeed! If your husband's first wife suddenly appeared from the grave and came to live in the house with you, do you suppose you'd be able to look on the bright side?

**Madame Arcati**   I resent your tone, Mrs Condomine, I really do.

**Ruth**   You most decidedly have no right to – you are entirely to blame for the whole horrible situation.

**Madame Arcati**   Kindly remember that I came here the other night on your own invitation.

**Ruth**   On my husband's invitation.

**Madame Arcati**   I did what I was requested to do, which was to give a séance and establish contact with the other side – I had no idea that there was any ulterior motive mixed up with it.

**Ruth**   Ulterior motive?

**Madame Arcati**    Your husband was obviously eager to get in touch with his former wife. If I had been aware of that at the time I should naturally have consulted you beforehand – after all 'Noblesse oblige'!

**Ruth**    He had no intention of trying to get in touch with anyone – the whole thing was planned in order for him to get material for a mystery story he is writing about a homicidal medium.

**Madame Arcati** (*drawing herself up*)    Am I to understand that I was only invited in a spirit of mockery?

**Ruth**    Not at all – he merely wanted to make notes of some of the tricks of the trade.

**Madame Arcati** (*incensed*)    Tricks of the trade! Insufferable! I've never been so insulted in my life. I feel we have nothing more to say to one another, Mrs Condomine – Good-bye. (*Turns away.*)

**Ruth**    Please don't go – please—

**Madame Arcati** (*turns and faces* **Ruth**)    Your attitude from the outset has been most unpleasant, Mrs Condomine. Some of your remarks have been discourteous in the extreme and I should like to say without umbrage, that if you and your husband were foolish enough to tamper with the unseen for paltry motives and in a spirit of ribaldry, whatever has happened to you is your own fault and, to coin a phrase, as far as I'm concerned you can stew in your own juice!

**Madame Arcati** *goes majestically from the room.*

**Ruth** ( *puts out cigarette in ash-tray on small table*)    Damn – Damn – Damn!

*After a moment or two* **Charles** *comes in with* **Elvira**.

**Charles**    What on earth was Madame Arcati doing here?

**Ruth**    She came to tea.

**Charles**    Did you ask her?

**Ruth**   Of course I did.

**Charles**   You never told me you were going to.

**Ruth**   You never told me you were going to ask Elvira to
live with us.

**Charles**   I didn't.

**Elvira** (*sauntering over to the tea-table*)   Oh, yes, you did,
darling – it was your sub-conscious.

**Charles**   What was the old girl so cross about – she
practically cut me dead.

**Ruth**   I told her the truth, about why we invited her the
other night.

**Charles**   That was quite unnecessary and most unkind.

**Ruth**   She needed taking down a bit, she was blowing
herself out like a pouter pigeon.

**Charles**   Why did you ask her to tea?

**Elvira**   To get me exorcised, of course. Oh, dear, I wish I
could have a cucumber sandwich – I did love them so.

**Charles**   Is that true, Ruth?

**Ruth**   Is what true?

**Charles**   What Elvira said.

**Ruth**   You know perfectly well I can't hear what Elvira
says.

**Charles**   She said that you got Madame Arcati here to
try to get her exorcised. Is that true?

**Ruth**   We discussed the possibilities.

**Elvira** (*sits in arm-chair with her legs over left arm*)   There's a
snake in the grass for you.

**Charles**   You had no right to do such a thing without
consulting me.

**Ruth**   I have every right – this situation is absolutely impossible and you know it.

**Charles**   If only you'd make an effort and try to be a little more friendly to Elvira we might all have quite a jolly time.

**Ruth**   I have no wish to have a jolly time with Elvira.

**Elvira**   She's certainly very bad-tempered, isn't she? I can't think why you married her.

**Charles**   She's naturally a bit upset – we must make allowances.

**Elvira**   I was never bad-tempered though, was I, darling? Not even when you were beastly to me—

**Charles**   I was never beastly to you.

**Ruth** (*exasperated*)   Where is Elvira at the moment?

**Charles**   In the chair by the table.

**Ruth**   Now look here, Elvira – I shall have to call you Elvira, shan't I? I can't very well go on saying Mrs Condomine all the time, it would sound too silly. . . .

**Elvira**   I don't see why.

**Ruth**   Did she say anything?

**Charles**   She said she'd like nothing better.

**Elvira** (*giggling*)   You really are sweet, Charles, darling – I worship you.

**Ruth**   I wish to be absolutely honest with you, Elvira. . . .

**Elvira**   Hold on to your hats, boys!

**Ruth**   I admit I did ask Madame Arcati here with a view to getting you exorcised and I think that if you were in my position you'd have done exactly the same thing – wouldn't you?

**Elvira**   I shouldn't have done it so obviously.

**Ruth**   What did she say?

**Charles**   Nothing – she just nodded and smiled.

**Ruth** (*with a forced smile*)   Thank you, Elvira – that's generous of you. I really would so much rather that there were no misunderstandings between us. . . .

**Charles**   That's very sensible, Ruth – I agree entirely.

**Ruth** (*to* **Elvira**)   I want, before we go any further, to ask you a frank question. Why did you really come here? I don't see that you could have hoped to have achieved anything by it beyond the immediate joke of making Charles into a sort of astral bigamist.

**Elvira**   I came because the power of Charles's love tugged and tugged and tugged at me. Didn't it, my sweet?

**Ruth**   What did she say?

**Charles**   She said that she came because she wanted to see me again.

**Ruth**   Well, she's done that now, hasn't she?

**Charles**   We can't be inhospitable, Ruth.

**Ruth**   I have no wish to be inhospitable, but I should like to have just an idea of how long you intend to stay, Elvira?

**Elvira**   I don't know – I really don't know! (*She giggles.*) Isn't it awful?

**Charles**   She says she doesn't know.

**Ruth**   Surely that's a little inconsiderate?

**Elvira**   Didn't the old spiritualist have any constructive ideas about getting rid of me?

**Charles**   What did Madame Arcati say?

**Ruth**   She said she couldn't do a thing.

**Elvira** (*rises and crosses to window*)   Hurray!

**Charles**   Don't be upset, Ruth dear – we shall soon adjust ourselves, you know – you must admit it's a unique experience – I can see no valid reason why we shouldn't get a great deal of fun out of it.

**Ruth**  Fun! Charles, how can you – you must be out of your mind!

**Charles**  Not at all – I thought I was at first – but now I must say I'm beginning to enjoy myself.

**Ruth** (*bursting into tears*)  Oh, Charles – Charles. . . .

**Elvira**  She's off again.

**Charles**  You really must not be so callous, Elvira – try to see her point a little—

**Ruth**  I suppose she said something insulting. . . .

**Charles**  No, dear, she didn't do anything of the sort.

**Ruth**  Now look here, Elvira. . . .

**Charles**  She's over by the window now.

**Ruth**  Why the hell can't she stay in the same place?

**Elvira**  Temper again – my poor Charles, what a terrible life you must lead.

**Charles**  Do shut up, darling, you'll only make everything worse.

**Ruth**  Who was that 'darling' addressed to – her or me?

**Charles**  Both of you.

**Ruth** *rises*.

**Ruth** (*stamping her foot*)  This is intolerable!

**Charles**  For heaven's sake don't get into another state.

**Ruth** (*furiously*)  I've been doing my level best to control myself ever since yesterday morning and I'm damned if I'm going to try any more, the strain is too much. She has the advantage of being able to say whatever she pleases without me being able to hear her, but she can hear me all right, can't she, without any modified interpreting?

**Charles**  Modified interpreting! I don't know what you

mean.

**Ruth**   Oh, yes, you do – you haven't told me once what she really said – you wouldn't dare. Judging from her photograph she's the type who would use most unpleasant language. . . .

**Charles**   Ruth – you're not to talk like that.

**Ruth**   I've been making polite conversation all through dinner last night and breakfast and lunch to-day – and it's been a nightmare – and I am not going to do it any more. I don't like Elvira any more than she likes me and what's more I'm certain that I never could have, dead or alive. If, since her untimely arrival here the other evening, she had shown the slightest sign of good manners, the slightest sign of breeding, I might have felt differently towards her, but all she has done is try to make mischief between us and have private jokes with you against me. I am now going up to my room and I shall have my dinner on a tray. You and she can have the house to yourselves and joke and gossip with each other to your heart's content. The first thing in the morning I am going up to London to interview the Psychical Research Society and if they fail me I shall go straight to the Archbishop of Canterbury. . . .

*Exit* **Ruth**.

**Charles** (*making a movement to follow her*)   Ruth . . .

**Elvira**   Let her go – she'll calm down later on.

**Charles**   It's unlike her to behave like this – she's generally so equable.

**Elvira**   No, she isn't, not really, her mouth gives her away – it's a hard mouth, Charles.

**Charles**   Her mouth's got nothing to do with it – I resent you discussing Ruth as though she were a horse.

**Elvira**   Do you love her?

**Charles**   Of course I do.

**Elvira**   As much as you loved me?

**Charles**   Don't be silly – it's all entirely different.

**Elvira**   I'm so glad. Nothing could ever have been quite the same, could it?

**Charles**   You always behaved very badly.

**Elvira**   Oh, Charles!

**Charles**   I'm grieved to see that your sojourn in the other world hasn't improved you in the least.

**Elvira** (*curls up in right end of sofa*)   Go on, darling – I love it when you pretend to be cross with me. . . .

**Charles**   I'm going up to talk to Ruth.

**Elvira**   Cowardy custard.

**Charles**   Don't be idiotic. I can't let her go like that – I must be a little nice and sympathetic to her.

**Elvira**   I don't see why! If she's set on being disagreeable I should just let her get on with it.

**Charles**   The whole business is very difficult for her – we must be fair.

**Elvira**   She should learn to be more adaptable.

**Charles**   She probably will in time – it's been a shock—

**Elvira**   Has it been a shock for you too, darling?

**Charles**   Of course – what did you expect?

**Elvira**   A nice shock?

**Charles**   What do you want, Elvira?

**Elvira**   Want? I don't know what you mean.

**Charles**   I remember that whenever you were over-poweringly demure it usually meant that you wanted something.

**Elvira**   It's horrid of you to be so suspicious. All I want is to be with you.

**Charles**  Well you are.

**Elvira**  I mean alone, darling. If you go and pamper Ruth and smarm her over, she'll probably come flouncing down again and our lovely quiet evening together will be spoilt.

**Charles**  You're incorrigibly selfish.

**Elvira**  Well, I haven't seen you for seven years – it's only natural that I should want a little time alone with you – to talk over old times. I'll let you go up just for a little while if you really think it's your duty.

**Charles**  Of course it is.

**Elvira** (*smiling*)  Then I don't mind.

**Charles**  You're disgraceful, Elvira.

**Elvira**  You won't be long, will you? You'll come down again very soon?

**Charles**  I shall probably dress for dinner while I'm upstairs – you can read the *Tatler* or something.

**Elvira**  Darling, you don't have to dress – for me.

**Charles**  I always dress for dinner.

**Elvira**  What are you going to have? I should like to watch you eat something really delicious. . . .

**Charles** (*moves up to door*)  Be a good girl now – you can play the gramophone if you like.

**Elvira** (*demurely*)  Thank you, Charles.

**Charles** *goes out.*

**Elvira** *gets up, looks in the gramophone cupboard, finds the record of 'Always' and puts it on.*

*She starts to waltz lightly round the room to it.*

**Edith** *comes in to fetch the tea-tray. She sees the gramophone playing* *by itself and so she turns it off and puts the record back in the cupboard. While she is picking up the tray* **Elvira** *takes the record out and puts it on again.*

**Edith** *gives a shriek, drops the tray and rushes out of the room.* **Elvira** *continues to waltz gaily.*

*Curtain.*

### Scene Three

*The time is evening several days later.*

*When the curtain rises* **Mrs Bradman** *is sitting in an arm-chair.* **Ruth** *is standing by the window drumming on the pane with her fingers.*

**Mrs Bradman**    Does it show any signs of clearing?

**Ruth**    No, it's still pouring.

**Mrs Bradman**    I do sympathise with you, really I do – it's really been quite a chapter of accidents, hasn't it?

**Ruth**    It certainly has.

**Mrs Bradman**    That happens sometimes, you know – everything seems to go wrong at once – exactly as though there were some evil forces at work. I remember once when George and I went away for a fortnight's holiday not long after we were married – we were dogged by bad luck from beginning to end – the weather was vile – George sprained his ankle – I caught a terrible cold and had to stay in bed for two days – and to crown everything the lamp fell over in the sitting-room and set fire to the treatise George had written on hyperplasia of the abdominal glands.

**Ruth**    How dreadful! (*Absently.*)

**Mrs Bradman**    He had to write it all over again – every single word.

**Ruth**    You're sure you wouldn't like a cocktail or some sherry or anything?

**Mrs Bradman**   No, thank you – really not – George will be down in a minute and we've got to go like lightning – we were supposed to be at the Wilmots' at seven and it's nearly that now.

**Ruth** (*coming away from the window*)   I think I'll have a little sherry – I feel I need it. (*Moves up to table and pours sherry.*)

**Mrs Bradman**   Don't worry about your husband's arm, Mrs Condomine – I'm sure it's only a sprain.

**Ruth**   It's not his arm I'm worried about.

**Mrs Bradman**   And I'm sure Edith will be up and about again in a few days. . . .

**Ruth**   My cook gave notice this morning.

**Mrs Bradman**   Well, really! Servants are awful, aren't they? Not a shred of gratitude – at the first sign of trouble they run out on you – like rats leaving a sinking ship.

**Ruth**   I can't feel that your simile was entirely fortunate, Mrs Bradman.

**Mrs Bradman** (*flustered*)   Oh, I didn't mean that, really I didn't!

**Dr Bradman** *comes in.*

**Dr Bradman**   Nothing to worry about, Mrs Condomine – it's only a slight strain. . . .

**Ruth**   I'm so relieved.

**Dr Bradman**   He made a good deal of fuss when I examined it – men are much worse patients than women, you know – particularly highly strung men like your husband.

**Ruth**   Is he so highly strung, do you think?

**Dr Bradman**   Yes, as a matter of fact I wanted to talk to you about that. I'm afraid he's been overworking lately.

**Ruth** (*frowning*)   Overworking?

**Dr Bradman**  He's in rather a nervous condition – nothing serious, you understand—

**Ruth**  What makes you think so?

**Dr Bradman**  I know the symptoms. Of course the shock of his fall might have something to do with it, but I certainly should advise a complete rest for a couple of weeks—

**Ruth**  You mean he ought to go away?

**Dr Bradman**  I do. In cases like that a change of atmosphere can work wonders.

**Ruth**  What symptoms did you notice?

**Dr Bradman**  Oh, nothing to be unduly alarmed about – a certain air of strain – an inability to focus his eyes on the person he is talking to – a few rather marked irrelevancies in his conversation.

**Ruth**  I see. Can you remember any specific example?

**Dr Bradman**  Oh, he suddenly shouted 'What are you doing in the bathroom?' and then, a little later, while I was writing him a prescription he suddenly said 'For God's sake behave yourself!'

**Mrs Bradman**  How extraordinary.

**Ruth** (*nervously*)  He often goes on like that – particularly when he's immersed in writing a book—

**Dr Bradman**  Oh, I am not in the least perturbed about it really – but I do think a rest and a change would be a good idea.

**Ruth**  Thank you so much, Doctor. Would you like some sherry?

**Dr Bradman**  No, thank you – we really must be off.

**Ruth**  How is poor Edith?

**Dr Bradman**  She'll be all right in a few days – she's still recovering from the concussion.

**Mrs Bradman**   It's funny, isn't it, that both your housemaid and your husband should fall down on the same day, isn't it?

**Ruth**   Yes, if that sort of thing amuses you.

**Mrs Bradman** (*giggling nervously*)   Of course I didn't mean it like that, Mrs Condomine.

**Dr Bradman**   Come along, my dear – you're talking too much as usual.

**Mrs Bradman**   You are horrid, George.

**Mrs Bradman** *rises and crosses to* **Ruth**.

Good-bye, Mrs Condomine—

**Ruth** (*shaking hands*)   Good-bye.

**Dr Bradman** (*also shaking hands*)   I'll pop in and have a look at both patients some time to-morrow morning.

**Ruth**   Thank you so much.

**Charles** *comes in. His left arm is in a sling.* **Elvira** *follows him in.*

**Dr Bradman**   Well – how does it feel?

**Charles**   All right.

**Dr Bradman**   It's only a slight sprain, you know.

**Charles**   Is this damned sling really essential?

**Dr Bradman**   It's a wise precaution – it will prevent you using your left hand except when it's really necessary.

**Charles**   I had intended to drive into Folkestone this evening.

**Dr Bradman**   It would be much better if you didn't.

**Charles**   It's extremely inconvenient—

**Ruth**   You can easily wait and go to-morrow Charles.

**Elvira**   I can't stand another of those dreary evenings at home, Charles – it'll drive me dotty – and I haven't seen a movie for seven years. . . .

**Charles**    Let me be the first to congratulate you.

**Dr Bradman** (*kindly*)    What's that, old man?

**Ruth** (*with intense meaning*)    Charles, dear – try to be sensible I implore you.

**Charles**    Sorry – I forgot.

**Dr Bradman**    You can drive the car if you promise to go very slowly and carefully. Your gear change is on the right, isn't it?

**Charles**    Yes.

**Dr Bradman**    Well, use your left hand as little as possible.

**Charles**    All right.

**Ruth**    You'd much better stay at home.

**Dr Bradman**    Couldn't you drive him in?

**Ruth** (*stiffly*)    I'm afraid not – I have lots to do in the house and there's Edith to be attended to.

**Dr Bradman**    Well, I'll leave you to fight it out among yourselves. (*To* **Charles**.) But remember if you do insist on going – carefully does it – the roads are very slippery anyhow. Come along, Violet.

**Mrs Bradman**    Good-bye again – good-bye, Mr Condomine.

**Charles**    Good-bye.

**Charles** *follows the* **Bradmans** *off.*

**Ruth** (*left alone, at fire, speaks to* **Elvira** *right down stage*)    You really are infuriating, Elvira – surely you could wait and go to the movies another night.

**Elvira** *takes rose out of vase on centre table and throws it at* **Ruth** *and runs out of windows.*

**Ruth** (*picking up the rose and putting it back in the vase*)   And
stop behaving like a schoolgirl – you're old enough to know
better.

**Charles** (*comes in*)   What?

**Ruth** (*puts rose back in vase*)   I was talking to Elvira.

**Charles**   She isn't here.

**Ruth**   She was a moment ago – she threw a rose at me.

**Charles**   She's been very high-spirited all day. I know this
mood of old. It usually meant that she was up to
something.

*Pause.* **Ruth** *shuts door and then comes across below sofa to*
**Charles**.

**Ruth**   You're sure she isn't here?

**Charles**   Quite sure.

**Ruth**   I want to talk to you.

**Charles**   Oh God!

**Ruth**   I must – it's important.

**Charles**   You've behaved very well for the last few days,
Ruth – you're not going to start making scenes again, are
you?

**Ruth**   I resent that air of patronage, Charles. I have
behaved well, as you call it, because there was nothing else
to do, but I think it only fair to warn you that I offer no
guarantee for the future. My patience is being stretched to
its uttermost.

**Charles**   As far as I can see the position is just as difficult
for Elvira as it is for you – if not more so. The poor little
thing comes back trustingly after all those years in the other
world and what is she faced with? Nothing but brawling
and hostility!

**Ruth**   What did she expect?

**Charles**   Surely even an ectoplasmic manifestation has the right to expect a little of the milk of human kindness?

**Ruth**   Milk of human fiddlesticks.

**Charles**   That just doesn't make sense, dear.

**Ruth** (*comes to* **Charles** *and leans over him*)   Elvira is about as trusting as a puff-adder.

**Charles**   You're granite, Ruth – sheer unyielding granite.

**Ruth**   And a good deal more dangerous into the bargain.

**Charles**   Dangerous? I never heard anything so ridiculous. How could a poor lonely wistful little spirit like Elvira be dangerous?

**Ruth**   Quite easily – and she is. She's beginning to show her hand.

**Charles**   How do you mean – in what way?

**Ruth**   This is a fight, Charles – a bloody battle – a duel to the death between Elvira and me. Don't you realise that?

**Charles**   Melodramatic hysteria.

**Ruth**   It isn't melodramatic hysteria – it's true. Can't you see?

**Charles**   No, I can't. You're imagining things – jealousy causes people to have the most curious delusions.

**Ruth** (*pause*)   I am making every effort not to lose my temper with you, Charles, but I must say you are making it increasingly difficult for me.

**Charles**   All this talk of battles and duels—

**Ruth**   She came here with one purpose and one purpose only – and if you can't see it you're a bigger fool than I thought you.

**Charles**   What purpose could she have had beyond a natural desire to see me again? After all you must remember that she was extremely attached to me, poor child.

**Ruth**   Her purpose is perfectly obvious. It is to get you to herself for ever.

**Charles**   That's absurd – how could she?

**Ruth**   By killing you off, of course.

**Charles**   Killing me off. You're mad!

**Ruth**   Why do you suppose Edith fell down the stairs and nearly cracked her skull?

**Charles**   What's Edith got to do with it?

**Ruth**   Because the whole of the top stair was covered with axle grease – Cook discovered it afterwards.

**Charles**   You're making this up, Ruth. . . .

**Ruth**   I'm not. I swear I'm not. Why do you suppose when you were lopping that dead branch off the pear tree that the ladder broke? Because it had been practically sawn through on both sides?

**Charles** (*rises*)   But why should she want to kill me? I could understand her wanting to kill you, but why me?

**Ruth**   If you were dead it would be her final triumph over me. She'd have you with her for ever on her damned astral plane and I'd be left high and dry. She's probably planning a sort of spiritual re-marriage. I wouldn't put anything past her.

**Charles** (*really shocked*)   Ruth!

**Ruth**   Don't you see now?

**Charles**   She couldn't be so sly, so wicked – she couldn't.

**Ruth**   Couldn't she just?

**Charles**   I grant you that as a character she was always rather light and irresponsible but I would never have believed her capable of low cunning—

**Ruth**   Perhaps the spirit world has deteriorated her.

**Charles**   Oh Ruth!

**Ruth**   For heaven's sake stop looking like a wounded spaniel and concentrate – this is serious.

**Charles**   What are we to do?

**Ruth**   You're not to let her know that we suspect a thing – behave perfectly ordinarily – as though nothing had happened. I'm going to Madame Arcati immediately – I don't care how cross she is, she's got to help us – even if she can't get rid of Elvira she must have some technical method of rendering her harmless. If a trance is necessary she shall go into a trance if I have to beat her into it. I'll be back in half an hour – tell Elvira I've gone to see the vicar—

**Charles**   This is appalling. . . .

**Ruth**   Never mind about that – remember now, don't give yourself away by so much as a flick of an eyelid—

**Elvira** *comes in from the garden.*

**Charles**   Look out. . . .

**Ruth**   What?

**Charles**   I merely said it's a nice look out.

**Elvira**   What's a nice look out?

**Charles**   The weather, Elvira – the glass is going down and down and down – it's positively macabre.

**Elvira**   I find it difficult to believe that you and Ruth, at this particular moment, can't think of anything more interesting to talk about than the weather.

**Ruth** (*rises*)   I can't stand this any more. I really can't.

**Charles**   Ruth dear – please. . . .

**Elvira**   Has she broken out again?

**Ruth**   What did she say?

**Charles**  She asked if you had broken out again.

**Ruth**  How dare you talk like that, Elvira?

**Charles**  Now then, Ruth. . . .

**Ruth** (*with dignity*)  Charles and I were not talking about the weather, Elvira, as you so very shrewdly suspected. I should loathe you to think that we had any secrets from you.

**Ruth** *addressing* **Elvira** *up stage.* **Charles** *motions that she is behind her.* **Ruth** *turns and addresses her down stage.* **Elvira** *crosses below her to above sofa.*

(*Repeats.*)  And so I will explain exactly what we were talking about. I was trying to persuade him *not* to drive you into Folkestone this evening, it will be bad for his arm and you can perfectly easily wait until to-morrow. However as he seems to be determined to place your wishes before mine in everything, I have nothing further to say. I'm sure I hope you both enjoy yourselves.

*She goes out and slams the door.*

**Elvira**  Oh, Charles – have you been beastly to her?

**Charles**  No – Ruth doesn't like being thwarted any more than you do.

**Elvira**  She's a woman of sterling character. It's a pity she's so ungiving.

**Charles**  As I told you before – I would rather not discuss Ruth with you – it makes me uncomfortable.

**Elvira**  I won't mention her again. Are you ready?

**Charles**  What for?

**Elvira**  To go to Folkestone of course.

**Charles**  I want a glass of sherry first.

**Elvira**  I don't believe you want to take me at all.

**Charles**  Of course I want to take you, but I still think it would be more sensible to wait until to-morrow – it's a filthy night.

**Elvira** (*crosses and flings herself into arm-chair – crossly*)   How familiar this is.

**Charles**   In what way familiar?

**Elvira**   All through our married life I only had to suggest something for you immediately to start hedging me off—

**Charles**   I'm not hedging you off, I merely said . . .

**Elvira**   All right – all right – we'll spend another cosy intimate evening at home with Ruth sewing away at that hideous table centre and snapping at us like a terrier.

**Charles**   Ruth is perfectly aware that the table centre is hideous. It happens to be a birthday present for her mother—

**Elvira**   It's no use trying to defend Ruth's taste to me – it's thoroughly artsy craftsy and you know it.

**Charles**   It is not artsy craftsy.

**Elvira**   She's ruined this room – look at those curtains and that awful shawl on the piano. . . .

**Charles**   Lady Mackinley sent it to us from Burma.

**Elvira**   Obviously because it had been sent to her from Birmingham.

**Charles** (*crosses to right of* **Elvira**)   If you don't behave yourself I shan't take you into Folkestone ever.

**Elvira** (*coaxingly*)   Please, Charles – don't be elderly and grand with me! Please let's go now.

**Charles**   Not until I've had my sherry.

**Elvira**   You are tiresome, darling – I've been waiting about for hours. . . .

**Charles**   A few more minutes won't make any difference then. (*He pours himself out some sherry.*)

**Elvira** (*petulantly, flinging herself into a chair*)   Oh, very well.

**Charles**   Besides the car won't be back for half an hour at least.

**Elvira** (*sharply*)   What do you mean?

**Charles** (*sipping his sherry nonchalantly*)   Ruth's taken it – she had to go and see the vicar. . . .

**Elvira** (*jumping up – in extreme agitation*)   What!!

**Charles**   What on earth's the matter?

**Elvira**   You say *Ruth*'s taken the car?

**Charles**   Yes – to go and see the vicar – but she won't be long.

**Elvira** (*rises*)   Oh, my God! – Oh, my God!

**Charles**   Elvira!

**Elvira**   Stop her – you must stop her at once. . . .

**Charles**   Why – what for? . . .

**Elvira** (*jumping up and down*)   Stop her – go out and stop her immediately.

**Charles**   It's too late now – I heard her go a couple of minutes ago. . . .

**Elvira** (*retreats backwards slowly towards window* – **Charles** *comes to her*)   Oh Oh Oh Oh!!!

**Charles**   What are you going on like this for? What have you done?

**Elvira** (*frightened*)   Done! – I haven't done anything—

**Charles**   Elvira – you're lying.

**Elvira** (*backing away from him*)   I'm not lying – what is there to lie about?

**Charles**   What are you in such a state for?

**Elvira** (*almost hysterical*)   I'm not in a state – I don't know what you mean. . . .

**Charles**  You've done something dreadful—

**Elvira**  Don't look at me like that, Charles – I haven't – I swear I haven't. . . .

**Charles** (*striking his forehead*)  My God the car!

**Elvira**  No, Charles – no. . . .

**Charles**  Ruth was right – you did want to kill me – you've done something to the car. . . .

**Elvira** (*howling like a banshee*)  Oh – oh – oh – oh!

**Charles** (*steps towards her again*)  What did you do – answer me?

*At this moment the telephone rings.*

**Charles** (*at telephone*)  Hallo – hallo – yes, speaking. . . . I see . . . the bridge at the bottom of the hill . . . thank you— No, I'll come at once.

*He slowly puts back the receiver. As he does so the door bursts open.* **Elvira** *stands facing door.*

**Elvira** (*obviously retreating from someone*)  Well, of all the filthy low-down tricks. (*She shields her head with her hands and screams.*) Ow – stop it – Ruth – leave go—

*She runs out of the room and slams the door. It opens again immediately and slams again.* **Charles** *stares aghast.*

*Curtain.*

# Act Three

**Scene One**

*The time is evening a few days later.*

**Charles** *is standing before the fire drinking his after-dinner coffee. He is in deep mourning. He finishes his coffee, puts the cup down on the mantelpiece, lights a cigarette and settles himself comfortably in an arm-chair. He adjusts a reading lamp and with a sigh of well-being, opens a novel and begins to read it. There is a ring at the front-door bell. With an exclamation of annoyance he puts down the book, gets up and goes out into the hall. After a moment or so* **Madame Arcati** *comes in.* **Charles** *follows her and shuts the door.* **Madame Arcati** *is wearing the strange, rather barbaric evening clothes that she wore in Act I.*

**Madame Arcati**   I hope you will not consider this an intrusion, Mr Condomine.

**Charles**   Not at all – please sit down, won't you?

**Madame Arcati**   Thank you. (*She sits.*)

**Charles**   Would you like some coffee – or a liqueur?

**Madame Arcati**   No, thank you. I had to come, Mr Condomine.

**Charles** (*politely*)   Yes?

**Madame Arcati**   I felt a trmendous urge – like a rushing wind and so I hopped on my bike and here I am.

**Charles**   It was very kind of you.

**Madame Arcati**   No, no, no – not kind at all – it was my duty – I know it strongly.

**Charles**   Duty?

**Madame Arcati**   I reproach myself bitterly, you know.

**Charles**   Please don't – there is no necessity for that. (*Sits* *in arm-chair.*)

**Madame Arcati**   I allowed myself to get into a huff the other day with your late wife. I rode all the way home in the grip of temper, Mr Condomine – I have regretted it ever since.

**Charles**   My dear Madame Arcati . . .

**Madame Arcati** (*holding up her hand*)   Please let me go on. Mine is the shame, mine is the blame – I shall never forgive myself. Had I not been so impetuous – had I listened to the cool voice of reason – much might have been averted. . . .

**Charles**   You told my wife distinctly that you were unable to help her – you were perfectly honest – Over and above the original unfortunate mistake I see no reason for you to reproach yourself.

**Madame Arcati**   I threw up the sponge – in a moment of crisis I threw up the sponge instead of throwing down the gauntlet. . . .

**Charles**   Whatever you threw, Madame Arcati, I very much fear nothing could have been done – it seems that circumstances have been a little too strong for all of us.

**Madame Arcati**   I cannot bring myself to admit defeat so easily – it is gall and wormwood to me – I could have at least concentrated – made an effort.

**Charles**   Never mind.

**Madame Arcati**   I do mind. I cannot help it. I mind with every fibre of my being. I have been thinking very carefully, I have also been reading up a good deal during the last few dreadful days. . . . I gather that we are alone?

**Charles** (*looking round*)   My first wife is not in the room, she is upstairs lying down, the funeral exhausted her. I imagine that my second wife is with her but of course I have no way of knowing for certain.

**Madame Arcati**   You have remarked no difference in

the texture of your first wife since the accident?

**Charles** No, she seems much as usual, a little under the weather, perhaps, a trifle low spirited, but that's all.

**Madame Arcati** Well that washes that out.

**Charles** I'm afraid I don't understand.

**Madame Arcati** Just a little theory I had. In the nineteenth century there was a pretty widespread belief that a ghost who participated in the death of a human being, disintegrated automatically—

**Charles** How do you know that Elvira was in any way responsible for Ruth's death?

**Madame Arcati** Elvira – such a pretty name – it has a definite lilt to it, hasn't it? (*She hums for a moment.*) Elvira – El-vi-ira. . . .

**Charles** (*rather agitated*) You haven't answered my question. How did you know?

**Madame Arcati** It came to me last night, Mr Condomine – it came to me in a blinding flash – I had just finished my Ovaltine and turned the light out when I suddenly started up in bed with a loud cry – 'Great Scott!' I said – 'I've got it!' – after that I began to put two and two together. At three in the morning – with my brain fairly seething – I went to work on my crystal for a little but it wasn't very satisfactory – cloudy, you know—

**Charles** (*moving about uneasily*) I would be very much obliged if you would keep any theories you have regarding my wife's death to yourself, Madame Arcati. . . .

**Madame Arcati** My one desire is to help you. I feel I have been dreadfully remiss over the whole affair – not only remiss but untidy.

**Charles** I am afraid there is nothing whatever to be done.

**Madame Arcati** (*triumphantly*) But there is – there is! (*She*

*produces a piece of paper from her bag and brandishes it.*) I have
found a formula – here it is! I copied it out of
Edmondson's *Witchcraft and its Byways.*

**Charles** (*irritably*)   What the hell are you talking about?

**Madame Arcati** (*rises*)   Pluck up your heart, Mr
Condomine . . . all is not lost!

**Charles** (*rises*)   Now look here, Madame Arcati—

**Madame Arcati**   You are still anxious to de-materialise
your first wife, I suppose?

**Charles** (*in a lower voice, with a cautious look towards the
door*)   Of course I am – I'm perfectly furious with her
but—

**Madame Arcati**   But what?

**Charles**   Well – she's been very upset for the last few
days – you see apart from me being angry with her which
she always hated even when she was alive, Ruth, my
second wife, has hardly left her side for a moment – you
must see that she's been having a pretty bad time what
with one thing and another. . . .

**Madame Arcati**   Your delicacy of feeling does you credit
but I must say, if you will forgive my bluntness, that you
are a damned fool, Mr Condomine.

**Charles** (*away to left by gramophone. Stiffly*)   You are at
liberty to think whatever you please.

**Madame Arcati**   Now, now, now – don't get on your
high horse – there's no sense in that, is there? I have a
formula here that I think will be able to get rid of her
without hurting her feelings in the least. It's extremely
simple and requires nothing more than complete
concentration from you and a minor trance from me – I
may even be able to manage it without lying down.

**Charles**   Honestly I would rather—

*At this moment the door opens and* **Elvira** *comes quickly into the* *room. She is obviously very upset.*

**Elvira**    Charles—

**Charles**    What on earth's the matter?

**Elvira** (*seeing* **Madame Arcati**)    Oh! What's she doing here?

**Charles**    She came to offer me her condolences.

**Elvira**    They should have been congratulations.

**Charles**    Please don't say things like that, Elvira – it is in the worst possible taste. Madame Arcati – allow me to introduce my first wife Elvira—

**Madame Arcati**    How do you do?

**Elvira**    What does she want, Charles – send her away. (*She walks about the room.*)

**Madame Arcati**    In what part of the room is she at the moment?

**Charles**    She's moving about rather rapidly. I'll tell you when and where she settles.

**Elvira**    She's the one who got me here in the first place, isn't she?

**Charles**    Yes.

**Elvira**    Well, please tell her to get me away again as soon as possible – I can't stand this house another minute.

**Charles**    Really, Elvira – I'm surprised at you.

**Elvira** (*nearly in tears*)    I don't care how surprised you are – I want to go home – I'm sick of the whole thing.

**Charles**    Don't be childish, Elvira.

**Elvira**    I'm not being childish – I mean it.

**Madame Arcati** (*by fireplace. Sniffing*)    Very interesting – very interesting – I smell ectoplasm strongly!

**Elvira**    What a disgusting thing to say.

**Madame Arcati**   Where is she now?

**Charles**   Here – close to me.

**Madame Arcati** (*mystically – stretching out her hands*)   Are you happy, my dear—?

**Elvira** (*stamping her foot*)   Tell the silly old bitch to mind her own business.

**Madame Arcati** (*in a sing-song voice*)   Was the journey difficult? Are you weary?

**Elvira**   She's dotty.

**Charles**   Just a moment, Madame Arcati. . . .

**Madame Arcati** (*with her eyes shut*)   This is wonderful – wonderful—

**Elvira**   For God's sake tell her to go into the other room, Charles, I've got to talk to you.

**Charles**   Madame Arcati. . . .

**Madame Arcati**   Just a moment. I almost have contact – I can sense the vibrations – this is magnificent. . . .

**Charles**   Go on, Elvira – don't be a spoilsport – give her a bit of encouragement.

**Elvira**   If you'll promise to get her into the other room.

**Charles**   All right.

**Elvira** *crosses to* **Madame Arcati** *and blows gently into her ear.*

**Madame Arcati** (*jumping*)   Yes, yes – again – again—

**Elvira** (*blowing in the other ear*)   How's that?

**Madame Arcati** (*clasping and unclasping her hands in a frenzy of excitement*)   This is first-rate – it really is first-rate. Absolutely stunning!

**Charles**   I'm so glad you're pleased.

**Elvira**   Please get rid of her. Ruth will be in in a minute.

**Charles**  Madame Arcati, would you think it most frightfully rude if I asked you to go into the dining-room for a moment? My first wife wishes to speak to me alone.

**Madame Arcati**  Oh, must I? It's so lovely being actually in the room with her.

**Charles**  Only for a few minutes – I promise she'll be here when you come back.

**Madame Arcati**  Very well. Hand me my bag, will you – it's on the settee.

**Elvira** (*picking it up and handing it to her*)  Here you are.

**Madame Arcati** (*taking it and blowing her a kiss*)  Oh, you darling – you little darling.

**Madame Arcati** *humming ecstatically, goes into the dining-room and shuts the door.*

**Elvira**  How good is she really?

**Charles**  I don't know.

**Elvira**  Do you think she really could get me back again?

**Charles**  But, my dear child . . .

**Elvira**  And don't call me your dear child – it's smug and supercilious.

**Charles**  There's no need to be rude.

**Elvira**  The whole thing's been a failure – a miserable dreary failure – and oh! what high hopes I started out with.

**Charles**  You can't expect much sympathy from me, you know. I am perfectly aware that your highest hope was to murder me.

**Elvira**  Don't put it like that, it sounds so beastly.

**Charles**  It is beastly. It's one of the beastliest ideas I've ever heard.

**Elvira**  There was a time when you'd have welcomed the chance of being with me for ever.

**Charles**   Your behaviour has shocked me immeasurably, Elvira – I had no idea you were so unscrupulous.

**Elvira** (*bursting into tears*)   Oh, Charles. . . .

**Charles**   Stop crying.

**Elvira**   They're only ghost tears – they don't mean anything really – but they're very painful.

**Charles**   You've brought all this on yourself, you know.

**Elvira**   That's right – rub it in. Anyhow it was only because I loved you – the silliest thing I ever did in my whole life was to love you – you were always unworthy of me.

**Charles**   That remark comes perilously near impertinence, Elvira.

**Elvira**   I sat there, on the other side, just longing for you day after day. I did really – all through your affair with that brassy-looking woman in the South of France I went on loving you and thinking truly of you – then you married Ruth and even then I forgave you and tried to understand because all the time I believed deep inside that you really loved me best . . . that's why I put myself down for a return visit and had to fill in all those forms and wait about in draughty passages for hours – if only you'd died before you met Ruth everything might have been all right – she's absolutely ruined you – I hadn't been in the house a day before I realised that. Your books aren't a quarter as good as they used to be either.

**Charles** (*incensed*)   That is entirely untrue. . . . Ruth helped me and encouraged me with my work which is a damned sight more than you ever did.

**Elvira**   That's probably what's wrong with it.

**Charles**   All you ever thought of was going to parties and enjoying yourself.

**Elvira**   Why shouldn't I have fun? I died young, didn't I? .

**Charles**   You needn't have died at all if you hadn't been idiotic enough to go out on the river with Guy Henderson and get soaked to the skin.

**Elvira**   So we're back at Guy Henderson again, are we?

**Charles**   You behaved abominably over Guy Henderson and it's no use pretending that you didn't.

**Elvira**   Guy adored me – and anyhow he was very attractive.

**Charles**   You told me distinctly that he didn't attract you in the least.

**Elvira**   You'd have gone through the roof if I'd told you that he did.

**Charles**   Did you have an affair with Guy Henderson?

**Elvira**   I would rather not discuss it if you don't mind.

**Charles**   Answer me – did you or didn't you?

**Elvira**   Of course I didn't.

**Charles**   You let him kiss you though, didn't you?

**Elvira**   How could I stop him – he was bigger than I was.

**Charles** (*furiously*)   And you swore to me—

**Elvira**   Of course I did. You were always making scenes over nothing at all.

**Charles**   Nothing at all—

**Elvira**   You never loved me a bit really – it was only your beastly vanity.

**Charles**   You seriously believe that it was only vanity that upset me when you went out in the punt with Guy Henderson?

**Elvira**   It was not a punt – it was a little launch.

**Charles**   I didn't care if it was a three-masted schooner

. you had no right to go!

**Elvira**  You seem to forget *why* I went! You seem to forget that you had spent the entire evening making sheep's eyes at that overblown harridan with the false pearls.

**Charles**  A woman in Cynthia Cheviot's position would hardly wear false pearls.

**Elvira**  They were practically all she was wearing.

**Charles**  I am pained to observe that seven years in the echoing vaults of eternity have in no way impaired your native vulgarity.

**Elvira**  That was the remark of a pompous ass.

**Charles**  There is nothing to be gained by continuing this discussion.

**Elvira**  You always used to say that when you were thoroughly worsted.

**Charles**  On looking back on our married years, Elvira, I see now, with horrid clarity, that they were nothing but a mockery.

**Elvira**  You invite mockery, Charles – it's something to do with your personality, I think, a certain seedy grandeur.

**Charles**  Once and for all, Elvira—

**Elvira**  You never suspected it but I laughed at you steadily from the altar to the grave – all your ridiculous petty jealousies and your fussings and fumings—

**Charles**  You were feckless and irresponsible and morally unstable – I realised that before we left Budleigh Salterton.

**Elvira**  Nobody but a monumental bore would have thought of having a honeymoon at Budleigh Salterton.

**Charles**  What's the matter with Budleigh Salterton?

**Elvira**  I was an eager young bride, Charles – I wanted glamour and music and romance – all I got was potted palms, seven hours every day on a damp golf course and a three-piece orchestra playing 'Merrie England'.

**Charles**   It's a pity you didn't tell me so at the time.

**Elvira**   I did – but you wouldn't listen – that's why I went out on the moors that day with Captain Bracegirdle. I was desperate.

**Charles**   You swore to me that you'd gone over to see your aunt in Exmouth!

**Elvira**   It was the moors.

**Charles**   With Captain Bracegirdle?

**Elvira**   With Captain Bracegirdle.

**Charles** (*furiously*)   I might have known it – what a fool I was – what a blind fool! Did he make love to you?

**Elvira** (*sucking her finger and regarding it thoughtfully*)   Of course.

**Charles**   Oh, Elvira!

**Elvira**   Only very discreetly – he was in the cavalry, you know. . . .

**Charles**   Well, all I can say is that I'm well rid of you.

**Elvira**   Unfortunately you're not.

**Charles**   Oh yes I am – you're dead and Ruth's dead – I shall sell this house lock, stock and barrel and go away.

**Elvira**   I shall follow you.

**Charles**   I shall go a long way away – I shall go to South America – you'll hate that, you were always a bad traveller.

**Elvira**   That can't be helped – I shall have to follow you – you called me back.

**Charles**   I did *not* call you back!

**Elvira**   Well somebody did – and it's hardly likely to have been Ruth.

**Charles**  Nothing in the world was further from my thoughts.

**Elvira**  You were talking about me before dinner that evening.

**Charles**  I might just as easily have been talking about Joan of Arc but that wouldn't necessarily mean that I wanted her to come and live with me.

**Elvira**  As a matter of fact she's rather fun.

**Charles**  Stick to the point.

**Elvira**  When I think of what might have happened if I'd succeeded in getting you to the other world after all – it makes me shudder, it does honestly . . . it would be nothing but bickering and squabbling for ever and ever and ever. I swear I'll be better off with Ruth – at least she'll find her own set and not get in my way.

**Charles**  So I get in the way, do I?

**Elvira**  Only because I was idiotic enough to imagine that you loved me, and I sort of felt sorry for you.

**Charles**  I'm sick of these insults – please go away.

**Elvira**  There's nothing I should like better – I've always believed in cutting my losses. That's why I died.

**Charles**  Of all the brazen sophistry—

**Elvira**  Call that old girl in again – set her to work – I won't tolerate this any longer – I want to go home.

**Elvira** *starts to cry.*

**Charles**  For heaven's sake don't snivel.

**Elvira** (*stamping her foot*)  Call her in – she's got to get me out of this.

**Charles** (*going to the dining-room door*)  I quite agree – and the sooner the better. (*He opens the door.*) Madame Arcati – would you please come in now?

**Charles** *goes out.* **Madame Arcati** *comes in followed by* **Charles**.

**Madame Arcati** (*eagerly*)   Is the darling still here?

**Charles** (*grimly*)   Yes, she is.

**Madame Arcati**   Where – tell me where?

**Charles**   Over by the piano – blowing her nose.

**Madame Arcati** (*approaches piano above* **Elvira**)   My dear – oh, my dear—

**Elvira**   Stop her fawning on me, Charles, or I shall break something.

**Charles**   Elvira and I have discussed the whole situation, Madame Arcati, and she wishes to go home immediately.

**Madame Arcati**   Home?

**Charles**   Wherever she came from.

**Madame Arcati**   You don't think she would like to stay a few days longer – while I try to get things a little more organised?

**Elvira**   No – no – I want to go now.

**Madame Arcati**   I could come and be here with her – I could bring my crystal—

**Elvira**   God forbid!

**Charles**   We are both agreed that she must go as soon as possible. Please strain every nerve, Madame Arcati – make every effort – you said something about a formula – what is it?

**Madame Arcati** (*reluctantly*)   Well – if you insist—

**Charles**   I most emphatically do insist.

**Elvira** (*wailing*)   Oh, Charles . . .

**Charles**   Shut up.

**Madame Arcati**   I can't guarantee anything, you know –

I'll do my best but it may not work.

**Charles**   What is the formula?

**Madame Arcati**   Nothing more than a little verse really – it fell into disuse after the seventeenth century – I shall need some pepper and salt—

**Charles**   There's some pepper and salt in the dining-room – I'll get it.

*He goes.*

**Madame Arcati**   We ought of course to have some Shepherd's Wort and a frog or two but I think I can manage without.

**Madame Arcati** *talks to* **Elvira** *as though she were standing by piano.*

You won't be frightened, dear, will you? It's absolutely painless.

**Charles** (*coming back with the cruet*)   Will this be enough?

**Madame Arcati**   Oh yes – I only need a little – put it on the table please. Now then, let me see— (*She fumbles in her bag for the paper and her glasses.*) Ah, yes— (*To* **Charles**.) Sprinkle it, will you – just a soupçon – there, right in the middle—

**Charles** *does so.*

**Elvira**   This is going to be a flop – I can tell you that here and now.

**Madame Arcati**   Now a few snapdragons out of that vase, there's a good chap.

**Charles** *brings flowers.*

**Charles**   Here you are.

**Elvira**   Merlin does all this sort of thing at parties and bores us all stiff with it.

**Madame Arcati**   Now then – the gramophone – in the

old days of course they used a zither or reed pipes – we'd better have the same record we had before, I think.

**Elvira**   I'll get it.

**Elvira** *gets record and gives it to* **Madame Arcati**, *then crosses to mantelpiece.*

**Charles**   Whatever you think best, Madame Arcati.

**Madame Arcati** (*watching, fascinated*)   Oh, if only that Mr Emsworth of the Psychical Research Society could see this – he'd have a fit, he would, really! Don't start it yet, dear. Now then – sit down, please, Mr Condomine, rest your hands on the table but don't put your fingers in the pepper – I shall turn out the lights myself— Oh, shucks, I'd nearly forgotten— (*She goes to the table and makes designs in the sprinkled pepper and salt with her forefinger.*) One triangle – (*She consults the paper.*) One half circle and one little dot – there!

**Elvira**   This is waste of time – she's a complete fake.

**Charles**   Anything's worth trying.

**Elvira**   I'm as eager for it to succeed as you are – don't make any mistake about that. But I'll lay you ten to one it's a dead failure.

**Madame Arcati**   Now, if your wife would be kind enough to lie down on the sofa—

**Charles**   Go on, Elvira—

**Elvira** (*lying down*)   This is sheer nonsense – don't blame me if I get the giggles.

**Charles**   Concentrate – think of nothing.

**Madame Arcati** (*she faces* **Elvira**'s *feet instead of her head*) That's right – quite right – hands at the sides – legs extended – breathe steadily – one two – one two – one two – is she comfortable?

**Charles**   Are you comfortable, Elvira?

**Elvira**   No.

**Charles**   She's quite comfortable.

**Madame Arcati**   I shall join you in a moment, Mr
Condomine – I may have to go into a slight trance, but if
I do, pay no attention – Now first the music and away we
go! (*Crosses to gramophone and starts it.*)

**Madame Arcati** *turns on the gramophone and stands quite still
by the side of it with her hands behind her head for a little – then
suddenly, with great swiftness, she runs to the door and switches out
the lights. Her form can dimly be discerned moving about in the
darkness.* **Charles** *gives a loud sneeze.*

**Elvira** (*giggling*)   Oh dear – it's the pepper.

**Charles**   Damn!

**Madame Arcati**   Hold on to yourself – concentrate—

**Madame Arcati** *recites in a sing-song voice.*
   'Ghostly spectre – ghoul or fiend
   Never more be thou convened
   Shepherd's Wort and Holy Rite
   Banish thee into the night.'

**Elvira**   What a disagreeable little verse.

**Charles**   Be quiet, Elvira.

**Madame Arcati** (*pulls up chair down stage left and sits opposite*
**Charles**)   Sshh! (*There is silence.*) Is there anyone there? . . .
Is there anyone there? – one rap for yes – two raps for
no— Is there anyone there? . . . (*The table gives a loud bump.*)
Aha— Good Stuff! Is that you, Daphne? . . . (*The table gives
another bump.*) I'm sorry to bother you, dear, but Mrs
Condomine wants to return. (*The table bumps several times very
quickly.*) Now then, Daphne. . . . Did you hear what I said?
(*After a pause the table gives one bump.*) Can you help us? . . .
(*There is another pause, then the table begins to bump violently
without stopping.*) Hold tight, Mr Condomine – it's trying to
break away— Oh – oh – oh – (*The table falls over with a
crash. She falls off chair and pulls over table on to her.*)

**Charles**   What's the matter, Madame Arcati? – are you

hurt?

**Madame Arcati** (*wailing*)   Oh – oh – oh—

**Charles** *rushes to door and turns on lights then back to* **Madame Arcati** *and kneels above her.*

**Charles**   What on earth's happening?

**Madame Arcati** *is lying on the floor with the table upside down on her back.* **Charles** *hurriedly lifts it off.*

**Charles** (*shaking her*)   Are you hurt, Madame Arcati?

**Elvira** (*rises and comes and looks at* **Madame Arcati** *then crosses back to fireplace*)   She's in one of her damned trances again and I'm here as much as ever I was.

**Charles** (*shaking* **Madame Arcati**)   For God's sake wake up.

**Elvira**   Leave her alone – she's having the whale of a time.

**Madame Arcati** (*moaning*)   Oh – oh – oh—

**Elvira**   If I ever do get back I'll strangle that bloody little Daphne. . . .

**Madame Arcati** (*sitting up suddenly*)   What happened?

**Charles**   Nothing – nothing at all.

**Madame Arcati** *rises.* **Charles** *rises and picks up table.*

**Madame Arcati** (*dusting herself*)   Oh, yes, it did – I know something happened.

**Charles**   You fell over – that's all that happened.

**Madame Arcati**   Is she still here?

**Charles**   Of course she is.

**Madame Arcati**   Something must have gone wrong.

**Elvira**   Make her do it properly. I'm sick of being messed about like this.

**Charles**   Be quiet – she's doing her best.

**Madame Arcati**   Something happened – I sensed it in my trance – I felt it – it shivered through me.

*Suddenly the window curtains blow out almost straight and* **Ruth** *walks into the room. She is still wearing the brightly-coloured clothes in which we last saw her but now they are entirely grey. So is her hair and her skin.*

**Ruth** (*enters from windows and goes straight to* **Charles** *centre*)   Once and for all, Charles – what the hell does this mean?

*The lights fade.*


## Scene Two

*When the lights go up again several hours have elapsed.*

*The whole room is in slight disarray. There are birch branches and evergreens laid on the floor in front of the doors and crossed birch branches pinned rather untidily on to the curtains. The furniture has been moved about a bit. On the Bridge table there is a pile of playing-cards,* **Madame Arcati**'s *crystal and a Ouija board. Also a plate of sandwiches and two empty beer mugs.*

**Madame Arcati** *is asleep on the sofa.* **Ruth** *is leaning on the mantelpiece.* **Charles** *sitting on back of sofa.* **Elvira** *sitting on piano-stool above séance table.*

**Ruth**   Well – we've done all we can – I must say I couldn't be more exhausted.

**Elvira**   It will be daylight soon.

*The clock strikes five, very slowly.*

**Ruth**   That clock's always irritated me – it strikes far too slowly.

**Charles**   It was a wedding present from Uncle Walter.

**Ruth**   Whose Uncle Walter?

**Charles**   Elvira's.

**Ruth**   Well all I can say is he might have chosen something a little more decorative.

**Elvira**   If that really were all you could say, Ruth, I'm sure it would be a great comfort to us all.

**Ruth** (*grandly*)   You can be as rude as you like, Elvira. I don't mind a bit − as a matter of fact I should be extremely surprised if you weren't.

**Elvira** (*truculently*)   Why?

**Ruth**   The reply to that is really too obvious.

**Charles**   I wish you two would stop bickering for one minute.

**Ruth**   This is quite definitely one of the most frustrating nights I have ever spent.

**Elvira**   The reply to that is pretty obvious, too.

**Ruth**   I'm sure I don't know what you mean.

**Elvira**   Skip it.

**Ruth** (*crosses to* **Elvira**)   Now listen to me, Elvira. If you and I have got to stay together indefinitely in this house − and it looks unpleasantly likely − we had better come to some sort of an arrangement.

**Elvira**   What sort of an arrangement?

**Charles**   You're *not* going to stay indefinitely in this house.

**Ruth**   With you, then − we shall have to be with you.

**Charles**   I don't see why − why don't you take a cottage somewhere?

**Ruth**   You called us back.

**Charles**   I've already explained until I'm black in the face that I did nothing of the sort.

**Ruth**   Madame Arcati said you did.

**Charles**   Madame Arcati's a muddling old fool.

**Elvira**   I could have told you that in the first place.

**Ruth**   I think you're behaving very shabbily, Charles.

**Charles**   I don't see what I've done.

**Ruth**   We have all agreed that as Elvira and I are dead that it would be both right and proper for us to dematerialise again as soon as possible. That, I admit. We have allowed ourselves to be subjected to the most humiliating hocus-pocus for hours and hours without complaining. . . .

**Charles**   Without complaining?

**Ruth**   We've stood up – we've lain down – we've concentrated. We've sat interminably while that tiresome old woman recited extremely unflattering verses at us. We've endured five séances – we've watched her fling herself in and out of trances until we're dizzy and at the end of it all we find ourselves exactly where we were at the beginning. . . .

**Charles**   Well, it's not my fault.

**Ruth**   Be that as it may, the least you could do is to admit failure gracefully and try and make the best of it – your manners are boorish to a degree.

**Charles** (*rises*)   I'm just as exhausted as you are. I've had to do all the damned table tapping, remember.

**Ruth**   If she can't get us back, she can't and that's that. We shall have to think of something else.

**Charles**   She *must* get you back – anything else is unthinkable.

**Elvira**   There's gratitude for you!

**Charles**   Gratitude?

**Elvira**   Yes, for all the years we've both devoted to you –
you ought to be ashamed.

**Charles**   What about all the years I've devoted to you?

**Elvira**   Nonsense – we've waited on you hand and foot –
haven't we, Ruth? – You're exceedingly selfish and always
were.

**Charles**   In that case I fail to see why you were both so
anxious to get back to me.

**Ruth**   You called us back. And you've done nothing but
try to get rid of us ever since we came – hasn't he, Elvira?

**Elvira**   He certainly has.

**Ruth**   And now, owing to your idiotic inefficiency, we find
ourselves in the most mortifying position – we're neither
fish, flesh nor fowl nor whatever it is.

**Elvira**   Good red herring.

**Ruth**   It can't be.

**Charles**   Well, why don't you do something about it?
Why don't you go back on your own?

**Ruth**   We can't – you know perfectly well we can't.

**Charles**   Isn't there anybody on the other side who can
help?

**Ruth**   How do I know? I've only been there a few days
. . . ask Elvira.

**Elvira**   I've already told you that's no good – if we got
Cagliostro, Mesmer, Merlin, Gil de Retz and the Black
Douglas in a row they couldn't do a thing – the impetus
has got to come from here. . . . Perhaps darling Charles
doesn't want us to go quite enough.

**Charles**   I certainly do.

**Elvira**   Well, you must have a very weak will then. I
always suspected it.

**Ruth**   It's no use arguing any more – wake up, Madame Arcati.

**Elvira**   Oh, not another séance – please not another séance.

**Charles**   Please wake up, Madame Arcati. . . .

**Ruth**   Shake her.

**Charles**   It might upset her.

**Ruth**   I don't care if it kills her.

**Charles**   Please wake up, Madame Arcati. . . .

**Madame Arcati** (*waking*)   What time is it?

**Charles**   Ten past five!

**Madame Arcati**   What time did I go off? (*She sits up.*)

**Charles**   Over an hour ago.

**Madame Arcati** (*reaching for her bag*)   Curious . . . very curious. Forgive me for a moment, I must just make a note of that for my diary. (*She takes a book out of her bag and scribbles in it.*) Are they still here?

**Charles**   Yes.

**Madame Arcati**   How disappointing.

**Charles**   Have you any suggestions?

**Madame Arcati** (*rising briskly*)   We mustn't give up hope – chin up – never give in – that's my motto.

**Ruth**   This schoolgirl phraseology's driving me mad.

**Madame Arcati**   Now then. . . .

**Charles**   Now then what?

**Madame Arcati**   What do you say we have another séance and really put our shoulders to the wheel? – Make it a real rouser?

**Elvira**   For God's sake not another séance.

**Madame Arcati**  I might be able to materialise a
trumpet if I tried hard enough – better than nothing, you
know – I feel as fit as a fiddle after my rest.

**Elvira**  I don't care if she materialises a whole symphony
orchestra – I implore you not to let her have another
séance.

**Charles**  Don't you think, Madame Arcati, that perhaps
we've had enough séances? After all they haven't achieved
much, have they?

**Madame Arcati**  Rome wasn't built in a day, you know.

**Charles**  I know it wasn't, but . . .

**Madame Arcati**  Well then – cheer up – away with
melancholy.

**Charles**  Now listen, Madame Arcati . . . before you go
off into any further trances I really think we ought to
discuss the situation a little.

**Madame Arcati**  Good – an excellent idea – and while
we're doing it I shall have another of these delicious
sandwiches – I'm as hungry as a hunter. (*Crosses to table and
gets sandwich.*)

**Charles**  Would you like some more beer?

**Madame Arcati**  No, thank you – better not.

**Charles**  Very well – I think I'll have a small whisky-and-
soda.

**Madame Arcati**  Make it a double and enjoy yourself.

**Charles** *goes to the drink table and mixes himself a whisky-and-
soda.*

**Ruth**  One day I intend to give myself the pleasure of
telling Madame Arcati exactly what I think of her.

**Charles**  She's been doing her best.

**Madame Arcati**  Are the girls getting despondent?

**Charles**   I'm afraid they are, rather.

**Madame Arcati**   We'll win through yet – don't be downhearted. (*Sits on sofa.*)

**Ruth**   If we're not very careful she'll materialise a hockey team.

**Madame Arcati**   Now then, Mr Condomine – the discussion – fire away.

**Charles** (*crosses and sits on pouffe down stage right*)   Well, my wives and I have been talking it over and they are both absolutely convinced that I somehow or other called them back.

**Madame Arcati**   Very natural.

**Charles**   I am equally convinced that I did not.

**Madame Arcati**   Love is a strong psychic force, Mr Condomine – it can work untold miracles – a true love call can encompass the universe—

**Charles** (*hastily*)   I'm sure it can but I must confess to you frankly that although my affection for both Elvira and Ruth is of the warmest I cannot truthfully feel that it would come under the heading that you describe.

**Elvira**   I should just think not indeed.

**Madame Arcati**   You may not know your own strength, Mr Condomine.

**Charles** (*firmly*)   I did *not* call them back – either consciously or sub-consciously.

**Madame Arcati**   But, Mr Condomine. . . .

**Charles**   That is my final word on the subject.

**Madame Arcati**   Neither of them could have appeared unless there had been somebody – a psychic subject – in the house, who wished for them . . .

**Charles**   Well, it wasn't me.

**Elvira**  Perhaps it was Doctor Bradman – I never knew he cared.

**Madame Arcati**  Are you sure? – Are you really sure?

**Charles**  Absolutely positive.

**Madame Arcati** (*throws sandwich over her head and rises*)  Great Scott, I believe I've been barking up the wrong tree!

**Charles**  How do you mean?

**Madame Arcati**  The Sudbury case!

**Charles**  I don't understand.

**Madame Arcati**  There's no reason why you should – it was before your day – I wonder – oh, I wonder . . .

**Charles**  What was the Sudbury case? I wish you'd explain.

**Madame Arcati**  It was the case that made me famous, Mr Condomine – it was what you might describe in theatrical parlance as my first smash hit! I had letters from all over the world about it – especially India.

**Charles**  What did you do?

**Madame Arcati**  I de-materialised old Lady Sudbury after she'd been firmly entrenched in the private chapel for over seventeen years.

**Charles**  How? – Can you remember how?

**Madame Arcati**  Chance – a fluke – I happened on it by the merest coincidence.

**Charles**  What fluke – what was it?

**Madame Arcati**  Wait – all in good time. (*She begins to walk about the room.*) Now let me see – who was in the house during our first séance?

**Charles**  Only the Bradmans, Ruth and me, and yourself.

**Madame Arcati**  Ah, yes – yes – to be sure – but the

Bradmans weren't here last night, were they?

**Charles**   No.

**Madame Arcati**   Quickly – my crystal—

**Charles** (*gets crystal from table and gives it to* **Madame Arcati**)   Here . . .

**Madame Arcati** (*shaking it crossly*)   Damn the thing, it gives me the pip. It's cloudy again. (*She looks again.*) Ah! – that's better – it's there again – it's there again – I'm beginning to understand.

**Charles**   I wish I was. What's there again?

**Madame Arcati**   A bandage . . . a white bandage – hold on to a white bandage. . . .

**Charles**   I haven't got a white bandage.

**Madame Arcati**   Shhh!

**Elvira**   She's too good, you know – she ought to be in a circus.

**Madame Arcati** *runs across and leaps on to pouffe. She advances to the middle of the room and raises her arms slowly – she begins to intone.*

**Madame Arcati**
Be you in nook or cranny answer me,
Be you in Still-room or closet answer me,
Be you behind the panel, above the stairs
Beneath the eaves – waking or sleeping,
Answer me!
That ought to do it or I'm a Dutchman.

**Charles**   Do what?

**Madame Arcati**   Hush – wait—

**Madame Arcati** *crosses to window and picks up bunch of garlic and crosses to writing-desk, making cabalistic signs. She picks up one of the birch branches and waves it solemnly to and fro.*

**Ruth** (*rises and comes to gramophone down stage left*)   For God's sake don't let her throw any more of that garlic about – it nearly made me sick last time.

**Charles**   Would you like the gramophone on or the lights out or anything?

**Madame Arcati**   No, no – it's near – it's very near—

**Elvira**   If it's a ghost I shall scream.

**Ruth**   I hope it's nobody we know – I shall feel so silly.

*Suddenly the door opens and* **Edith** *comes into the room. She is wearing a pink flannel dressing-gown and bedroom slippers. Her head is bandaged.*

**Edith**   Did you ring, sir?

**Madame Arcati**   The bandage! The white bandage!

**Charles**   No, Edith.

**Edith**   I'm sorry, sir – I could have sworn I heard the bell – or somebody calling – I was asleep – I don't rightly know which it was. . . .

**Madame Arcati**   Come here, child.

**Edith**   Oh! (*She looks anxiously at* **Charles**.)

**Charles**   Go on – go to Madame Arcati – it's quite all right.

**Madame Arcati**   Who do you see in this room, child?

**Edith**   Oh dear. . . .

**Madame Arcati**   Answer please.

**Edith** (*falteringly*)   You, Madame. (*She stops.*)

**Madame Arcati**   Go on.

**Edith**   The Master.

**Madame Arcati**   Anyone else?

**Edith**   Oh, no, Madame. . . .

**Madame Arcati** (*inflexibly*)   Look again.

**Edith** (*imploringly, to* **Charles**)  I don't understand, sir –
I—

**Madame Arcati**  Come, child – don't beat about the
bush – look again.

**Elvira** *moves across to fireplace.* **Ruth** *follows.* **Edith** *follows
them with her eyes.*

**Ruth**  Do concentrate, Elvira, and keep still.

**Elvira**  I can't. . . .

**Madame Arcati**  Do you see anyone else now?

**Edith** (*slyly*)  Oh no, Madame.

**Madame Arcati**  She's lying.

**Edith**  Oh, Madame!

**Madame Arcati**  They always do.

**Charles**  They?

**Madame Arcati** (*sharply*)  Where are they now?

**Edith**  By the fireplace— Oh!

**Charles**  She can see them – do you mean she can see
them?

**Madame Arcati**  Probably not very clearly – but
enough—

**Edith** (*bursting into tears*)  Let me go – I haven't done
nothing nor seen nobody – let me go back to bed.

**Madame Arcati**  Give her a sandwich.

**Charles** *goes to table and gets sandwich for* **Edith**.

**Edith** (*drawing away*)  I don't want a sandwich. I want to
go back to bed.

**Charles** (*handing* **Edith** *the plate*)  Here, Edith.

**Madame Arcati**  Nonsense – a big healthy girl like you
saying no to a delicious sandwich – I never heard of such a

thing – sit down.

**Edith** (*to* **Charles**)   Please, sir, I . . .

**Charles**   Please do as Madame Arcati says, Edith.

**Edith** (*sitting down and sniffing*)   I haven't done nothing wrong.

**Charles**   It's all right – nobody said you had.

**Ruth**   If she's been the cause of all this unpleasantness I'll give her a week's notice to-morrow.

**Elvira**   You may not be here to-morrow—

**Madame Arcati**   Look at me, Edith.

**Edith** *obediently does so.*

**Madame Arcati**   Cuckoo – cuckoo – cuckoo—

**Edith** (*jumping*)   Oh dear – what's the matter with her? Is she barmy?

**Madame Arcati**   Here, Edith – this is my finger – look – (*She waggles it.*) Have you ever seen such a long, long, long finger – look now, it's on the right – now it's on the left – backwards and forwards it goes – see – very quietly backwards and forwards – tic-toc – tic-toc – tic-toc.

**Elvira**   The mouse ran up the clock.

**Ruth**   Be *quiet* – you'll ruin everything.

**Madame Arcati** *whistles a little tune close to* **Edith***'s face – then she snaps her fingers.* **Edith** *looks stolidly in front of her without flinching.* **Madame Arcati** *stands back.*

**Madame Arcati**   Well – so far so good – she's off all right.

**Charles**   Off?

**Madame Arcati**   She's a Natural – just the same as the Sudbury case – it really is the most amusing coincidence. Now then – would you ask your wives to stand close together, please.

**Charles**   Where?

**Madame Arcati**   Over there by you.

**Charles**   Elvira – Ruth—

**Ruth**   I resent being ordered about like this.

**Elvira**   I don't like this at all – I don't· like any of it – I feel peculiar.

**Charles**   I'm afraid I must insist.

**Elvira**   It would serve you right if we flatly refused to do anything at all.

**Madame Arcati**   Are you sorry for having been so mischievous, Edith?

**Edith** (*cheerfully*)   Oh yes, Madame.

**Madame Arcati**   You know what you have to do now, don't you, Edith?

**Edith**   Oh yes, Madame.

**Ruth**   I believe it's going to work whatever it is – Oh, Charles.

**Charles**   Shhh!

**Ruth**   This is good-bye, Charles.

**Elvira**   Tell her to stop for a minute – there's something I want to say before I go.

**Charles**   You should have thought of that before – it's too late now.

**Elvira**   Of all the mean, ungracious—

**Ruth**   Charles – Listen a moment. . . .

**Madame Arcati** (*in a shrill voice*)   Lights!

**Madame Arcati** *rushes to the door and switches off the lights. In the dark* **Edith** *is singing 'Always' in a very high cockney voice.*

**Elvira** (*in the dark*)   I saw Captain Bracegirdle again,

Charles – several times – I went to the Four Hundred with him twice when you were in Nottingham, and I must say I couldn't have enjoyed it more . . . etc.

**Ruth**　Don't think you're getting rid of us quite so easily, my dear – you may not be able to see us but we shall be here all right – I consider that you have behaved atrociously over the whole miserable business, and I should like to say here and now . . . etc.

*Her voice fades into a whisper and then disappears altogether.*

**Madame Arcati** (*exultantly*)　Splendid – Hurrah! – We've done it! That's quite enough singing for the moment, Edith.

**Charles** (*after a pause*)　Shall I put on the lights?

**Madame Arcati**　No, I will.

**Charles** *crosses to window and pulls curtains. Daylight floods into the room.* **Ruth** *and* **Elvira** *have disappeared.* **Edith** *is sitting still on the chair.*

**Charles**　They've gone – they've really gone.

**Madame Arcati**　Yes – I think we've really pulled it off this time.

**Charles**　You'd better wake her up, hadn't you? She might bring them back again.

**Madame Arcati** (*clapping her hands in* **Edith**'*s face*)　Wake up, child!

**Edith** (*nearly jumping out of the chair*)　Good 'Eavens! Where am I?

**Charles**　It's all right, Edith – you can go back to bed now.

**Edith**　Why, it's morning.

**Charles**　Yes – I know it is.

**Edith**　But I *was* in bed – how did I get down 'ere?

**Charles**　I rang, Edith – I rang the bell and you

answered it – didn't I, Madame Arcati?

**Edith**  Did I drop off? Do you think it's my concussion again? Oh dear!

**Charles**  Off you go, Edith, and thank you very much. (*He presses a pound note into her hand.*) Thank you very much, indeed.

**Edith**  Oh, sir, whatever for? (*She looks at him in sudden horror.*) Oh, sir!

*She bolts from the room.*

**Charles** (*surprised*)  What on earth did she mean by that?

**Madame Arcati**  Golly, what a night! I'm ready to drop in my tracks.

**Charles**  Would you like to stay here – there's the spare room, you know.

**Madame Arcati**  No, thank you – each to his own nest – I'll pedal home in a jiffy – it's only seven miles.

**Charles**  I'm deeply grateful to you, Madame Arcati. I don't know what arrangements you generally make, but I trust you will send in your account in due course.

**Madame Arcati**  Good heavens, Mr Condomine – it was a pleasure – I wouldn't dream of such a thing.

**Charles**  But really I feel that all those trances . . .

**Madame Arcati**  I enjoy them, Mr Condomine, thoroughly. I always have since a child.

**Charles**  Perhaps you'd give me the pleasure of lunching with me one day soon?

**Madame Arcati**  When you come back – I should be delighted.

**Charles**  Come back?

**Madame Arcati** *crosses to table and kneels to pick up cards on floor.*

**Madame Arcati** (*lowering her voice*)  Take my advice, Mr Condomine, and go away immediately.

**Charles**  But, Madame Arcati! You don't mean that . . . ?

**Madame Arcati**  This must be an unhappy house for you – there must be memories both grave and gay in every corner of it – also— (*She pauses.*)

**Charles**  Also what?

**Madame Arcati** (*thinking better of it*)  There are more things in heaven and earth, Mr Condomine. (*She places her finger to her lips.*) Just go – pack your traps and go as soon as possible. (*Rises and goes to* **Charles**.)

**Charles** (*also in lowered tones*)  Do you mean that they may still be here?

**Madame Arcati** (*she nods and then nonchalantly whistles a little tune*)  Quien sabe, as the Spanish say. (*She collects her bag and her crystal.*)

**Madame Arcati** *goes to table and collects crystal, cards and Ouija board.*

**Charles** (*looking furtively round the room*)  I wonder – I wonder. I'll follow your advice, Madame Arcati. Thank you again.

**Madame Arcati**  Well, good-bye, Mr Condomine – it's been fascinating – from first to last – fascinating. Do you mind if I take just one more sandwich to munch on my way home? (*Gets sandwich from table.*)

**Charles**  By all means.

**Madame Arcati** *goes to the door.* **Charles** *follows her to see her safely out.*

**Madame Arcati** (*as they go*)  Don't trouble – I can find my way. Cheerio once more and Good Hunting!

**Charles** *watches her into the hall and then comes back into the room. He prowls about for a moment as though he were not sure that he was alone.*

**Charles** (*comes in. Softly*)   Ruth – Elvira – are you there?
(*A pause.*) Ruth – Elvira – I know damn well you're there –
(*Another pause.*) I just want to tell you that I'm going away so
there's no point in your hanging about any longer – I'm
going a long way away – somewhere where I don't believe
you'll be able to follow me – in spite of what Elvira said I
don't think spirits can travel over water. Is that quite clear,
my darlings? You said in one of your more acid moments,
Ruth, that I had been hag-ridden all my life! How right
you were – but now I'm free, Ruth dear, not only of
Mother and Elvira and Mrs Winthrop Llewelyn, but free of
you too and I should like to take this farewell opportunity
of saying I'm enjoying it immensely—

*The vase on mantelpiece falls on to hearth-stone and smashes.*

Aha – I thought so – you were very silly, Elvira, to
imagine that I didn't know all about you and Captain
Bracegirdle – I did. But what you didn't know was that I
was extremely attached to Paula Westlake at the time!

*The picture above piano crashes to the ground.*

I was reasonably faithful to you, Ruth, but I doubt if it
would have lasted much longer – you were becoming
increasingly domineering, you know, and there's nothing
more off-putting than that is there?

*The clock strikes sixteen very quickly.*

Good-bye for the moment, my dears. I expect we are
bound to meet again one day, but until we do I'm going to
enjoy myself as I've never enjoyed myself before.

*A sofa cushion is thrown into the air towards* **Charles**.

You can break up the house as much as you like – I'm
leaving it anyhow. Think kindly of me and send out good
thoughts—

*The curtains are pulled up and down and the gramophone lid opens
and shuts. The overmantel begins to shake and tremble as though
someone were tugging at it.*

Nice work, Ruth – get Elvira to help you . . . persevere.

*A figure from above right book-shelves falls off on to floor.*

Good-bye again – parting is such *sweet* sorrow!

*A vase from book-shelves up stage falls. The curtains falls.*
*Gramophone starts playing 'Always' very quickly and loudly. He goes*
*out of the room just as the overmantel crashes to the floor and the*
*curtain pole comes tumbling down.*

*Curtain.*